THE MIRROR STEAMED OVER

THE MIRROR STEAMED OVER

LOVE AND POP IN LONDON, 1962

ANTHONY BYRT

AUCKLAND
UNIVERSITY
PRESS

First published 2020
Auckland University Press
University of Auckland
Private Bag 92019
Auckland 1142
New Zealand
www.press.auckland.ac.nz

ISBN 978 1 86940 910 4

Published with the assistance of Creative New Zealand

creative nz
Arts Council of New Zealand Toi Aotearoa

A catalogue record for this book is available from the National Library of New Zealand

Design by Kalee Jackson
Cover image: David Hockney and Barrie Bates in Cornwall, October 1961, photo: Ron Fuller, courtesy of the Ron Fuller estate
This book was printed on FSC® certified paper
Printed in China by Everbest Printing Investment Ltd

For Kyra

The source of all art, the source of all creativity, is love. If anybody thinks there is something more important, I would like to know what it is.

— DAVID HOCKNEY

Suddenly, you're from nowhere, you're brand new. I became British – I was created there in 1962. I could say: 'Billy Apple was born in London,' and a lie detector wouldn't twitch.

— BILLY APPLE

CONTENTS

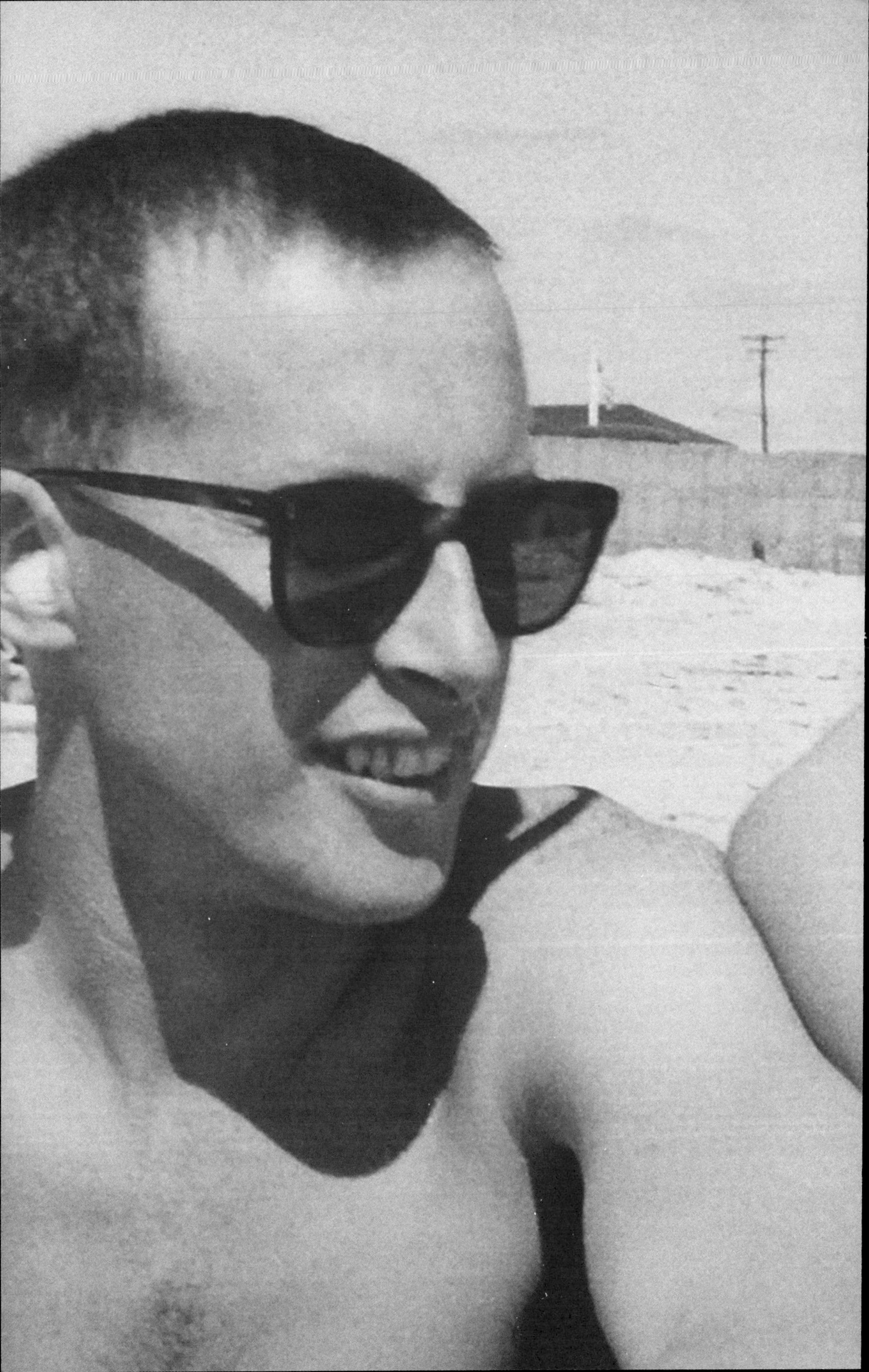

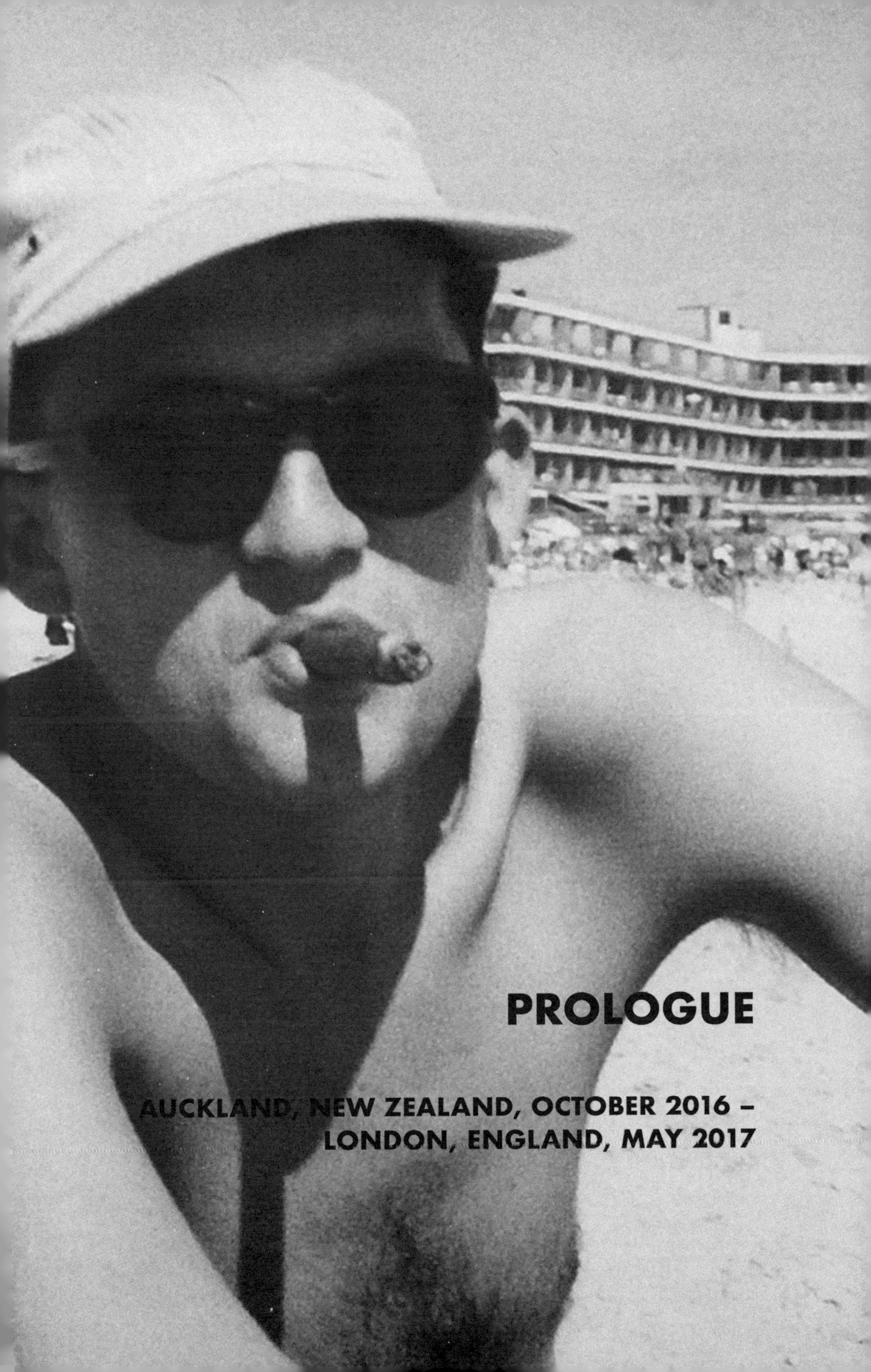

PROLOGUE

AUCKLAND, NEW ZEALAND, OCTOBER 2016 – LONDON, ENGLAND, MAY 2017

JUST AFTER his twenty-fourth birthday, he is already recognisable as the artist the world will know and celebrate, shirtless on the beach with a cap perched on his head, a cigar held in place by pursed lips. The sun is high and his broad, flattish nose protrudes from the cap's umbrella of shadow. The cigar's silhouette drops dead straight from the wet lips, slicing his chin in two.

One skinny arm presses against that of his friend, who is also bare-chested but slightly more solid, with the hint of a strong bicep. The friend, with no hat, already has the high hairline of a man who'll lose most of it later. Both have narrow patches of hair on their chests. The smoker is the woollier of the two, but only just. Their sunglasses are near-identical, as if bought together on the day: a two-for-one special on a nearby boardwalk. Behind them, in the distance, people mill in front of a seaside hotel, but no one comes near them: two perfect hipsters stuck together in their own American universe.

Billy Apple, sitting in his Auckland dining room, looks at the photo for what must be the thousandth time. But the context, today, is abrasively different: a Christie's auction catalogue, half a page given over to the image of him and David Hockney – the cigar smoker – together on a New York beach in the summer of 1961. The pages around the photo are dedicated to the Hockney work in the sale: *Figure in a Flat Style*, 1961. Apple remembers Hockney making it when they were students together at London's Royal College of Art (RCA) from 1959 to 1962.

Apple has a double ambivalence about seeing his younger self – when he was still known by his birth name, Barrie Bates – in the catalogue.

First, he has long been aggrieved about his comparative absence from histories of 1960s British art, and here his cultural status is reduced to Hockney's travel buddy. The second reason, though, is more complex. He was the publisher's source – he gave Christie's the image, and in that way asserted his existence while also relegating himself to secondary player, a walk-on role in his more famous friend's story.

In 2015, I'd written a long profile of Apple, and the magazine had run the photo as part of a grid of four – all of them images of Bates and Hockney together that summer, on the beach, and at Coney Island. In the first of the photos, they stand on a balcony overlooking the amusement park. Hockney, in his trademark specs, bites his index finger coquettishly. Bates, next to him, looks into the middle distance. Dusk light shadows their faces. You can, though, make out the badges they're wearing ('buttons', as Apple calls them). Hockney has two pinned to his white t-shirt. The first simply reads 'DAVID'; the one beneath it, 'I LIKE BOYS'. Bates doesn't have a name badge (the button-vendor probably didn't have the unusual spelling of 'Barrie') but does have a counterbalancing 'I LIKE GIRLS' hanging from his shirt. The badges are meant for cheeky teens escaping their parents' watch into the world of fairground flirtations. Bates and Hockney, in their mid-twenties, are already too old for them: innocent declarations turned leery and sexual, Hockney's bold at a time when homosexuality was still illegal, Bates's more conventional, and even, perhaps, worn a little nervously next to his friend's.

We sit at Apple's dining table, drinking coffee. Early summer sunlight unfurls through the sash window and flops across worn yellow Formica. Outside, I can see the northern stand of Eden Park, just a block away. As Apple turns the catalogue's pages, he lands on an entry for another of his contemporaries, a guy who became so successful he bought a castle in Scotland. He points at the reserves and rages about what a mediocre artist the man was. I laugh. It defuses him; he grins too, the same smile as the young man's on the beach.

I've known Apple since I was twenty-three, the age he was when he first left New Zealand in 1959 as Bates, and headed to the RCA to study graphic design. Just over three years later he became Billy Apple: the living, breathing 'brand' that has come to define everything he's made and done since. Apple is now in his eighties (although he likes to date himself based on the creation of his new identity: by that measure, he turned fifty in 2012). It's at this age that artists start to talk more, in private at least, about legacies, about looking back so they can be sure of their place in the future, their work entering the canon so as to give them a kind of immortality. Apple, though, takes this idea more seriously than that. Since 2009, he's been working on a project called *The Immortalisation of Billy Apple®* with the geneticist Craig Hilton. Apple's cells have been virally immortalised, and are multiplying into the many billions in an American human-tissue collection. Pieces of him will literally live forever. He loves to keep up with how his cells are multiplying.

Apple is obsessed with numbers, and that includes dates. He has another set of photographs of Bates and Hockney together in October 1961, at the wedding of an RCA student, near Mevagissey in Cornwall. In the images, the pair aren't long back from New York. In one, Hockney and Bates square up to the camera. Hockney's hair is longer than he usually has it, peroxided blonde, dark regrowth just pushing through. He's wearing a Union Jack waistcoat and no tie. Bates, by contrast, has his hair cropped short, and he wears the same sunglasses he had on that day at the beach. In the background, a man runs past the door of his Mini van: Michael Kullman, the RCA's General Studies tutor, who will play a vital role in Hockney's and Bates's story before the academic year is out. His car will also become part of one of Hockney's best-known paintings.

For years, Apple had been unable to remember the exact details of the wedding, until he finally recalled that the groom was a classmate of theirs called 'Adams'. I tracked down Michael Adams in the Seychelles. Apple was right; it was his wedding. Adams told me that the Union Jack waistcoat had actually been his – Hockney borrowed it and never gave it back. When Adams saw Hockney at the wedding, he asked him why he'd bleached his hair. 'Because gentlemen prefer blondes!' was the reply. Later that night, Adams remembers, Bates played jazz on the church bells, much to the approval of the vicar. Apple doesn't remember that, but does recall almost freezing to death, sleeping on the floor of a stone building with Hockney. A year or so later, I track down a photo of it: an annex to Rose Cottage on Cornwall's Heligan Estate, where many of the wedding guests stayed.

All of these details, for Apple, take secondary importance to knowing the date and time of the ceremony. As he gets older, this obsession with a correct timeline seems less about accuracy than about placing himself in the world; knowing exactly where he was, never alone but always in relation – to people, to ideas, to moments and histories. It's the same reason he still has every passport he's ever been issued, from the New Zealand one given to Bates before he boarded a boat for London, to his American ones as the naturalised 'Billy Apple' (he is still a US citizen).

Apple is pleased to know the new details of the wedding. So, as I usually do in these moments, I push him again on the nature of his relationship with Hockney. He has always been forthcoming, to a point. He and Hockney are still in touch, emailing each other occasionally, or catching up when Apple shows with his London dealer and Hockney happens to be in town at the same time. But between 1959 and 1962 there were periods when they were very close. Hockney, the Northern boy, and Bates, from the former colonies, were both outsiders when they arrived at the RCA. Hockney remembers meeting Bates because the New Zealander had started to spend much of his time hanging out in the Painting School, and that he thought he was a 'fascinating and droll character'. The pair became friends. They stayed up late in their studios together. They travelled together. They made work together. They bleached their hair together. And, in 1962, they almost failed art school together.

Did they sleep together? Apple says no. But Bates's girlfriend at the time, the soon-to-be-published novelist Ann Quin, seemed to enjoy poking fun at how close the men were. Channelling Bates's voice as she described the impact of his 1961 trip to New York with Hockney, she wrote:

> And all those pretty boys, sure is easy to go queer over there. No he's not, sure he's slept around with men, that doesn't make him camp though. Anyway, makes a change doesn't it? Called round at 2am before going to Paris, guess he was in love with me at one time. Went round together in New York, until he shacked up with this guy. Yeh we went blonde together, dyed it overnight at some party, so they told me. This crazy negro got into my bed, naked, slithering like a fish on a marble slab. Yeh I guess I almost went queer, didn't want to get too involved. These slobs over here, they might look camp, but that's as far as it goes, they don't know how to swing man.

I Google photos of Quin on my phone and bring one up. In it, she's caught in a kind of rapture, eyes turned upwards, her mouth open, a cigarette in her right hand. She has a round face, thick, dark hair, heavy eyebrows and everything in frenetic animation, the glow from an arched window blasting her with backlight. There's another one from the same photo shoot, less energetic, in which she sits in a chair reading pages of typed manuscript. I show them to Apple, but it's not how he remembers her. The photographs are, I later discover, taken too late: Bates and Quin had already parted ways by then.

I show him a more solemn image, a close portrait of her taken on the three-quarter angle, with short hair and an impassive stare, a high-necked sweater creeping upward and closing her in. It's the image from the cover of an edition of her first novel, *Berg*.

'That's her,' Apple says. 'That's what she looked like then.'

When Apple had first talked to me about Quin – in 2015, for the magazine profile – he'd said:

> We had a relationship. She researched and wrote my thesis for me, as a conversation between Vincent van Gogh and Larry Rivers at the Five Spot Jazz Club. It was called 'Pop Corn'. In those days, they handed out topics for people's dissertations. If you're in the Graphic Design School, they give you van Gogh, because they think you're a bit fucking stupid. So I did it the way I'd do any business. You get the best writer around and away you go. She ghosted the whole bloody thing. But boy, did she piece it together.

He'd gone on to recount a few stark character traits, including one I squeamishly included about Quin pissing in public between parked cars in Kensington. And he'd told me about her death – Quin drowned at Brighton in 1973. Two-and-a-half paragraphs and then the article moved on: a precocious cartoon lover half-formed in a magazine feature.

Apple – or Bates, as he was – met Quin when she was the secretary to Carel Weight, the head of the RCA's Painting School. He recalls that they were together during the 1961/62 academic year – Bates's and Hockney's final year of study, in which both men collided with the college's authorities and launched themselves into the London art scene. Later, Quin would publish four novels. *Berg* – a novel about a man who changes his name so he can murder his estranged father – came out in 1964, but she'd written it while she was employed at the RCA. She also wrote several things for and *as* Bates, including letters and his RCA dissertation – that imaginary conversation between van Gogh and Larry Rivers.

Those photographs – of the two men in New York, and, just a few months later, standing alongside each other, supremely confident at a friend's wedding – are cracks in the orthodox histories of the RCA's '1959 generation'. Though I'd always known that Barrie Bates was integral to that moment, the images of him and Hockney together – intimate, perhaps a little rivalrous, but above all performative – suggested something I hadn't fully grasped until I saw that auction catalogue: that, at the time, these young men weren't just thinking deeply about what they made but also about *who they were*.

The fact that Quin was, at the same time, writing a novel about a man riven with anxieties about his own identity suggested that, rather than simply going through a process of 'finding themselves', these young artists and writers were beginning to explore, and play with, the cultural and artistic potentials of 'the self' – and that the way they were doing this was different from the generation before them. Of course, they weren't alone in this: many of their contemporaries, on both sides of the Atlantic, were becoming key figures in Pop art's accelerating trajectory, which shunned the idea that one's subjectivity was the outer expression of an inner universe, and instead favoured the notion that the self was something produced out in the world – both a subject and an object – in relation to the social and cultural forces exerted on it.

As the art historian Christina Barton has convincingly argued, Bates, in his transformation to Apple, took this a step further. She writes that for Bates, 'identity [was not] some inner essence, but a set of superficial signs' and that this 'riposte to modernist depth' has contributed to his marginal status in histories of the period. Despite the fact that Hockney maintained a commitment to conventional working methods like painting and drawing, and despite his status as arguably the most recognisable figure of the era, his own reinvention offered a similar challenge. Beyond the surface effects and Pop potentials of mass consumerism, both he and Bates intuited a much larger cultural revolution underway: namely, that the liberated individual, acting in his or her self-interest – sexually, creatively, politically, economically – was becoming the new unit around which British and American society would be organised. After the war years and more than a decade of austerity in Britain, this liberation was simultaneously a progressive ideal and a huge opportunity for Bates and Hockney to create, and self-consciously perform, new selves.

Over the following decades, similar strategies would be taken up by everyone from Andy Warhol and Gilbert & George to Jeff Koons and the Young British Artists (YBAs). Hockney's blonde hair and Bates's disappearance and replacement by Billy Apple (also marked by peroxiding his hair) were early, and essential, expressions of this new approach to being. The questions they were asking of themselves were still fundamentally existential, but what had shifted was the perspective: from the interior self as felt and then expressed in one's work, to the carefully constructed and observable individual reflected back in the mirror.

But why did these two young men in particular undergo such significant transformations, and in such a short period of time? In Bates's case, his relationship with Quin was certainly one part of it. Quin wrote with an extraordinary inventiveness and fearlessness about sex, mistaken identities, reflections, ventriloquism and love triangles. Her struggles with mental illness were often crippling, but a young existentialist psychiatrist called R. D. Laing would at least help her, and many of her generation, see that their problems were generated just as much from without as within, as responses to a restrictive society. Madness, in Laing's formulation, was a struggle with ontological insecurity – a problem of recognising one's subjectivity, one's identity, one's naming as an individual – in relation to others and the world. Quin seemed to recognise that Bates was on the cusp of just such an ontological change, and began to wrap language around it for him.

In Hockney's case, his decision to make work about his sexuality was key to his transformation. His best works from that time – the Love paintings, *We Two Boys Together Clinging*, the 'Demonstrations of Versatility', 'A Rake's Progress' – are all about his status as a young gay man in a country where consensual sex between men was still criminal. They are, in this sense, works about a young man discovering his identity, one that, in his hands, would oscillate between the heartfelt and the performed: within a year of his graduating in July 1962, he wasn't just a celebrated young talent in London, but a recognisable figure – a celebrity.

Something immense had happened in New York in 1961 which accelerated both men's new and quite radical approaches to individualism and identity over the year that followed. A few months after Apple and I sat together looking at that Christie's catalogue, I travelled to London. My sense was that those photographs were a potential portal into a book project, but I didn't yet have enough raw material to be fully convinced. At that time, Tate Britain was staging a major Hockney retrospective. Though it charted the full breadth of his remarkable career, I was most interested in the works he made during his time at the RCA, which tracked both his new confidence about his sexuality and his eventual transformation into the public figure and celebrity, 'David Hockney'.

On the same trip, I'd also arranged to spend some time in the RCA's archives. With Apple's permission, I was given access to Barrie Bates's student file. As the college's archivist Neil Parkinson brought it over to me, he grinned. It was, he told me, considerably thicker than many of the student files from the period. Parkinson also has an enthusiasm for the RCA's Hockney years, so he knew Bates's reputation. Bates was regarded as one of the most talented graphic design students the RCA had ever encountered. He was also considered, by many of the college's faculty and staff, to be a giant pain in the arse. The many letters in his file – most of which were between RCA faculty, and which Apple had no idea existed – documented their professional conundrum: what to do with such a gifted student with such an inbuilt capacity for self-destruction.

I also read Ann Quin's staff file: much thinner, but still with useful information about how she was living while she was with Bates, and while she was writing *Berg*. Information about Quin's life before the novel was published in 1964 is fairly scarce. But as her file showed, she was there at the RCA, at ground zero, from 1959 to 1962, working in the very department that produced the painters Hockney, Peter Phillips, R. B. Kitaj, Derek Boshier, Adrian Berg – surely a significant name in Quin's literary evolution – Frank Bowling and Patrick Caulfield.

Into this mix, in November 1961, entered a seminal American figure: the ostensible subject of 'Pop Corn', Bates's and Quin's collaboration on his dissertation – Larry Rivers. Caught between Abstract Expressionism and Pop, Rivers has never quite fitted into neat art histories. But he was, in his own way, an archetype of his era: a saxophone-playing occasional actor and sometime heroin user who was also one of the essential painters of the 1950s New York School, and who briefly captured the popular American imagination by winning one of the country's most iconic TV game shows. He was also a man with an invented name. And that November he gave a talk at the RCA that would change the direction of Bates's work forever. He would also meet Hockney and Quin.

In December 1961, the BBC broadcast a version of Rivers' lecture, in two parts. I managed to track down the first part in the BBC's archives. There's a brief silence at the start, then Rivers' voice cuts through, unmistakable: his lecture delivered deadpan, in a New York accent so thick as to be almost absurd – the working-class painter-hero. Then, after eleven minutes, the recording stops dead. Both exhilarated and deeply frustrated, I'd at least heard some of the parts Apple had remembered as having had such a dramatic impact on Bates. A year later, on a British Library microfiche, I located a radio transcript of the entire thing. As much as it was a classic 'artist talk', it was also a kind of manifesto for contemporaneity: an invitation to the young artists assembled at the RCA to forget the past – both art history's and their own – and make art of their times. It was, significantly, I think, given its legacy, titled 'A Self-Portrait'.

When I returned to Auckland, I was convinced there was a book in this material. At its heart, this is a love story: a speculative biography of a moment in which a group of talented young people found each other, fell in love, slept together, worked together and remade themselves. In doing so, they made some extraordinary things. Bates and Hockney, each in their own ways, transformed themselves precisely by understanding that they *weren't* the central protagonists in their own lives – that they were in fact the products, and embodiments, of a profound period of social change. This understanding allowed them to develop toolkits to start performing new identities, building their public selves as figures formed in relation – to ideas, to mass communication, to technological and social transformation, and to the new freedoms of individualism.

The story's three main characters – Bates, Quin and, perhaps most controversially, the 'David Hockney' who existed before he blonded his hair and put on a gold jacket – are all dead or long disappeared. This book, then, is built around the fragments and clues and artefacts they left behind: in particular, Hockney's and Bates's work from the period; Quin's writings; Rivers' RCA lecture and his autobiography; documents from the RCA's archive; and letters, photographs and ephemera in Billy Apple's Auckland archive (he is, thankfully for my purposes, an obsessive hoarder).

I have also tried as much as possible to read, look at and listen to the things these young artists and writers were engaging with: the specific advertising campaigns coming out of Madison Avenue; films like Shirley Clarke's *The Connection*; publications like the *New Yorker*, *Esquire*, *Eros* and *ARK*; jazz recordings; exhibition catalogues; books and articles by the likes of R. D. Laing, Norman Mailer, Marshall McLuhan, James Baldwin and Nat Hentoff. Throughout, I've consistently treated these as primary materials of the moment rather than secondary resources about it – because they weren't just recording the new world emerging around them but actually helping to make and shape it.

I have brought these sources together with some of the well-known biographies and histories of the period in an attempt to fully understand the intellectual and creative electricity coursing through the culture. I'm convinced that, in this moment, there are vital clues to how the sixties subsequently evolved, not just in terms of the high Pop of Andy Warhol's New York and 'Swinging London', but in the very idea of the free, artistic individual – a schizophrenic character who still lies at the heart of our society, simultaneously buffeted by social and political winds but expected to somehow slice through them and show us something new about ourselves.

That figure is part trickster, part moralist, part public intellectual and part celebrity. It has cut an essential path through our cultural landscape for the past sixty years and tells us a great deal, I think, about the origins of the individualism that still shapes the contemporary world, socially, sexually and economically. And Hockey and Bates laid two of the earliest stones along that path. This, then, is the story of their extraordinary transformation, in London, in 1962 – and of how a young writer called Ann Quin, and an American painter called Larry Rivers, contributed to it.

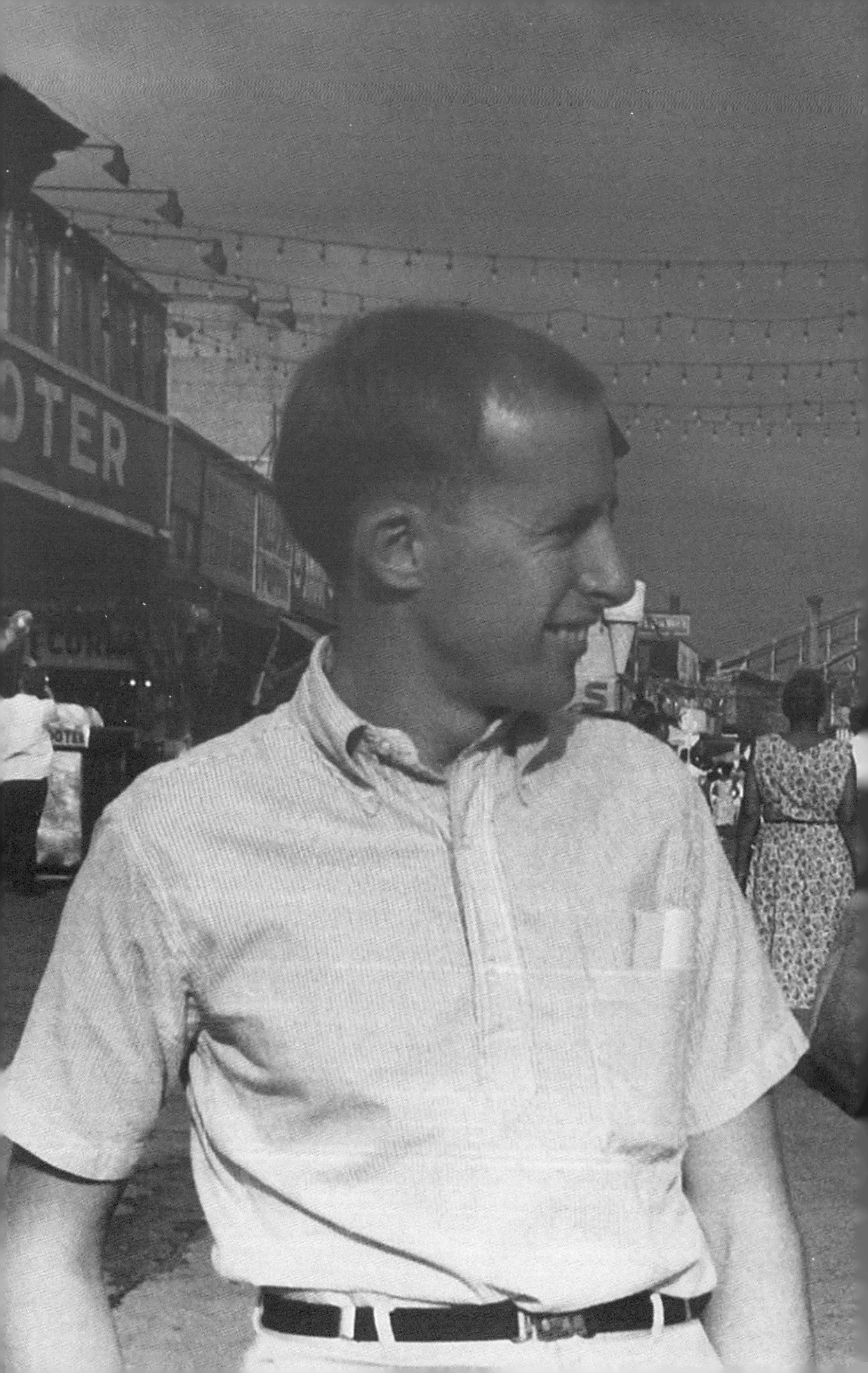

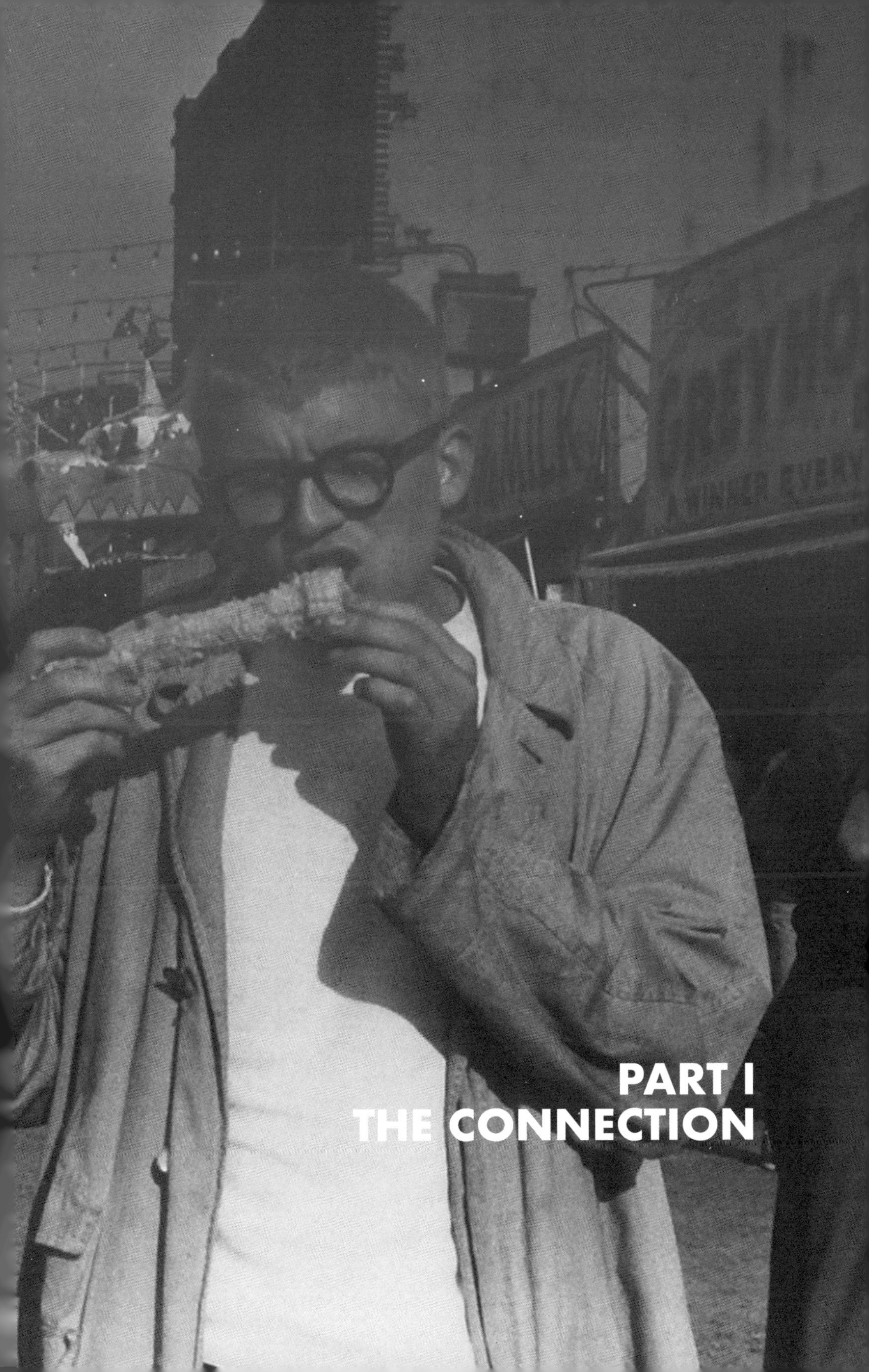

PART I
THE CONNECTION

1 a.m. Tues. morning

Darling,

Man are my eyeballs stinging and boy am I seeing everything yellow well maybe I ought to try slashing something off my flesh it weighs heavily – fingers like stalks soaked with mighty tempests – after a weekend drought . . . . . . Christ could I get really sloshed right now and be laid by you a dozen and a half times with Sandra somewhere over the edge . . . reminds me I wouldn't mind a trip to down under wearing my 'Bizarre' dress and SOFT (clinging) black-black leather coms and outerwear etcetera etcetera – though Dorse would do?

— ANN QUIN TO BARRIE BATES, EARLY 1962

IN SUCH a crowded room, the paintings aren't really visible at a distance. Instead, you have to shunt your way forward, politely but assertively, shoulders wide enough to establish contemplative space, because this is Hockney's 2017 blockbuster retrospective and Tate always lets too many people in for its big exhibitions. It's also a bottleneck, one of the earliest rooms – the one filled with the paintings that made Hockney's name in 1961 and 1962: works that established him as one of the most significant painters to emerge in Britain since Francis Bacon. In 1962 Bacon was the existential Establishment, and Hockney was the hot, young, Poppy thing. Fifty-five years later, Hockney is as Establishment as Establishment comes: arguably the most popular 'serious' British artist of the past half-century, if not of all time, even if he has spent much of his life on the other side of the Atlantic.

That popularity is down to his work, of course. But it is also down to the man himself: the Yorkshire-inflected affability and straight-talking; the legacy of that peroxided blonde hair; and, as he ages, the cloth caps and cardigans and canes and signature specs. Hockney isn't just a great artist but an embodiment of what much of the British public imagines an artist nearing the end of his career should be: like someone's kooky granddad, losing his hearing but maintaining his humour and charm, painting dog portraits and Yorkshire landscapes and doodling on an iPad.

It's a far cry from Bacon's tortured-genius persona, which stuck with him until his death in 1992. But perhaps the way each man aged in the public's mind's eye isn't so surprising, because the twenty years between them were more like a century. Towards the end of World War II, Bacon began to make what became some of his best work, and masterpiece after masterpiece came in the brutal decade of austerity that followed the war. By the time Hockney got to the RCA in 1959, the British economic gloom had started to lift. Two years later, everything was pure potential: both in British society, which was going through a series of cultural and sexual changes that would find their full expression later in the decade, and in Hockney's own work.

The transformation in Hockney's work, when viewed chronologically at the Tate exhibition and in the accompanying catalogue, is swift and profound. The slightly humdrum semi-abstractions of *Love Painting* and *Shame*, both 1960, quickly give way to the altogether more promising *The Third Love Painting*, 1960, in which a lumpy torso with wisps of paint like hair springing from it is surrounded by phrases resembling bathroom graffiti, both ominous and erotic: 'my brother is only 17'; 'ring me anytime at home'; 'I am he that aches with amorous love'. Love and shame have matured quickly into a deeper articulation of the space between physical desire, danger – both legal and violent – and care. That lumpy torso is then doubled, articulated and joined with limbs the following year in *We Two Boys Together Clinging*, 1961: Hockney's tribute to Walt Whitman, Cliff Richard and his outed self.

The paintings tumble out of him: *The Cha Cha That Was Danced in the Early Hours of 24th March 1961*, 1961, in which he paints his crush, Peter Crutch, holding a handbag; *Cleaning Teeth, Early Evening (10PM) W11*, 1962, in which two giant heads with legs and Colgate tubes for cocks, one of them chained down, squirt toothpaste into each other's mouths; and the 'Demonstrations of Versatility': *A Grand Procession of Dignitaries in the Semi-Egyptian Style*, 1961; *Tea Painting in an Illusionistic Style*, 1961, *Figure in a Flat Style*, 1961; and *Flight into Italy – Swiss Landscape*, 1962, in which a Mini van with three figures races through the Alps, the words 'thats [*sic*] Switzerland that was' trailing in its wake. Works that made not just Hockney but a generation, changing the terms of conversation for British painting.

'Ten or eleven years ago,' the RCA's principal Robin Darwin wrote in the college's 1959 Annual Report,

> students were older than they are now, the sequence of their education had been interrupted by war or national service; they had known experiences and discharged responsibilities far outside the orbit of their interests, and returning to them they were primarily concerned in the rediscovery of themselves as individuals. As artists they were less self-confident, but in all other ways they were more mature. By these same tokens perhaps they were less experimental in their ideas. The student of today is less easy to teach because the chips on his shoulder, which in some instances are virtually professional epaulettes, make him less ready to learn; yet this refusal to take ideas on trust, though it may not be congenial to the tutor, may in the long run prove to be a valuable characteristic.

It's unclear whether Darwin knew exactly what he and his faculty had recruited for the 1959 student intake when he wrote this. But the likes of Bates and Hockney were unquestionably part of a new pattern in the RCA's most gifted recruits. The college had recently produced the Pop pioneers Peter Blake and Joe Tilson, and the abstractionists Robyn Denny and Richard 'Dick' Smith. All four were key figures in a new and progressive London art scene that took its inspiration from America. Smith was the first visual artist to receive a Harkness Fellowship, in 1959, which gave him two years in the States, where he made connections with the New York art scene that would help his own career as well as the eventual trajectories of some of the 1959 RCA intake.

Marco Livingstone has argued that this group – and Smith in particular – represented a significant change in British painting. 'In severing the links with landscape still so prevalent in British art,' he wrote in 1992, 'replacing such references with allusions to the built environment and the man-made world of the mass media, Smith and his colleagues laid the basis for an essentially urban avant-garde art that constituted a real break with native tradition. The one thing Smith was not prepared to sacrifice, however, was the intimacy of the personal mark.'

That so much new thinking emerged around this time at the RCA initially seems surprising, given some of the faculty teaching there. The Painting School, for example, was run by Carel Weight, a gifted painter of suburban scenes and portraits who had also served as an official war artist. Despite the seemingly conservative subject matter, Derek Boshier (one of the 1959 painting intake) remembered Weight and his work fondly: 'I was a great fan of Carel Weight's paintings,' he said in a 2013 interview, 'we all were, all the faculty and all the students admired his work I think . . .' Weight's teaching team, though, was dominated by a figurative, post-war stuffiness: landscape enthusiasts Roger de Grey and Robert Buhler, and Ruskin Spear, a painter of portraits and London pub scenes. In technical terms, they were all immensely talented. In terms of subject matter and execution, though, their work already belonged to a bygone era.

The much younger Sandra Blow, who joined the faculty in 1961, was a welcome relief: she was an important figure in contemporary British abstraction, as well as a seriously fashionable figure within the London art world. At the start of the sixties Blow's work still showed the influence of the year she'd spent in Rome in 1947–48 with her lover Alberto Burri. As Michael McNay wrote in a 2006 obituary for Blow, 'Burri remade Blow in his image.' Paintings like Blow's *Composition II*, 1960, clearly illustrate this, its black, white and muddy colour scheme, with just a hint of red, owing much to Burri's similarly hued works from the 1950s. She was, though, developing her own voice and reputation: she'd been exhibiting in London since 1951 and New York since 1957, and in 1958 she was included in the Central Pavilion exhibition at the Venice Biennale. It appears she'd made an impression on Ann Quin, too: 'Christ could I get really sloshed right now and be laid by you a dozen and a half times,' she wrote to Bates in early 1962, 'with Sandra somewhere over the edge . . .' It seems likely that the glamorous Blow, then working in the department where Quin was secretary, is the 'Sandra' she was referring to.

Hockney claimed in 1976 that '[t]he staff said that the students in that year were the worst they'd had for many, many years. They didn't like us; they thought we were a little bolshy, or something . . .' Events towards the end of their first year seemed to bear out this animosity. That collective bolshiness was apparently too much for Darwin, and, demanding the Painting School make an example, Allen Jones – who would become such an important figure in British Pop – was booted out of the RCA. 'They stuck a pin in the list,' Jones recalled in 2013, 'and it was my name that came out of that.' Jones says that it was a dreadful moment for him – because he'd done nothing to deserve such treatment, but also because it could have had a major impact on his future livelihood. Artists who graduated from the Slade, the Royal Academy or the RCA were instantly placed on a graduate pay scale for teaching jobs, which is what many had to do to make a living. Jones says it was like having his 'legs cut off'. He went and did a teaching diploma instead, but stayed closely connected to the RCA painters he'd briefly studied alongside, and to the emerging London scene they were starting to shape.

But neither Jones's expulsion nor Hockney's recollections of the faculty's antipathy towards his cohort capture the dramatic way the Darwin-era RCA had transformed post-war art education in Britain. Darwin had become the RCA's principal in 1948, and immediately set about modernising it by hiring professional artists and designers. The idea was to create a postgraduate college with strong links to industry (particularly in design), where students could specialise in narrow fields – typography, say, or silversmithing and jewellery – that prepared them for a life of work in their chosen disciplines. While this doesn't seem particularly radical now, it was a major shift from the comparatively fusty pre-war years during which the RCA had a reputation as a training ground for art teachers and not much else. Implicitly, it was an acknowledgement of a new British creative economy, in a world of mass communication and new technologies that had been supercharged by wartime innovations.

Arguably the clearest and most successful example was the school Bates entered in 1959: Graphic Design, run by Richard Guyatt. Under Guyatt's guidance, the school had leapt to the forefront of transatlantic design, and was notable for its industry-leading publication, *ARK*. Guyatt was also sufficiently attuned to his students to recognise the New Zealander Bates's singular, unusual gifts – and would become a central figure in Bates's early development.

As Hockney biographer Christopher Simon Sykes points out, Hockney and his British classmates were also among the first to benefit from the 1944 Education Act. Towards the end of the war, this new legislation transformed primary and secondary education in the UK, making higher levels of education more accessible to the working classes and requiring the provision of school meals. It raised the school leaving age to fifteen and put in place the 11-plus exam, which determined the secondary pathways children would follow. Crucially, this was a meritocratic system: in principle, smart kids who did well, no matter their economic background, ended up going to grammar schools. Hockney was one of those smart kids, earning a scholarship to Bradford Grammar – one of the oldest and best schools of its type in England – in 1948.

Bradford is an essential part of the Hockney mythology. While it's easy to emphasise the wartime grimness he grew up in (the Hockney household had narrowly missed being bombed by the Germans), it's also significant that the Hockneys valued education. Hockney grew up in a house with books, and went to the theatre (including to see the opera) and to museums – albeit the ones in and around Bradford and Leeds (he didn't visit London until he was sixteen). His parents Laura and Kenneth were bright, and both knew that schooling was the key to their children's future success. Hockney's older brother Paul had also won a scholarship to Bradford Grammar.

Even at this early stage in his biography writers run into an issue, which Chris Stephens, the curator of Hockney's 2017 Tate retrospective, describes diplomatically: 'The Hockney literature,' he writes, 'has . . . been dominated by [Hockney's] own view of his art and its development, and this has naturally served to isolate it from broader accounts.' Hockney, in other words, has cast his own shadow over how we might understand his early evolution. And this stretches all the way back to the boy entering grammar school for the first time. It unfurls to its full length in Hockney's 1976 'autobiography' – in reality, a story of his early years edited from conversations with Nikos Stangos – published when he was just thirty-nine, a book that cements the view of him as the avuncular Yorkshireman, and creates a kind of *Beano*-esque English aura around his adolescence.

The Hockney-as-cheeky-teen narrative goes something like this: David enters Bradford Grammar with a scholarship, which means he's placed in one of the top forms. To his dismay, he discovers that he's able to study art for only about ninety minutes a week. The bottom class, by contrast, gets far more time in the art rooms. So he comes up with a cunning plan to fail his way down the forms. This is much to the alarm of the school, and his parents, but it works, and he turns himself into a decidedly average academic achiever. We do, though, get flashes of the future great artist: the posters he makes for school events, some early paintings. And, most of all, caricatures: exercise books filled with daydreamy doodles and comical portraits which, combined with his status as class clown, hatred of sports days and love of slapstick-style self-deprecation, keep his classmates endlessly entertained.

There's no reason to doubt this is based in truth. But in its distillation, and its repetition by his later biographers, it's become a winking shorthand, hindsight perfectly revealing the obscenely gifted, precocious, gay (there are comical accounts of his time in the Boy Scouts) superstar he'll become in the early sixties. More complex is what happens after he leaves Bradford Grammar for Bradford School of Art in September 1953.

Hockney had actually sought permission to leave grammar school much earlier to join the junior arm of the art school. But the Director of Schools in Bradford turned him down, insisting, much to Hockney's distress, that he finish his secondary education first.

At Bradford School of Art he begins his serious training as an artist, particularly in conventional drawing techniques. This would become foundational to his place as one of the great draughtsmen of twentieth-century British art. He also became part of a close group of talented painters, including John Loker, Peter Kaye, Dave Oxtoby and, most of all, Norman Stevens, who would go to the RCA ahead of Hockney, warning his own classmate, Adrian Berg, about the talented kid who was on his way in 1959.

Hockney was taught at Bradford by Derek Stafford, a recent graduate of the RCA and still in his twenties. Stafford encouraged Hockney and his classmates to travel outside of Bradford to see as much art as they could: to Wakefield and to Leeds, and particularly to London. The group would either hitchhike or get cheap day-return tickets and stretch that day as far as they could, leaving just after midnight and coming back on the last train before the clock ticked over twenty-four hours later. It was on these trips that Hockney first encountered London's gallery scene, and the Tate Gallery, and, perhaps most importantly in terms of his future development, the National Gallery.

Hockney's performative self-awareness found an early manifestation in Bradford. For a time, he modelled himself on Stanley Spencer, at that moment the archetypally eccentric English artist. According to biographer Peter Webb, Hockney 'imitated the painter by walking about wearing a bowler hat and long woolly scarf, in a heavy black overcoat with drooping shoulders, carrying an old umbrella and pushing a pram containing his painting materials'. It was a look topped off by Hockney's signature National Health Service spectacles. Though it may have been a passing phase, it's evidence of a very young artist already thinking not just about his work but about how to manifest his presence as an artist in public.

Hockney took his exams for the National Diploma in Design in the summer of 1957 and, unsurprisingly, smashed them, receiving a first-class diploma with honours. At the encouragement of Stafford, he had applied to the RCA and Slade postgraduate programmes. He travelled to London to take the entrance exams, and met Derek Boshier there. Both young men were accepted to the RCA. The Slade had given Hockney the nod, too. Stafford encouraged him to choose the RCA.

But before he could take up his place, he had the small matter of his National Service to complete. Like his father, Hockney registered as a conscientious objector, and completed most of his service working in hospitals, delaying his entry to the RCA until the 1959/60 academic year.

There are strong parallels between Hockney's backstory and that of the young man who would, at the end of 1962, disappear forever and be replaced by Billy Apple: Barrie Bates.

Bates was a year and a half older than Hockney, born in Auckland on 31 December 1935. Bates's parents also had middle-class ambitions for their kids. In fact, his mother Marija, who had aspired to be a ballerina, was already middle class, but married Bates's more working-class father Albert, a telephone mechanician who worked for the post and telegraph service. Like Hockney's father Kenneth, Albert was also a hobbyist artist: a part-time watercolourist who recognised his boy had some talent and encouraged him to attend Saturday morning art classes. There are parallels between their mothers, too: where Laura Hockney was a religious, teetotalling vegetarian, Marija was meticulous to the point of neurosis, insisting on the utmost cleanliness in herself and her children. Both families were large: Bates was one of four siblings, Hockney was one of five.

For Hockney, grammar school offered a way up and out of his blue-collar surrounds. In Auckland, Mount Albert Grammar, which Bates attended, was more egalitarian but offered similar opportunities. The two boys' experiences at secondary school were, however, very different. Hockney was clearly an over-achiever who, as he tells it, began to wilfully under-achieve so he could spend more time in the art room. He was also popular with his schoolmates. Bates, by contrast, hated school, and as Apple tells it, was bullied so much that he convinced the school's principal he should be allowed to arrive late and leave early. Even with this accommodation, he didn't see things through, leaving the school after three years, at age fifteen, without a qualification.

For many young New Zealand men of his era, leaving school young wasn't the end of the world. In the early fifties, New Zealand was a wealthy country that had modelled itself as a kind of classless utopia: still unmistakably tied to Britain, but without all the pesky societal stratification. Bates lived with his grandparents for a while, helping them around their property, then got a job in 1953 as a lab assistant in a paint factory. Soon after, he got his first break in Auckland's advertising industry, as a messenger. And in 1956 he was taken on as a trainee graphic designer for the department store chain, the Farmers Trading Company. While there he redesigned the company's logo, which Farmers kept for three decades – a strange ghost of Bates himself, well and truly outlasting the man who disappeared in 1962.

Bates took evening art classes at Auckland City Art Gallery and Elam School of Fine Arts. This gave him a dual life, bouncing between the advertising and art worlds, which he would carry with him to the RCA, and which would continue, after he became Apple, until 1990 when he finally returned to New Zealand. This is also where the parallels with Hockney pick up again, because, as with Derek Stafford, it was an RCA graduate who first gave Bates the desire to study at the London institution. The RCA-trained artist Robert Ellis joined the teaching staff at Elam in 1957. Prior to that, he'd taught at Yeovil School of Art, where one of his students had been a young painter called Derek Boshier.

In 1958, Ellis encouraged Bates to put together a portfolio for submission to the RCA, despite the fact he had no formal qualifications. This wasn't a particularly unusual pathway for talented New Zealand artists: William 'Bill' Culbert was nearing the end of his own time at the RCA just as Bates was applying. The New Zealand government supported these students with travelling scholarships of £500 per year – a pretty generous sum compared to what the likes of Hockney and Boshier, as domestic students, received. Bates applied for the scholarship but was turned down. It wasn't until the RCA – and in particular Richard Guyatt – saw the portfolio and was so impressed by it that Bates got the money, albeit a lesser amount of £400.

This augured well for the twenty-three-year-old Aucklander: he had the recommendation of a gifted RCA graduate in Robert Ellis; he had a direct contact with Boshier and his family; and, perhaps most significantly, his work had already made an impact on Guyatt, who would become so important to his early trajectory as an artist and designer, both as a defender and mentor.

Although there's no question Auckland was almost as far away from London as one could get, it wasn't, in the 1950s, a complete backwater. In terms of modern art, the city had experienced a major overhaul through both the influx of British staff to Elam – not just Ellis, but others like Michael Nicholson – and the Auckland City Art Gallery's engagement with, and collection of, European and British modernism under the leadership of Peter Tomory, who took up the directorship in 1956. Local painters were also beginning to make their presence felt as genuine modernists – most notably Colin McCahon, who would become the giant of New Zealand art over the next three decades until his death in 1987.

There were coffee bars, a growing sexual freedom, jazz records and fashion, and international influence in art and design. As Christina Barton notes, Bates himself had already started to receive recognition, having had some of his design work published internationally, in the 1958–59 edition of *Modern Publicity*, while the Dutch émigré Kees Hos wrote a favourable article about him in the influential New Zealand magazine *Home and Building* in July 1959. Bates, then, was no hick. He was, though, an extremely complicated young man: gifted, but with no qualifications to his name and a history of being bullied at school. He set off for London with a well-established chip on his shoulder, massive ambitions and serious points to prove. The colonial wasn't going to let his colonial baggage hold him, or drag him, back.

Bates travelled to Australia in July 1959, and took an ocean liner from there to England, arriving in early September. The Boshiers picked him up and took him back to the pub they ran in Basingstoke. He and Boshier then headed up to London, and moved into a flat at 83 Warwick Road, ready for the start of their first term at the RCA – where Boshier would once again encounter the young man from Bradford he'd first met when they were both interviewed back in 1957, and whom Bates would meet for the first time.

An important cast of characters was beginning to assemble at the RCA that autumn: Bates, Hockney, Boshier, Allen Jones, Peter Phillips, R. B. Kitaj, Frank Bowling and Peter Crutch. At the college already were Hockney's Bradford colleague Norman Stevens, Adrian Berg, Pauline Boty and Ridley Scott (Scott was a year ahead of Bates in Graphic Design, and the pair struck up a friendship). And among the support staff there was Ann Quin, who started that October as Carel Weight's secretary.

Quin was until recently a relatively obscure figure in 1960s British culture. But the 2018 publication of *The Unmapped Country: Stories & Fragments*, edited by Jennifer Hodgson, has led to a resurgence of British interest in Quin, and via her estate new details have emerged about her.

Much of what is known about Quin's early life comes from a brief autobiography published in *London Magazine* in July 1966. 'Bound by perverse securities in a Convent, RC Brighton for eight years,' she wrote:

> Taking that long to get over. The Holy Ghost. The Trinity. The Reverend Mother. I was not a Catholic. I was sent to a convent to be brought up 'a lady'. To say gate and not giate – the Sussex accent I had picked up from the village school in my belly-rubbing days had to be eliminated by How Now Brown Cow, if I wanted to make my way in the world. According to Mother.

Her mother, Anne Reid, was wrong. Quin, from the time she moved to London from Brighton as a young woman in the 1950s to her death in 1973, would make her way in the world as one of the most talented writers of her generation. That way, though, was ferociously difficult: only a small group of readers, writers, critics and editors truly understood her significance in her own lifetime, and her battles with mental illness were debilitating. Still, her mother was right about one thing: a recording of Quin from the late sixties illustrates that the How Now Brown Cow worked – her deeper-than-average voice has none of the Sussex inflection the nuns were so keen to drill out of her.

As is the case with other talented women of her generation who died young (Pauline Boty, for instance, who died aged twenty-eight in 1966), Quin has, for a long time, largely been known as a footnote in other people's stories – including those of two writers with whom she had brief affairs, the American poet Robert Creeley and the British novelist Henry Williamson – or as a kind of curiosity in the history of experimental British fiction. Quin published four novels and wrote a cluster of short stories and fragments, and some of her letters have ended up in other people's archives: among them, those of her publisher Marion Boyars; the Carmelite friar Brocard Sewell, who was part of the 1960s British literary scene; and Apple, a natural hoarder who still has pieces of writing Quin sent to Bates, and wrote as Bates, while they were together in 1961/62. Her employment records at the RCA largely square with her *London Magazine* account, as well as providing specific details about her life and livelihood around the time she wrote *Berg*.

Born 17 March 1936, Quin was raised by her mother Anne, whose married name was Ward (which is how she's listed on Quin's birth certificate) but who for all of Quin's life was known by her maiden name, Anne Reid. Reid had married young to a much older man, Philip Henry Ward. Ward was a captain in the merchant navy, working on boats between Mumbai and Port Said on the Suez Canal. The couple had a son, John Edward, in 1928. Around 1934, Ward retired and moved his young family back to the UK, to Brighton. Soon after their arrival, Reid left Ward and their son John. A year or so later, her daughter Ann Quin was born – the father listed on her birth certificate as Montague Nicholas Quin, an optician. There is no record of Reid ever divorcing Ward.

Quin and her mother lived in Ovingdean, a small village near Brighton (Ward and his son John had moved to Paington, Devon). As she wrote in *London Magazine*, Quin received a Catholic education at the Convent of the Blessed Sacrament, but had little time for her regular homework, preferring to immerse herself in books from the public library: Greek and Elizabethan dramatists, Dostoevsky, Woolf, Chekhov, Hardy and Lawrence (Lawrence's legacy would eventually come to play a particularly important role in her own work and trajectory).

Quin described herself as a teenager preoccupied with sex and physicality: wondering whether the nuns stripped completely to bathe, and being 'excited in getting into the Sixth Form, not only because the classroom windows overlooked the boys' college, but on the whole sinful world lay before me at the end of the year'. She also wrote that '[a]t fourteen I met my half-brother for the first time and fell desperately in love with him; he died five years later and I saw myself as Antigone. At eighteen I went up to London to spend Saturdays with my father . . . and pretended he was my lover.' The half-brother was John Ward. By the time the siblings first met around 1950, Ward was in his early twenties. He married in 1952, and had his own son, Jeremy, in 1953. John then died of polio in 1955. But with the two branches of the family reconnected, Jeremy maintained relationships with his aunt, Quin, and his grandmother, Reid, until both women died within months of each other in 1973. Jeremy describes Quin as having a complex, love-hate relationship with her mother, whom she referred to as 'Mother Courage'. He also says that his grandmother was fiery and could be a 'terrific snob', and would be 'spinning in her grave' at the suggestion, which has been made by several commentators, that Quin was working class.

The young Quin became fixated with the theatre, in which she was able 'to witness a fantasy world that relieved my many desires, frustrations'. She set her sights on becoming an actor. She got her first job as an assistant stage manager with a repertoire company, but left after a row with her boss – over a hem she'd sewn crooked. Soon after, she auditioned for the Royal Academy of Dramatic Art (RADA) – and this is where we get the first inkling of the crippling anxiety that formed part of her illness. 'I expected a stage,' she wrote, 'even a platform, instead a smallish room, brightly lit; ten or twelve people faced me. I began, froze, asked to start again, but was struck dumb, and rushed out, silently screaming, down Gower Street.'

In Brighton, Quin enrolled at Box's Commercial College, where she gained a certificate in shorthand and typing. This was pure expedience, a way to pay the bills and maintain her independence while she set her attention on the serious business of becoming a published writer. During a brief stint in a newspaper office in London, she got appendicitis, went home to Brighton and fell in love with a painter, whom she doesn't name. She took a job in a solicitor's office, which was incredibly dreary, '[b]ut the world of love awaited me every evening, I lived for that, would have gladly died for it. The job, the love, lasted two years.'

After both ended, she moved back to London, first working for a solicitor's office in 1956 and the first part of 1957, then in the foreign rights department of the publisher Hutchinson & Co. She found a flat in Soho and began to write a novel called *A Slice of the Moon*, 'about a homosexual, though at the time I had never met one, knew very little about queers (maybe I had read something in Proust?)'. She was barely able to cover food and rent. Still, she wrote, this was '[a] time when I worked the hardest at writing, more disciplined than I have ever done since.'

Quin worked on the novel for eighteen months, moved home to her mother's in Brighton to finish it, then sent it off to publishers, who duly rejected it. It was around this time that she first met Paddy Kitchen, another aspiring writer, who was working in an administrative role at the RCA. In her recollections of Quin published in 1979 (also in *London Magazine*), Kitchen says that they met through Joy Rendle, who was 'the mother of a friend' and was working with Quin at St Dunstan's in Ovingdean – a convalescent centre for blind or visually impaired veterans. Rendle had thought it would be interesting to introduce the two young writers. The 'friend' was Timothy Rendle, an architect working for the firm Casson Conder in London. Kitchen's first role at the RCA had been as a secretary to Hugh Casson, who, as well as running his private practice, was at the helm of the college's Interior Design School. (She later moved to Robin Darwin's office and became the college's assistant registrar.) Kitchen read the manuscript of *A Slice of the Moon*. 'The four characters intertwined in complex relationships which I did not understand, and therefore barely believed in,' she wrote. 'I was not used to the stamping ground of the psyche, where Ann was intuitively at home.' After *A Slice of the Moon* was rejected, Quin began another book called *Oscar*, which she described as 'a novel that developed into telephone directory length of very weird content, without dialogue'. Kitchen described it as 'an extraordinary gothic edifice, in which the weird and macabre were given an uncanny reality in an almost-London landscape'.

In September 1958, Quin wrote to Kitchen about getting work in London because she was leaving her job at St Dunstan's. She also described her frustrations as a young woman writer. 'Honestly don't the other sex have the best of both worlds', she wrote:

> They can quite happily go on with their creating yet have a wife, mistress, children etc. without it upsetting them too much, besides doesn't he get all the attention and comforts from the woman, ah it was a sad day when the seed entered the wrong ovum and I was conceived a girl, sure now I would have made a wonderful man besides people take more notice of a male writer no matter what blarney he gushes forth . . .

By the end of October, Quin had arranged a childcare job in Paris, with the hope that she would eventually get a job at NATO, where the money was good. This didn't work out, and she returned to the UK. She moved back to London and got a three-day-a-week job, and was living on a pittance. ('I fell in love with poverty-stricken painters who needed feeding as much as I did,' she wrote of this time, 'so that never lasted long.') But by May 1959 she couldn't face a summer working in a law firm's basement, and took a hotel job as a resident waitress in Mevagissey, Cornwall, instead.

There, Quin had a more severe episode than the RADA panic attack. She escaped the hotel in the early morning and,

> reached home speechless, dizzy, unable to bear the slightest noise. I lay in bed for days, weeks, unable to face the sun. If I went out into the garden I dug holes and lay in them weeping. I woke up in the middle of the night screaming, convinced my tears were rivers of blood, that my insides were being eaten away by an earwig that had crawled into my ear. I went to see a psychiatrist, going more from curiosity, and spent a few hours entertaining the horrified lady. I decided to climb back out of madness, the loneliness of going over the edge was worse than the absurdity of coping with day to day living.

Afterwards, Quin went to Paris for a month, then returned to London and 'found a part-time job as secretary in the painting department of an art college'. This was, of course, at the RCA, where her great friend

Paddy Kitchen already worked. Quin began her employment as Carel Weight's secretary in the Painting School on 9 October 1959 – the start of the 1959/60 academic year in which Hockney, Boshier, Phillips, Bowling, Kitaj and Jones were among the intake. Just ahead of them was a thirty-year-old painter, whose surname would eventually become essential to Quin: Adrian Berg. She worked part-time, from 9.30 a.m. until 1 p.m. daily, leaving the afternoons and evenings free to write.

Quin's initial address in her RCA file was 62 Redcliffe Road, not far from the art school, from where she 'was turned out because my typing late at night disturbed the landlady'. She was still working on *Oscar*, which she eventually sent out to publishers. Again, it was rejected. But an encouraging letter was enough for her to start a third. That book would become *Berg*, which Quin finished before she left the art school in December 1962, having written three or four versions of it. Calder, which in 1963 would become Calder & Boyars – publishers of experimental and highly risky fiction, including the works of Samuel Beckett, Alain Robbe-Grillet, Marguerite Duras, William Burroughs, Hubert Selby Jr and Nathalie Sarraute – accepted it. The first person to read it there was a young editor called Dulan Barber (Barber was also a writer, who later published under his own name, as well as under the pseudonym Owen Brookes for his horror fiction; he married Kitchen later in the 1960s). Barber loved Quin's manuscript, and *Berg* was scheduled for publication in 1964.

The RCA was a three-year graduate diploma, and many of the staff, like Quin and Kitchen, were the same age as most of the students: young people in their twenties. So they were bound to become entangled. Bates, when he got involved with Quin in 1961, was twenty-five – only a few months older than her. And in 1960 one of Bates's classmates, the painter Frank Bowling, began a relationship with Kitchen.

Like Quin, Bowling has had a recent and much-deserved rediscovery. In 2017, Munich's Haus der Kunst staged a major exhibition of his work, and in the summer of 2019 Tate gave him the full survey treatment in London. This late-arriving recognition has also begun the work of re-inserting him into the histories of the Hockney-era RCA, where he was clearly one of the college's most gifted painters. In fact, he won the silver medal for Painting in 1962 as Hockney won the RCA's overall gold.

Bowling was born in February 1934 in Bartica, British Guiana. He grew up in New Amsterdam and arrived in London, aged nineteen, in 1953, first living with an uncle and intending to study English literature, before being told at the Labour Exchange that he'd have to perform his military service if he wanted to work in Britain. Bowling enlisted in the RAF that autumn, hoping he'd get an education alongside his service. He didn't, and, clashing with his superiors regularly, was eventually given a dishonourable discharge in 1956. In the meantime he'd met Keith Critchlow, an artist who left the air force to study painting at the RCA. Bowling became close with the Critchlow family – Keith's mother Rosalind was a journalist, his father Jerry a painter – and this, as well as hanging out in fashionable pubs like Finch's on Fulham Road, would have helped him become a presence in London's literary and art scenes.

To pay the bills, Bowling began life-modelling, including for Jerry Critchlow and, eventually, at the RCA. This was when the prospect of being an artist finally trumped his desire to be a writer. He took a place at the Chelsea School of Art in 1958, then applied to the RCA. His portfolio got through a first round of assessment but failed a second, so Carel Weight stepped in, helping his former life model get a place at the City & Guilds of London Art School, where Bowling quickly developed his technical knowledge of drawing and painting. It was enough to earn him the place he'd wanted from the start, at the RCA, which is how he entered as part of the same intake as Hockney and Bates.

Bowling got on well with both men, perhaps because he was also an outsider: a migrant to London who'd had to work doubly hard to earn his spot. With Bates, there was also a strong Commonwealth connection. Apple remembers that Bowling was rarely at the art school itself, preferring to work in his own studio in Cedars Road, Clapham, but that he was a striking physical presence – not because he was black, but because he was a big, solid guy, who seemed to translate that physicality into the surface of his figurative paintings which, at that time, often dealt with explicitly sexual, inter-racial themes. Apple also recalls that Bowling would often have pieces of animal carcass in his studio which made their way as subject matter into his paintings. In an interview from around 2007, Derek Boshier remembered the same thing – a tin bath, under Bowling's work table, with blood in it, and animal heads.

This interest in viscera was undoubtedly connected to the influence of Bowling's friend and mentor, Francis Bacon (though the two men later fell out). Many of Bowling's works from this period have been lost or destroyed, but surviving paintings and documentation show just how significant Bacon's impact on the young painter was. Bowling, at the time, did something quite rare: translating the existential and painterly tortures of Bacon's best work into social comment, as well as a complex exploration of his own subjectivity and sexuality as a black man in Britain. The first strand is exemplified by *Beggar In the Window*, 1962, in which a Bacon-esque screaming figure is seen through a window frame (akin to the box-like structures Bacon often placed his screaming figures within). The theme of poverty had roots in Bowling's Guyanese background: as a child, his mother would regularly feed and bathe beggars, and make Bowling help. Bacon's influence is even more obvious in Bowling's triptych *A Mirror, Three Windows, a Door*, 1962, with its twisting figures, darkly sexual themes and visceral portrayal of childbirth.

Bowling was one of the 'Windrush' generation – those West Indians who began a mass migration to Britain from the Caribbean in 1948. Initially, numbers were small; in the year Bowling arrived, 1953, he was one of only about two thousand. But by the mid-1950s, around forty thousand non-white Commonwealth migrants were arriving in Britain each year. And that began to have a substantial effect on attitudes about race, class and 'Britishness', raising tensions between whites and blacks in the UK's cities.

For many white 'Teddy Boys', the central issue was black men dating white women: a classic miscegenation fear that had also plagued the American South since the days of slavery. Riots eventually came in late summer 1958: first with clashes between whites and blacks in Nottingham; second, and more seriously, with the Notting Hill riots in West London (not far from the RCA), in which armed white gangs roamed through the suburb, smashing windows, throwing petrol bombs into houses, and randomly attacking black men and the white women thought to be dating them. This was a test of Britain's openness, of its commitment to reciprocity towards the citizens of its former Empire. The political parallels with the present Brexit moment are eerie: an unjustified fear of the other, a sense that they 'were coming here and stealing our jobs', taking and sexually corrupting white British women, putting pressure on housing, and bringing with them thoroughly un-British attitudes from their home countries.

Bowling and Kitchen fell in love and decided to marry. This, in the opinion of the RCA's administration, was unacceptable, and so Bowling was expelled in 1960. The reason given was that staff–student relationships were inappropriate, though it doesn't seem unreasonable to suggest there was an underlying racial charge too, especially given the close memories of Nottingham and Notting Hill. According to Martin Gayford, Bowling had befriended Francis Bacon by this time, and the senior artist consoled the younger man by telling him that Darwin was the worst painter who had ever lived.

It's also interesting that it was Bowling, the student, who took the initial fall for their relationship, rather than Kitchen the staff member. Once again, Weight intervened on Bowling's behalf, securing a place for him at the Slade School instead. The issue was eventually resolved by Kitchen's own resignation. She headed to Chelsea College of Art, which gave the RCA an elegant excuse to re-admit Bowling – clearly one of the most talented young painters in London – in January 1961.

The bold sexuality of Bowling's work from this period seems to draw on many of these personal experiences, portrayed in a Bacon-esque register, with plenty of Goya thrown in the mix. From 1960 to 1962, Bowling worked on a series called 'Birthday', inspired by seeing a neighbour giving birth. In one of these paintings, *Birthday*, 1962, a prone woman, viewed through an open window frame, lies on a bed, reclining with her arms behind her head like Goya's *Nude Maja*. *Afternoon Nap I* and *II*, also 1962, continue the Goya reference: another reclining woman, this time on one half of a sofa, the other half taken up by her lover – a twisted figure lifted straight from Goya's *Saturn Devouring His Son*. The same woman appears to be the model for Bowling's much grimmer painting *The Abortion*, 1962, in which a couple – the white woman, with her black lover – are in bed together. Above them floats another woman and, next to her, a baby – and the painting's titular subject – still bleeding from its umbilical cord.

It seems fair to assume that the black man in the work is essentially a self-portrait, particularly given that Bowling, in 1962, also made a life-size portrait of himself as Othello: Shakespeare's 'Moor', driven mad by suspicions about his white wife's fidelity. Chris Stephens has written of the *Afternoon Nap* paintings that: 'Bowling was waiting for the birth of his first child and had been terrified by the scandal that erupted around the drug thalidomide that caused babies to be born with severely malformed limbs. Also resonating through this horrific reference might have been thoughts of the widespread hostility to mixed-race marriages . . . and the belief that such relationships could produce monstrous children.'

Bowling and Kitchen's son Dan was born on 20 January 1962. That same year, Bowling's second son Benjamin was born to another woman,

Claire Spencer. Kitchen's second novel, published in 1970 after she and Bowling had divorced, and pointedly titled *A Fleshly School*, draws on the romantic complexities of that time. One of its storylines is a relationship between a student, Elinor, and David, the art school's assistant registrar. The novel is dedicated to two people. One of them is Ann Quin.

Implicit in Robin Darwin's statement about 'the student of today' is that they were part of Harold Macmillan's 'Never Had It So Good' generation. The age of austerity in Britain after World War II had been long and brutal. Rationing of many goods continued into the early 1950s. But the idea of making individual sacrifices for the greater collective good also resulted in some of the great economic and cultural reforms of the country's modern history. The 1944 Education Act was one. The National Health Service and National Insurance were two more. So too was the massive reconstruction of a Blitzed Britain, particularly in and around London. The New Towns Act 1946 led to the creation of places like Stevenage, Basildon and Harlow, built and connected with good rail to the city so middle-class workers could get in and out easily. In the cities, meanwhile, whole neighbourhoods were rebuilt as social housing, resulting in the kinds of tower blocks and housing estates that have come to define so much of Britain's local authority architecture.

By the late 1950s, these changes were beginning to thoroughly embed themselves in the British psyche. Unemployment was at historic lows, Britain was embracing the consumerist tidal wave, and the economy was bumping along nicely but for the threat of rising inflation. Macmillan's Conservatives won re-election comfortably on 8 October 1959 – the day before Quin officially started work at the RCA. For the group entering the college that year, all of them too young to have served in the war, this was the new reality: an optimism that created a framework for a new individualism rather than a culture of collective sacrifice. Hockney, for instance, had found it much easier to be a conscientious objector than his father Kenneth had during the war itself; Bowling's dishonourable discharge hadn't scuppered his artistic aspirations; Quin was able to live as a single, working woman in London.

This individualism was based on the granting and protection of adult freedoms. And one of the most important of these freedoms was the right to one's sexuality.

In August 1954, the British government set up a committee, with the oversight of Sir John Wolfenden, to look at the question of whether the country's archaic laws against gay sex should be reformed. Until Wolfenden, any sexual act between men, even if consensual and in private, was illegal. The resulting report, published almost exactly three years later, represented a significant moment for the gay rights movement – even if it would take another decade for the British Parliament to finally change the law.

In the 1950s, one of the main arguments for keeping the existing law was that gay sex, even in private, posed a threat to the overall moral health of society. Another was the commonly held misbelief that homosexuality and paedophilia went hand in hand, as twin urges. And a third was that homosexuality was a 'disease' or 'illness' that should be dealt with through medical intervention. Perhaps the most notorious example of this, and one of a handful of high-profile cases that led to the establishment of Wolfenden's committee, was the conviction of the mathematician and computer scientist Alan Turing, and his subsequent chemical castration in 1952.

The Wolfenden Report rebutted all of these arguments. It found that rather than being an 'all or none' condition, homosexuality existed on a spectrum, from people who were exclusively gay to those who had latent tendencies even they weren't aware of. The report also stated that going through a homosexual phase was a perfectly normal part of adolescent development, rather than an aberration that should be suppressed or treated. Its authors drew on Alfred Kinsey's 1948 *Sexual Behavior in the Human Male* to support both points. The report declared that there was absolutely no evidence that homosexuality was a disease, mental or physical (refuting, too, the myth it was caused by abscesses on the brain). It also debunked the destructive belief that being gay stemmed from the trauma of being 'seduced' in youth, a key aspect of the idea that homosexuality and paedophilia were synonymous.

Wolfenden's final recommendations hinged on two factors: consent and the right to privacy. Having thrown out the idea that all homosexuals were paedophiles, the report argued that sexual contact between adults and youths, whether homosexual or heterosexual, should be dealt with the same way: as a crime. Public sex – again, one of the pervading popular characterisations of homosexuals, lurking in public bathrooms, waiting for prey – should similarly be dealt with as a crime. But the precise nature of the sexual contact, whether gay or straight, was irrelevant.

With these caveats in place, the report recommended that 'homosexual behaviour between consenting adults in private should no longer be a criminal offence'. This was based on a central principle, which would also become essential to the artistic censorship debates and trials that followed: that individual morality and criminality were different things. 'There remains one additional counter-argument which we believe to be decisive,' the committee wrote,

> namely, the importance which society and the law ought to give to individual freedom of choice and action in matters of private morality. Unless a deliberate attempt is to be made by society, acting through the agency of the law, to equate the sphere of crime with that of sin, there must remain a realm of private morality and immorality which is, in brief and crude terms, not the law's business.

On 29 June 1960, the Labour MP Kenneth Robinson brought a motion in the House of Commons to accept Wolfenden's recommendations and decriminalise private homosexual acts between consenting adults. 'It is a subject which touches deep and perhaps primitive instincts and which rouses strong emotions,' Robinson said in Parliament, 'but it is also a topic of some importance not only to the minority who are directly affected by the law but also to the rest of the community.' He also made an impassioned case for the fact that homosexuality is a normal part of any society:

> The majority of homosexuals are useful citizens who go about quite unrecognised and unsuspected by most of us.
>
> Homosexuality has existed in all societies from the primitive to the sophisticated and at all periods of history regardless of laws and of the rules of society. It has been condemned, condoned and even encouraged at different times and in different cultures.

Despite his argument, Robinson's motion was resoundingly thumped, 213 to 99. It wouldn't be until 1967 that the law would finally change.

By the autumn of 1959, then, it was clear that the 'Never Had It So Good' generation were beginning to live through, and accelerate, a series of profound and lasting changes in British life. The contradiction at the heart of these changes is that the collective sacrifices of the austerity years had laid the groundwork for the radical, and rapid, emergence of individual rights and a new sense of individualism: the right to a quality education no matter your background; the right to practise your sexuality freely; the right to love whomever you choose, no matter their skin colour; the right to a private morality, even when it ran counter to the dominant culture's agreed codes.

At a community level, these shifts can be seen as liberations: as progressive moves that improved the lives of entire groups of people. But they were also forms of 'libertarianism'. This was particularly the case with Kinsey's ideas about the role of sex in shaping society – that individuals being free to pursue their sexuality would lead to a healthier collective community. This emphasis on individual happiness wasn't dissimilar to a growing capitalist logic in the post-austerity era that placed the individual at the heart of a new economic system. Provided the individual was doing no harm to anyone else, the argument went, they should be left free from government interventions in their decisions. The separation of morality from criminality, as proposed in the Wolfenden Report, was another revolutionary expression of this new spirit of personal liberty.

Between 1959 and 1961, this new libertarianism, both creative and sexual, would be put to the test in the courts, and in the studios of the RCA. And, for Bates and Hockney in particular, it would become transformational: not just a way to finally be who they were, but to be who they wanted to be.

'Made a lamentable start + very much a "mixed up kid". However eventually settled down and produced some excellent work – v. contemporary + chic. Incoherent but his eye right on the ball.'

This was Richard Guyatt's assessment of Bates at the end of his first year at the RCA. Bates's personal discombobulation had extended to his initial living arrangements: he didn't live at the Warwick Road flat with Derek Boshier for long. Apple says the comings and goings were more than he could cope with; Hockney biographer Peter Webb writes that the flat was a popular late-night hangout for RCA students once the local pubs and cafés had closed. Bates moved to a small flat by himself, around the corner in Warwick Gardens. While there, he reconnected with the Australian Phillip Russell, who he had first befriended on the ship that had brought them both to the UK. Russell had a job as a London pharmaceuticals rep, and the pair decided to get a flat together.

This was at 35A Cornwall Gardens, in South Kensington. They were eventually joined there by an Australian journalist called Peter Bell-Smith.

One of the perks of Russell's job that Bates and his art school pals were happy to exploit was that he had a company car (Apple remembers a party at the flat during which two guests tumbled out of the house fighting, and left a dent in the car's hood). It was also at this flat that, Apple recalls, Bates had a relationship with the improbably named Joy Knightley, who lived a few doors down. A few doors up from Bates was an Egyptian journalist whom Knightley was also involved with. Apple says the arrangement suited everybody just fine, and ended only when he headed to New York with Hockney in July 1961.

Bates quickly built a reputation at the RCA, largely because he'd become heavily involved in creating the visual language of the college's daily student life, including making posters for the RCA's jazz and film societies. Bates was a nut for both art forms, and the posters gave him the chance to develop singular responses to their visual potentials.

In this regard, Bates had as much to live up to as Hockney and the other painters did in the department that had produced Robyn Denny, Richard Smith, Joe Tilson and Peter Blake in recent years. Guyatt had built one of the most sophisticated graphic design programmes in the world, and this was underpinned by *ARK*: notionally a student magazine but one, as art historian Thomas Crow points out, that broke down barriers between fine art, commercial design and critical writing as early as the mid-fifties, and seemed to presage many of the kinds of printing techniques and tricks later ascribed to Andy Warhol and American Pop. This was particularly the case in a spread by David Collins and Richard Smith to accompany Smith's essay 'Man and He-Man' from 1957, in which the actor Glenn Ford is shown reaching for a gun in his holster, printed so that three identical images of him overlap in a kind of triple-vision, which beats Warhol's iconic Elvis to the draw by five years.

In 1995, Alex Seago published an in-depth analysis of *ARK*'s impact on mid-century British culture, from its inception in 1950 through to its peak circulation of around three thousand copies in 1963. This, he argues, was a period of huge transformation, particularly in the way young artists thought about images and their social and cultural function in an emerging era of mass communication. 'If the rise of image consciousness was one of the most obvious symptoms of the revolution in English culture during the 1950s and 1960s,' Seago writes, 'then the School of Graphic Design at the Royal College of Art bore a good deal of responsibility for that cultural transformation.'

ARK was at the heart of this, almost always edited by an RCA painting student, but art-directed and laid out by students from Graphic Design. This collaborative spirit was partly a consequence of proximity: the Graphic Design and Painting schools shared their location, in the Victoria & Albert Museum. But, from the mid-fifties on, it was also a consequence of sympathy, at least when it came to some of the RCA's most ambitious students. Strong connections began to emerge between students in the two schools, especially those with an interest in American visual culture. Seago points out that credit for this belonged not just with the students but with Darwin and Guyatt too. The new professionalism that they promoted, and their desire to elevate the perception of 'commercial arts' to a status similar to that of painting, created some of the most important cross-fertilisations of the period – including the connections between Hockney and Bates.

Bates, always a believer in his own abilities, was unintimidated, and threw himself into poster-making and advertising ideas in Guyatt's school. It was doubtless this work that Guyatt referred to as contemporary and chic. But that same year Bates was also beginning to develop a conceptually driven approach to his art practice. The turning point may well have been a trip he took to Spain in the April break of 1960, just before the last term of the year. In Alicante, he used photography to make what was arguably his first conceptual art work (and an early one in the history of conceptual art as a whole). The two images that survive from that work are now known as *Art Declared Found Activity (Lathering, Alicante Spain, April 1960)* and *Art Declared Found Activity (Shaving, Alicante Spain, April 1960)*, both 1960. In them we see a man being shaved.

In the first, he leans back in the barber's chair with eyes closed, a cloth protecting his front. A hand reaches in from the right edge of the frame, brushing shaving cream onto his chin. He's almost completely lathered; the white of the cream is a void in the centre of the picture, his bottom lip the only surface breaking through. The second image is much darker: two hands this time enter the frame from the left; the man's face is turned as one hand stretches the skin of his cheek taut while the other scrapes him with a cut-throat razor.

It's a banal, daily act. But via careful lighting, staging and framing, it's elevated into an artistic one. On one level, Bates's work is a knowing wink to the processes of painting: applying paint, scraping back, starting again. But just as crucial – especially for the image/text trajectory that would come to define so much of Bates's, then Apple's work – is the way he titled the images with the simple facts of the action, the location and the date. In contrast to his classmates over in Painting, Bates was claiming a stake in an alternative history of modern art: not the story of Picasso and Pollock and Bacon, but the legacy of Marcel Duchamp, the readymade, and Dada. Bates wasn't framing a found object as an art work as Duchamp had, but rather framing a found activity: what made it art was his declaration that it was so. The young artist couldn't have known it, but with these seemingly straightforward photos he'd laid down two guiding ideas that would shape his practice for the next fifty years: on the one hand, that the daily and the banal had validity as art material; and, on the other, that his art work's significance – or, perhaps, its art-ness – emerges in a complex interaction between word and image.

At the Cornwall Gardens flat, Bates took huge leaps forward as an artist. Early experiments extended the Spanish work, making full use of his flatmates and friends as subjects. In *Drunk (Earls Court Road, London, Winter 1960)*, 1960, he presents images in a grid, of Bell-Smith and another friend, Ahmad Jarr, wasted in the street together; a black man in a white jacket and a white man in a dark jacket going through all the emotions of drunkenness – confusion, disagreement, laughter, embrace.

In *Body Cleaning: Bathing and Shampooing (35A Cornwall Gardens, London, Winter 1960)*, 1960, there are twelve shots on a sheet, arranged in rows of four. In them Bell-Smith is doing exactly as the title suggests: soaping his hair with shampoo, looking at himself in a mirror as he brushes his teeth, lathering his face for a shave. In the penultimate image, the camera looks into the mirror at Bell-Smith's lathered face, the bath's taps doubled from two to four – the real ones and their reflections. In the final square, Bell-Smith hams up the fact that he's got shampoo in his eyes, squinting and sticking out his tongue.

The sequences of both works are more like sets of movie stills than photographs for an exhibition. *Body Cleaning* is also accompanied by a script, of sorts – a collaborative text between Bell-Smith and Bates, in the form of a dialogue:

> Hes a marvellous bloody writer . . . Trueman Capote
>
> Why?
>
> Jeez, you know he's just great, no detail, no full stops no nothing he just writes what he feels.
>
> Oh.
>
> Doesn't that impress you. Wouldn't you like to be able to do that.
>
> I can.
>
> Huh?
>
> I said I can.
>
> How, when where. What?
>
> Look around boy, look around.
>
> I am looking man.
>
> Look over there.
>
> What, that sign post-STOP, LOOK and LISTEN.
>
> Yeh! Look at it.
>
> I am.
>
> I could have written it.
>
> Gee. Jeez.

Yeh, or that, that one there.

Gents.

Yeh. Simple. Purpose and end. You have to have a purpose and you have to hand an end. When you have both you have finished.

Road Up, like for instance?

Yeh.

Jeez, Gee, God man, that's just grate.

Cant you spell.

Great!

Yeh.

Jeez.

Gee.

God man.

Its great.

Crazu.

Crazy man, cant you speel.

Yeh, cant type.

Type what type are you?

Jeez.

God.

Gee, don' know really. One of those (wave gand in suggestive tone=) you know.

Hih.

Huh.

Oh. Gtreat.

Jeez.

God.

Gee.

Despite its infuriating smartarsery and spelling mistakes, the text provides some clues about where Bates's practice was headed. Perhaps the most important aspect was its outsourcing: he knew Bell-Smith was a far better writer than he was. The reference to Capote is also significant: America, and American culture, were increasingly becoming Bates's fixation. The relationship between the Hip-sounding dialogue and the banal images also hints at the influences of the likes of Robert Frank and the Beats. But Bates's own ego starts to shine through, too: it's clear that he's the character claiming the perfection of signs like 'Gents' and STOP, LOOK and LISTEN. He was, after all, the RCA's graphic design star – the young man learning how to make image, text and typography work together to maximum effect.

During this time, Bates was torn about whether graphic design was the right path for him. In the summer break between his first and second years, he decided he wanted to change programmes and join Boshier, Phillips, Hockney, Kitaj and Bowling over in Painting. Carel Weight visited him at Cornwall Gardens, saw some paintings and gave him permission to make the switch.

Guyatt, though, made a counter-offer. If Bates stuck with graphic design, Guyatt would rig things so that he could roam free, making use of whatever technical expertise he saw fit from across the RCA's departments. The choice, for Bates, was an easy one: head off with Weight and the restrictions of paint and canvas, or capitalise on the full and extraordinary resources of the college, including Furniture Design, Engineering, Ceramics and Sculpture. He became, in his second year, a free-range student. It would change everything for him, and laid the foundations for fifty years of practice as Billy Apple. As Apple told me in 2012, this was the moment he began to think of himself as an 'art director': borrowing the language of the advertising world, he developed a new kind of artistic identity, one reliant not on the qualities of individual technique or touch but on the quality of his ideas.

The effects of this opportunity began to be felt immediately. Between 1960 and 1961, a deepening sophistication began to emerge in Bates's poster work, with subtle plays between text, image, visual pun and meaning, as well as recurring freehand forms that marked out a Bates poster like a signature. In early 1960, he had made a poster for a group exhibition called 'The Ring'. The exhibition, at the Bilston Art Gallery in the West Midlands, included four painters, two graphic designers (of which he was one) and one sculptor. The freehand drawing to illustrate the poster consisted of a near-perfect circle created in a few graphite loops. The four painters were represented by fingers (or possibly penises, or rockets) growing from the circle. Two more fingers, representing the graphic designers, have launched off the circle, while the biggest finger, representing the sculptor, disappears out of the frame.

Bates included several of his Jazz Society posters in the exhibition. But most remarkable, given their prescience, was his inclusion of a series of photographs. In three of them, arranged vertically, a young man stands, like William Tell, with an apple on his head. In another set of three, Bates himself appears with the other man, the two of them mouthing the apple from either side, the fruit the only obstacle to their mouths locking together in a passionate kiss. A local reviewer singled out Bates for praise, while also using his images as the platform for a pun that, while cheesy, seemed to recognise the gay sex/original sin tension in Bates's photographs: 'Barrie Bates shows some eye-catching themes for posters,' the reviewer writes. 'Indeed, it is here that the extravagant modern treatment bears greatest fruit.'

A Jazz Society poster Bates made for a playing of Miles Davis' *Kind of Blue* was, like the album, the height of modal elegance: a pale-blue sheet with the text typed simply in lower-case Gill Sans. For a Film Society screening of the 1957 western *The Tin Star* in February 1961, Bates printed an image of a crushed tin can – which he'd had manufactured in the Engineering School – its top opened jaggedly, pierced by several holes (made to look like they were from bullets) to form a sheriff's star. It was printed using offset lithography – a contemporary technology used in the magazine industry.

Bullet holes was a motif Bates liked; soon after, he made a work called *B.E.A. Flight over East Berlin (1961)*, 1961, a painting of half a Union Jack which Bates then took to a rifle range and had shot through several times as a comment on Britain's role in the Cold War. (The Union Jack would eventually come back full circle in his poster 'A Union, Jack!' of 1962.)

In the March/April 1961 issue of the influential American graphic design journal *Print*, Bates's student society posters were included in its roundup of the state of European design. His poster for a playing of *The Ahmad Jamal Trio at the Pershing* – a large, painted blob with thick brushstrokes springing down from it, not too different from the finger-penis-rockets of the Bilston Gallery poster – featured prominently as an illustration, accompanied by a short explanatory text: 'a desert scene', it reads, 'an oasis and palm trees. In red, a palm plantation, the blue, a fountain or water hole. Pink paper to suggest heat and haze and to have an impact on the eye.' The Saharan feel seems to be based only on the fact that the American pianist Jamal had an Arabic name, given there are no obvious desert references in the music, or in the site of its recording: the Pershing in Chicago.

Bates developed the visual identity for the 1961 'Young Contemporaries' exhibition. The poster for the exhibition and cover for its catalogue was a motif connected to 'The Ring' and Ahmad Jamal posters: another hand-drawn circle, though this time in the form of a target that doubled just as effectively as an eyeball – a blue iris at its top, a band of scrawly red, and just below that, wisps of red, bloodshot lines. To emphasise its status as free-rolling, three-dimensional and disembodied, there's a blue shadow like a puddle at its base. There are shades of *Tin Star* and *B.E.A. Flight* too, with the catalogue's cover punctured by three holes.

This was the catalogue in which the critic and curator Lawrence Alloway made his first proclamations about the 1959 RCA intake: 'A group, seen here for the first time,' he wrote in his short introduction,

> is of artists (mainly at the Royal College) who connect their art with the city. They do so, not by painting factory chimneys or queues [surely a dig at the RCA's Painting faculty, among them Weight and Ruskin Spear], but by using typical products and objects, including the techniques of grafiti [*sic*] and the imagery of mass communications. For these artists the creative act is nourished on the urban environment they have always lived in. The impact of popular art is present, but checked by puzzles and paradoxes about the play of signs at different levels of signification in their work, which combines real objects, same size representation, sketchy notation, printing, and writing.

Alloway was pointing to the rise of Hockney, Boshier and Phillips as the emerging stars of British painting. But his words were just as relevant to Bates's graphic design. In fact, when it came to 'the play of signs at different levels of signification' and the combinations of real objects, same-size representation, printing and writing, Bates would eventually go much further than most of his contemporaries.

Much of Hockney's first-year work at the RCA, Apple recalls, was done under the influence of Alan Davie, a Scottish abstractionist by whom Hockney had been deeply impressed when he saw a substantial survey of Davie's work in Wakefield in 1958. More generally, though, Hockney and his contemporaries were grappling with the immense weight of American Abstract Expressionism, which had landed in London in the late fifties with a massive and influential thud.

The first major exhibition of Jackson Pollock's work in the UK was at London's Whitechapel Gallery in 1958. It was a touring show from the New York Museum of Modern Art's (MoMA) International Program. Rather than simply stage the show following American instructions, the Whitechapel's director Bryan Robertson commissioned the architect Trevor Dannatt to design the exhibition. In Dannatt's hands, the show turned into a modernist installation, with some of Pollock's monumental drip paintings installed on freestanding breezeblock walls. Dannatt also mounted paintings on black panels, and created a ceiling of suspended fabric.

Dannatt's environment was an attempt to build on the idea that Pollock's drip works had been made with the desire to completely immerse viewers in their surfaces. The artistry of both men – Pollock with his drips, Dannatt with his clever design – had a huge impact on the London art scene. Hockney saw the exhibition. So did Bowling. In 2013, Allen Jones also recalled its significance. As an undergraduate at the Hornsey School of Art, he visited the exhibition with fellow students. 'I remember looking at this show,' he said, 'and saying "I think we could sue Hornsey". We'd been five years at art school and had received absolutely no indication of the reality of the contemporary art world.'

The following year, in February 1959, the Tate Gallery presented 'The New American Painting', which included work by seventeen painters, among them Pollock, Mark Rothko, Franz Kline, Adolph Gottlieb, Arshile Gorky, Willem de Kooning, Clyfford Still and Grace Hartigan. London was the exhibition's last stop of eight cities across Western Europe. Like the Pollock exhibition, 'The New American Painting' had been organised by MoMA's International Program, under the auspices of MoMA's International Council. A crucial figure in both exhibitions was the American poet Frank O'Hara who, having got his first job at MoMA soon after his arrival in New York from Ann Arbor, Michigan in 1951 – on the membership desk, selling tickets and postcards – was given a permanent position as the International Program's administrative assistant in April 1955.

O'Hara got his first curatorial break when he was assigned to curate an exhibition for the Fourth Sao Paulo Biennial in September 1957. One half of it was a group show including works by Hartigan, Kline, Philip Guston and Larry Rivers. The other half was a retrospective of Pollock – which later toured Europe, including to the Whitechapel. The Pollock show owed much to MoMA's own retrospective of the painter's work, curated by Sam Hunter, which had opened just months after Pollock's death in 1956. O'Hara also acknowledged Hunter's work in his important monograph on Pollock published in 1959. As O'Hara's biographer Brad Gooch points out, the Pollock show and 'The New American Painting' often crossed paths on their respective European tours, and by early 1959, 'Abstract Expressionism had triumphed and was rivalling jazz as America's most influential cultural export.'

In his introduction to 'The New American Painting' exhibition catalogue, MoMA's Alfred H. Barr chose to emphasise the painters' shared intellectual concerns. 'Indeed one often hears Existentialist echoes in their words,' he wrote, 'but their "anxiety", their "commitment", their "dreadful freedom" concern their work primarily. They defiantly reject the conventional values of the society which surrounds them, but they are not politically *engagés* even though their paintings have been praised and condemned as symbolic demonstrations of freedom in a world in which freedom connotes a political attitude.'

Frances Stonor Saunders argued in the mid-nineties that 'The New American Painting' had actually been part of the CIA's wider programme to co-opt contemporary American art, and Abstract Expressionism in particular, as a weapon in the Cold War, even suggesting that its staging in London was the result of CIA money funnelled through a donor. The specific facts of the CIA's cultural programme are debated, but it is nonetheless clear that the US saw contemporary American painting's progressive values and aesthetics as fundamentally American and 'free'. It was also a useful counterpoint to Soviet totalitarianism, as expressed through orthodox socialist realism and state-controlled art. The Cold War's threat of nuclear annihilation was implicit in O'Hara's own assessment of why Pollock's 'action painting' was so significant. '[T]his new painting does have qualities of passion and lyrical desperation,' he wrote, 'unmasked and uninhibited, not found in other recorded eras; it is not surprising that faced with universal destruction, as we are told, our art should at last speak with unimpeded force and unveiled honesty to a future which may well be non-existent, in a last effort of recognition which is the justification of being.'

The quasi-political function of Abstract Expressionism is backed up anecdotally by Apple, who remembers that one of the prime spots to see contemporary American painting in London wasn't at a museum but at the US Embassy. Its iconic Eero Saarinen-designed building opened on Grosvenor Square in 1960. That the embassy was such an important place to encounter contemporary art from the States was largely due to its cultural officer, Stefan Munsing. A graduate of Cranbrook Academy of Art in Michigan (an institution that had counted among its teaching staff Charles Eames and Saarinen), Munsing was given his London posting in 1955. There he became close with Lawrence Alloway, and helped both Alloway, then at the Institute of Contemporary Arts (ICA), and the Whitechapel Gallery's director Bryan Robertson get grants from the embassy to travel to the USA. These trips would prove vital to the growing transatlantic art traffic in the late 1950s. Richard Smith, Joe Tilson and Allen Jones are among the artists who, like Apple, have acknowledged Munsing and the American Embassy as essential parts of the contemporary art scene at the time.

Apple also remembers another great place near the embassy to see contemporary American art: the apartment of the collector E. J. 'Ted' Power. Power had made his fortune as the co-founder and chairman of Murphy Radio and Television. Apple says that Power was extremely welcoming to young artists, often letting them up to his place to look at his collection. Apple recalls seeing Abstract Expressionism there, including works by Mark Rothko and Barnett Newman. This seems very likely, given that Power owned at least three Rothkos and, as James Finch has written, bought his first Newman after seeing 'The New American Painting' in 1959. Power also became a collector of British Pop, acquiring art by Patrick Caulfield, Peter Blake, Richard Hamilton, and Apple too. He eventually became a highly influential trustee at the Tate Gallery in the late 1960s, gifting the institution several works or selling to it at good prices.

Several successful British painters just ahead of the 1959 generation had embraced the promises of Abstract Expressionism, especially the RCA graduates Richard Smith and Robyn Denny with their colour-field works, and the more expressive Sandra Blow, the youngest and most definitely hippest member of the Painting School's faculty. 'In the 1960s,' Hockney wrote in his autobiography,

> the subject had been completely played down; abstraction had begun to dominate everything, and people firmly believed that this was the way painting had to go. There was no other way out, people thought. Even I felt that, and I still felt it even when I began to reject it in action; in theory I still couldn't reject it at all. I felt, well, I'm sure they're right, and I think I felt that even as late as 1966.

In retrospect, however, this battle between abstraction and representation, as it relates to Hockney at least, seems less important than larger questions at the time about morality and freedom. And for the young RCA painters, there was one London figure who posed these questions more than any other: Francis Bacon.

By 1959, Bacon had established himself as the giant of contemporary British painting. He'd represented the UK at the Venice Biennale in 1954 alongside Lucian Freud and Ben Nicholson. He'd already made iconic works like *Three Studies for Figures at the Base of a Crucifixion*, *c*. 1944, and his screaming popes inspired by Diego Velázquez. He had also made explicitly homoerotic paintings such as *Man Kneeling in Grass*, 1952, and *Two Figures in the Grass*, 1954. Bacon's existentialist angst was of a totally different order from the Americans' in 'The New American Painting', and was expressed through the tortures and contortions and erotic potentials of the male figure, rather than through abstract splashes or zips of paint.

In late March 1960, Bacon had an exhibition of recent paintings at London's Marlborough Fine Art. This was towards the end of Hockney's first year at the RCA, and the young artist was impressed by what he saw. The exhibition included several of Bacon's 'Head' paintings – relatively small canvases by Bacon's standards, between 30 and 60 centimetres square, that still capture the deep physicality of his painting: whorls of brushstrokes that twist into bruised and swollen cheeks; eyes that seem closed over by some vicious punch or sting; noses that glow red with the rush of blood. There was also *Study from Portrait of Pope Innocent X By Velásquez*, 1959: different from his earlier popes, this one offering more side-eye than scream, a lurid green throne blending into the equally garish background, a purple skullcap popping above a bulging forehead.

It may also have been significant for Hockney, who was on the cusp of making his own erotic breakthroughs in his paintings, that Bacon showed several clearly homoerotic works, all from 1959: *Sleeping Figure*, in which a naked man curls up on a chaise; another nude in *Seated Figure on a Couch*, his penis clearly visible; and *Two Figures in a Room*, in which one man crouches, his fist driving into the red floor, as another figure – a semblance made from a few brushstrokes, surrounded by a green aura – lies on his back, his knees raised.

These works are striking in their comparative simplicity, the background expressive scratchiness and silhouetted cages of Bacon's earlier popes and portraits replaced by solid areas of bright colour. The figures, too, are almost always made from paint in big strokes. This economy doesn't hide the work's heart, though: a deep, sexual charge that doesn't rely on screaming mouths or hanging carcasses to make their messages about Bacon's sexuality loud and clear.

There was one more major exhibition that year which would leave a significant mark on Hockney and the other young painters around him. In July 1960, the Tate Gallery opened what has been described as Britain's first 'blockbuster' exhibition: a major survey of Pablo Picasso's work. Picasso's relationship with Britain had begun fifteen years earlier when, at the end of 1945, the Victoria & Albert Museum staged a substantial exhibition of his paintings alongside those of Henri Matisse. It had 170,000 visitors in just five weeks, including a seventeen-year-old Joe Tilson, who in 2013 described seeing it as life-changing. It also substantially helped the curator and art historian Roland Penrose – who would eventually write Picasso's biography and curate the 1960 Tate exhibition – in his cause to establish a dedicated modern art gallery in London. This eventually became the ICA, which would play a vital role in establishing the credentials of the RCA painters.

Under Penrose's leadership, the ICA in 1956 staged a Picasso exhibition, called 'Picasso Himself', to mark the artist's seventy-fifth birthday. The Tate survey, though, was of a different magnitude, presenting two hundred and seventy works, of which Picasso had loaned about one hundred. Of huge importance to the show and its legacy was the fact that it included Picasso's entire 'Las Meninas' series – the staggering culmination of his battle with arguably the most important and difficult painting of all time by his countryman Diego Velázquez. Hockney visited the Picasso show around eight times; this would have happened in the summer break between his first and second years at the RCA, and just a few months after his encounter with Bacon's work at Marlborough.

The intensity of Hockney's responses to Bacon and Picasso took place at a moment when he was building a new confidence to paint subject matter that really mattered to him. He was guided in this by an older student at the RCA, R. B. Kitaj.

An American who was studying in England, Kitaj was certainly regarded by many of the younger painting students as the star of the Painting School. Bates didn't share their enthusiasm, with Apple recalling in 2013 that 'Ron Kitaj and I were at loggerheads with each other: he thought that what I was doing was about Madison Avenue. He was right, it was subject matter. While he was reading Classics, I was looking ahead, not backwards.'

Following Kitaj's counsel, Hockney began to make works about his own strong commitment to vegetarianism. The idea that his work could address a lived polemic rather than pure abstraction or the dour everyday realism of his teachers like Weight and Spear provided a crucial launching pad for the work that would later put Hockney on the British art map.

Two other older painters would also have a big impact on Hockney's decisions about the content of his work. The first was Kitaj's studio-mate who had been part of the 1958 intake, Adrian Berg. Like Hockney, Berg was gay. Both Christopher Simon Sykes and Peter Webb suggest that he gave the younger artist a new confidence to be free about his sexuality. Like Kitaj, Berg was also incredibly well read; he'd previously gained a place at Cambridge to study medicine, but switched to English literature instead. In a forewarning of what would happen to the 1959 cohort, Berg had at the end of his first year been placed on a list of students who faced probation. But, he wrote, '[t]he moment Ron Kitaj and David Hockney came I was no longer in the firing line.' Berg was scathing of the faculty, and in particular their decision to expel Allen Jones: 'I think they were jealous of anyone who was in competition with them,' he wrote, '[t]here was a strong feeling of us and them. These things were life and death at the time, and we were in an insecure position.'

Then, in the 1960/61 year, another American showed up in the Painting School: Mark Berger, thirty and with a year off from his teaching duties at Tulane University in New Orleans. Berger was also extremely comfortable with his sexuality, and – crucially for Hockney – arrived with an armful of American male physique magazines. Hockney was now surrounded by older men who were by turns political, distinctly literary and, in Berg's and Berger's cases, openly gay. Consequently, a new licence emerged in Hockney's work – and, perhaps most importantly, a sense of a project. What elevated that project wasn't just its openness about his sexuality. His paintings were also celebrations of the joys of adult, physical love. It was Bacon's confrontational sexuality freed from existential angst. Hockney's focus wasn't to torture the bodies he desired but rather to venerate them: early evidence of his later mantra that, '[t]he source of all art, the source of all creativity, is love. If anybody thinks there is something more important, I would like to know what it is.'

Over the course of 1960 and into 1961, Hockney's sexuality and painting each seemed to feed the other; the more out he was, the better the painting got. In *Love Painting*, 1960, which owes so much to the influences of Jean Dubuffet and Alan Davie, Hockney offers up just the suggestion of a phallus entering the picture from the right, surrounded by splashy paint that keeps the work close to gestural abstraction. *Shame*, 1960, uses its title to hint at the otherwise abstract work's real subject matter. But things move very quickly from there into the far bolder *The Third Love Painting*, 1960. A more directly phallic form springs up from the bottom of the picture, and Hockney begins to use graffiti to more explicit effect, elevating the kinds of gay messages and codes found in public bathrooms, many of them with a deeply personal resonance for Hockney himself: 'ring me anytime at home'; 'my brother is only 17' (which later becomes a work in its own right); 'come on David admit it'; and the more literary flourish, 'I am he that aches with amorous love'. There's also a knowing nod to Bacon, with the outline of the kind of cage the older artist used so often to ensnare his figures.

Adhesiveness, 1960, is an early example of Hockney making his literary and gay influences more explicit. In it, two crudely drawn figures (a sign that he was inching towards the fully fledged figuration he is most celebrated for) interlock. One, wearing a hat, appears to be biting the other's nose while penetrating him. Really, the nose is as much a penis too, the figures locked in a 69 position that Hockney would return to in later paintings. The figure in the hat has the numbers '23.23' written on it; the other, '4.8'. When transposed onto the alphabet, these are 'W.W' and 'D.H' – Walt Whitman and David Hockney – Hockney borrowing Whitman's own simple code, in which the poet swapped letters for numbers.

This became an essential device in many of Hockney's most important paintings of the period. In *Doll Boy*, 1960–61, a figure has his head bowed, the words 'doll boy' scrawled next to him and 'Queen' on the hem of his shirt. Just below that are the numbers '3.18', or, 'C.R.' – Cliff Richard, who Hockney had a crush on, and whose song 'Living Doll' had been the most successful UK single of 1959. *Doll Boy* and *The Third Love Painting* were both included in 'Young Contemporaries' in February 1961. The young art dealer John Kasmin saw Hockney's work there for the first time, bought *Doll Boy*, and subsequently resolved to launch him into the London art scene.

Hockney's critical success at the time of 'Young Contemporaries', Kasmin's support, and other sales (Cecil Beaton had bought *Adhesiveness*) seemed to give him a new clarity of direction. This found its expression in arguably his most important painting of the period, *We Two Boys Together Clinging*, 1961, a brilliant coming-together of all these disparate strands – love, sex, Cliff Richard, Walt Whitman. In it, two block figures with stick legs (strongly similar to Bates's Ahmad Jamal poster from around the same time) clutch each other, with lines of paint connecting their bodies. Their faces press together, one marked '4.8' – Hockney – with the word 'never' scrawled over his mouth. The work's title comes directly from a Whitman poem, but it's also a play on current events; Hockney was evidently most amused, given his fixation with Cliff Richard, by a headline about a mountaineering accident that read 'TWO BOYS CLING TO CLIFF ALL NIGHT'. Richard is present, in the form of Hockney's pet name for him, 'Doll Boy', with the numbers '4.2' prominent in the lower left corner. Whitman is there too, in a small way, the hem of the Hockney figure a jagged white line that reads like a succession of Ws.

There's a series of photos by Geoffrey Reeve – a textiles student who photographed the 1959 generation extensively – of Hockney and his studio-mate Derek Boshier in front of *We Two Boys*. Boshier's initials are, of course, also D.B, or 4.2, though he is adamant that the Doll Boy reference was always to Richard and not to him. In one image, he and Hockney ham it up, holding hands, looking at each other as though about to kiss. In another, Boshier, bug-eyed and trying to slip away from Hockney's grip, play-acts the sudden realisation that Hockney has designs on him.

In an interview with Sykes, Mark Berger suggested that the two figures in *We Two Boys* actually came out of an etching Hockney had made to illustrate Berger's gay fairy tale, *Gretchen and the Snurl* (Apple still has a copy of these illustrations in his Auckland archive). Hockney had begun to work in the Printmaking department when he was running out of money for paint and canvas, and had discovered that materials were freely supplied there. There, the talented student Ron Fuller taught him etching – which would become absolutely essential to Hockney's sky-rocketing status in the coming years.

The subject of many of Hockney's most iconic works from this time is his unrequited crush Peter Crutch, a straight student studying furniture design, whose presence in Hockney's paintings is usually marked with the numbers 16.3, standing in for his initials P.C. *The Most Beautiful Boy in the World*, 1961, offers up a naked figure in side profile, wearing the outline of a baby-doll nightie, 'D.Boy' crawling up his neck towards his chin. The painting's title crawls down his back to his buttocks, and a heart with a protruding tongue (a stand-in for Hockney) makes out with him. Above him, vertically, is an Alka-Seltzer box, with the numbers '69' just below it. Crutch is also the subject of *The Cha Cha That Was Danced in the Early Hours of 24th March 1961*, 1961, which is easily misread as Hockney's representation of a drag act but was, according to Peter Webb, the recollection of a moment at a party when Crutch was holding a handbag for someone.

Crutch seemed unflustered by Hockney's attentions, given that another sequence of photographs by Reeve shows him with *The Cha Cha*, and with Hockney's other homage to him, *Peter.C*. This was one of the first works in which Hockney attached two canvases together. The effect warps Crutch's body. He was a tall man, but Hockney used the smaller of the two canvases for his legs, tilting the balance. Hockney used block type to spell out PETER.C on the top canvas and PETER on the bottom. He also used printed letters in *The Fourth Love Painting*, 1961, to spell out 'I will love you at 8pm next Wednesday' (the '8' hand-painted) – again, the numbers '69' not far away.

Peter Crutch told Webb that Hockney was especially interested in mirrors and mirror images around this time. That fascination is at the core of one of Hockney's early etchings, *Mirror, Mirror on the Wall*, 1961, which includes quotes not from Whitman but from another gay poet Adrian Berg had introduced him to and whose work would hugely affect him, C. P. Cavafy.

That Hockney began to make openly gay work, filled with literary and personal references, in 1960 and 1961 was a brave act – especially in light of the House of Commons' resistance to Wolfenden's suggested reforms. But there were other important debates about artistic freedom and morality swirling in the culture at that moment. And these were brought to a head by the trials relating to D. H. Lawrence's *Lady Chatterley's Lover* on both sides of the Atlantic.

The American public's fascination in the 1950s with the Kinsey Reports illustrated how the battle for sex had begun to reshape the country's cultural life. Another key fight came at the end of the decade when the owner of Grove Press, Barney Rosset, published an unexpurgated edition of *Lady Chatterley's Lover* in the US. The book, written in 1928, had never been published in the States or the UK, because of its sexual content and language. On 30 April 1959, New York City's postmaster Robert K. Christenberry ordered the interception of twenty-four cartons of the Grove edition of *Chatterley* on the grounds that, as an obscene publication, it had been banned from being mailed thirty years earlier. The Post Office then took Grove to trial for having mailed the book.

Grove's defence lawyer was Charles Rembar, who was no stranger to obscenity accusations against books. He'd previously represented Norman Mailer after Mailer's publisher Rinehart & Company had refused to publish *The Deer Park*, 1955, on the grounds that it was obscene. Rinehart also claimed that Mailer's obscenity was an illegal act, which therefore voided their contract, which meant Mailer couldn't keep his advances for the book. Rembar threatened to test that in court, and Rinehart settled with Mailer instead (Mailer later published *The Deer Park* with Putnam).

The Post Office's case against *Chatterley* was a chance for Rembar not just to get Grove off the hook but to put a lasting dent in America's anti-obscenity laws and achieve a big win for freedom of expression, both for authors and their publishers. This was all the more pressing because in 1957, in the case of *Roth v. United States*, the Supreme Court had ruled against Samuel Roth, a New York publisher of erotica, who had defended his right to publish porn on First Amendment grounds.

The majority ruling in *Roth* was that anti-obscenity laws weren't inherently unconstitutional. Or, put another way, the First Amendment right to freedom of expression did not extend to the protection of smut. To assess whether a publication was dirty or not, the majority argued, the standard should be whether the work had been produced primarily for 'prurient interest', and that this should be judged by 'contemporary community standards' and what the 'average person' would make of it. The judgment by William J. Brennan Jr. used a statement from the American Law Institute to elaborate: 'A thing is obscene if, considered as a whole, its predominant appeal is to prurient interest, i.e., a shameful or morbid interest in nudity, sex, or excretion, and if it goes substantially beyond customary limits of candor in description or representation of such matters.' The trial of *Chatterley*, then, hinged on whether the novel fell foul of these criteria. In the wake of *Roth*, there was the possibility that the book's alleged obscenities tipped into 'shameful or morbid' territory, or that it reached beyond those 'customary limits of candor'.

The danger of *Roth*, as Rembar saw it, was that these descriptors – the average man, community standards, prurient, shameful, morbid – would eventually be widely used to suppress all sorts of risky artistic work: they were moral values which undermined constitutionally protected freedoms. *Chattlerley* was therefore a perfect book to test the law. The two major complaints against it were interlinked: first, Lawrence's graphic descriptions of the sex acts between Connie (Lady Chatterley) and the gamekeeper Oliver Mellors; and second, the language Lawrence has Mellors use to describe that sex, especially 'fuck' and 'cunt'. Rembar's defence was complex, and evolved over time, but eventually coalesced around specific themes, and these were to have a lasting effect on censorship debates.

The first was about Lawrence himself: on the one hand, his intent in *Chatterley*, and on the other, his literary status and the place of the novel within it. To answer these inter-related questions, Rembar called on literary experts Alfred Kazin and Malcolm Cowley, who both defended Lawrence as one of the most significant English writers to have ever lived. They also vigorously defended the literary merits of his descriptions of sex, on the grounds that Lawrence was a writer who believed sex between a man and a woman was a deeply spiritual act – not about prurience or promiscuity but about communion with another, and a reconnection of our bodies and minds in an increasingly mechanised age. And Lawrence's language, they said, was no different from that of many other highly esteemed literary figures who hadn't been subject to obscenity charges.

With Lawrence's credentials established, Rembar turned to the question of prurience. This was where his defence was at its most substantial and mature, because he argued that a normal interest in sex was not prurient. In other words, sex is a normal part of adult life, and what Lawrence was describing wasn't shameful, or morbid, or excessive of that normalcy. This, Rembar argued, also lanced the second part of the argument, around contemporary community standards. If sex is a normal part of adult life, it is also a normal part of communities.

Rembar also saw serious danger in the 'average person' hypothesis, arguing that one couldn't park this standard of judgement at the door of the average joe in the street – the guy with little to no interest in literary values, or who doesn't read books at all. Instead, he claimed, 'if books are to be judged by community standards, they should be the standards of those who read them, rather than the standards of the population at large'. In his recounting of the trial, though, Rembar did acknowledge that *Chatterley* was a book with a difference. 'An outstanding best-seller among books taken seriously as literature will have,' he wrote, 'in all editions, perhaps a million and a half buyers. The various editions of *Lady Chatterley's Lover* that came out in 1959 and '60 sold over six million copies. The average man, it was pretty clear, was buying because it was a dirty book.'

Rembar's defence, once the case got to the federal courts, hinged on his argument that the Postal Service had no special competence in literature, freedom of speech and constitutional law. In other words, it had no right to decide what Americans should, or shouldn't, be reading. In the end, this was the most convenient argument for the judges to accept, rather than the harder path of having to overturn the Supreme Court decision in *Roth*. In their judgments, though, the judges highlighted the problems with *Roth*'s 'community standards' language, and emphasised the importance of a work's literary merit: the seeds of a changing attitude that would prove vital when Rembar was called upon to defend Grove again – in the case against Henry Miller's *Tropic of Cancer*, which Grove published in 1961.

It wasn't until the US judgments in favour of *Chatterley* that Penguin published it in the UK for the first time, in 1960. This decision by Penguin's founder Allen Lane also led to the first prosecution under new legislation: the Obscene Publications Act, which had become law in 1959. The Act was hugely significant, because it created a 'public good' defence: if a work of literature or art could prove its cultural merit, it couldn't be removed from sale or censored. *Chatterley* became a test of the law. And 'public good' was exactly the defence Penguin relied on.

The trial opened at London's Old Bailey on 20 October 1960. Mollie Panter-Downes, who wrote a 'Letter from London' for the *New Yorker* for decades, sat through the six-day proceedings, which came to be defined, largely, by the old-fashioned bombast of the Crown's prosecutor, Mervyn Griffith-Jones. As Panter-Downes wrote:

> The plot, Mr. Griffith-Jones said, was little more than padding between what he called the 'bouts' of sexual intercourse – thirteen bouts in all, he advised them, and added that the hero and heroine hardly existed except as bodies. Now he came to Lawrence's deliberate experiment with the use of Anglo-Saxon four-letter words. Mr. Griffith-Jones had been counting them up, too, and his arithmetic rang through the court as baldly as a grocery list – this one thirty times, that one thirteen times, this and that six times each. If the jury registered any shock then, by the end of the case it was clearly regarding the items as neutrally as though they were indeed salt, pepper, or mustard.

Witness after expert witness streamed through the court. In the end, it took the jury only three hours to unanimously find Penguin not guilty: perhaps the best proof yet of how much contemporary 'community standards' had changed when it came to the artistic depiction of sex. But Charles Rembar made some interesting criticisms of the Old Bailey trial. Strongest among them was that the British case descended into a trial of Lady Chatterley herself, rather than the book: in other words, that the fact of her adultery was a sufficiently corruptible force to make the book fall on the wrong side of the 'public good' argument. Farcically, in Rembar's view, the trial had ended up turning on whether a fictional character had made a bad life decision; the question of Connie's virtue became a football to decide what met appropriate behavioural standards for the day. As Rembar put it, 'the issue was morality, and the question of freedom was thoroughly obscured'.

For many of the young artists at the RCA, this simultaneous freeing up of sexual attitudes and censorship laws gave their work a new potential for contemporaneity and political urgency. It also highlighted the growing cultural synergy between London and New York – a recognition that if a book is deemed acceptable for publication in one place, it should be in the other. Ann Quin – a big fan of Lawrence's work – would surely have been following *Chatterley*'s path through the courts, particularly given the role descriptions of sex would play in her first published book, *Berg*. For Hockney and his colleagues like Bowling, Kitaj, Berger and Berg too, there must have been something freeing about the trials' confirmation that sex and politics in art would be protected from censorship and the more conservative leanings of mass opinion.

But fierce debates still raged at the RCA about the moral corruptibility of the individual – not through encounters with pornography or sex-heavy novels, but with advertising and the mechanisms of mass communication. Richard Guyatt's successful design graduates were often viewed by their contemporaries in other schools as having been wooed by the pernicious temptations of mass culture. In the Summer 1960 issue of the RCA student newspaper *Newsheet*, for example, one student writing under the moniker 'H.D.' stated that:

> 'If Graphic Design is even to be raised above a hack level, designers must avoid plunging into such sentimental slush as surrounds many products. No one would tolerate such rubbish in any other art-form, and no matter how well you design, it's still hardly the height of personal integrity to tell lies for money.

Bates, as the rising star of Graphic Design, clearly had a commercial career path ahead of him, if he wanted it. He was unsure if he did: attracted to the potential of financial and professional success, but still wanting to be recognised as an artist first and foremost. This is why *For Sale*, 1961, is one of his most intriguing and subtle early works. The 'painting' is simply that – the words 'FOR SALE' printed in red lettering on a white canvas. Apple remembers Bates and Hockney making it together late one night, recalling that Hockney helped him print the canvas by pulling the lever on the printing press.

The fact Bates's work essentially names its own condition as an exchangeable commodity points to a tongue-in-cheek attitude towards his peers' critiques of the advertising industry. All artists crave sell-out shows, but as individuals they never want to be seen as 'sell-outs'. Bates's seminal work declared that it was *For Sale*; far from being an advertising lie, it told the bald truth about its cultural status. It was also starkly different from the Poppy snatches of Americana in paintings by the likes of Peter Blake and Peter Phillips. The two words that make up the work's content could just as easily have been applied to their maker, too: a young, gifted designer waiting for an offer for his services from the highest bidder.

The commercial pathway kept opening out in front of Bates. In early 1961, he entered the Layton Student Prize, a national design competition in which students were asked to respond to the thoroughly English theme: 'drink more tea'. Bates's response was his 'we all love tea' campaign. Using the ceramic, photographic and metal resources of the RCA, he designed a series of objects associated with tea drinking in the shapes of hearts: a tin tea-caddy with its heart-shaped lid open; spoons bent together to form a heart; a teacup with a heart-shaped handle; and, slightly cheesier, a kettle and teapot with their spouts nuzzling, the kettle's heart-shaped lid slightly ajar as if it's blown its heart-fluttered top. Under each image are the words, all in lower case, 'we all love tea'. Bates won the first prize of £250 (the runner-up prizes were a laughably measly £10 each). It was an enormous sum of money, given that his annual bursary from the New Zealand government at the time was £400.

Though it was a response to a specific brief rather than a completely original project, 'we all love tea' showed Bates the potential of his new licence to roam from Guyatt. In June 1961, *Advertiser's Weekly* ran a short interview with him about the campaign. Did the headline precede the visual treatment or vice-versa, the interviewer asked. What was the starting point? 'From enmeshed thoughts,' Bates answered, 'I conceived, first, a purely visual solution, but the subsequent copy line was, to my mind, more important than the original idea of resulting heart-shaped tea utensils. The final result was a conceptual idea and not a design idea. There was no starting point except in thought.'

Later, he provided more detail about how the work came to be: again, this would become a blueprint for future Bates/Apple projects. 'Did you art-direct the photography, or give the photographer the general idea and a free hand?' he was asked. 'In this case I closely directed the photography', Bates replied, 'using the photographer as an extension of myself. There was also close direction with other craftsmen who manufactured my photographic models to my specifications.'

The win was a massive boost for the young New Zealander: proof he was finding his feet as a designer, but also developing a working method that suited his belief that ideas were the most important aspects of art and, indeed, of being a good artist. But there was also the pragmatic fact of a windfall: he was suddenly flush. And it meant, when Hockney told him about cheap airfares to New York for the summer break, he was able to jump on them without a second thought.

The timing was serendipitous: Hockney had already begun making his Tea Paintings, the first of which had been shown at 'Young Contemporaries' alongside *Doll Boy* and *Adhesiveness* in February. *The Second Tea Painting*, 1961, had included a representation of a Typhoo Tea box – Hockney's preferred brand, which he kept in his studio – in the background, behind brushmarks and a floating heart that look like an obliterated reversal of the figure in *The Most Beautiful Boy in the World*.

But *Tea Painting in an Illusionistic Style*, 1961, was a major breakthrough: a painting made from several shaped two-dimensional canvases that, when assembled, look like an open three-dimensional box of Typhoo Tea. Making the composition even more complicated is the figure Hockney seated within this framework. The figure's backside, back and right shoulder spill over into the side panel, and the top of his head pops 'out' of the box and onto the canvas that represents the container's opening. The figure, then, represents the traditional 'illusionistic style' referenced in the title, but the canvas arrangement itself is a virtuosic piece of dimensional disorientation: an open, seemingly three-dimensional container sitting flat against the wall. Hockney described how difficult it was to make, writing that the Tea Paintings were 'as close to pop art as I ever came' and that:

> To make a painting of a packet of tea more illusionistic, I hit on the idea of 'drawing' it with the shape of the canvas. The stretcher is made up from sections and I made the stretchers myself. It was quite difficult stretching them all up – the back is almost as complicated as the front; it took me five

> days. I don't think anybody had done shapes before. . . . It's interesting, I spelt the word 'tea' wrong on the left-hand section . . . I am a bad speller, but to spell a three-letter word wrong!! But it's drawn in perspective and it was quite difficult to do. I took so long planning it that in my concern for flatness or abstraction I spelt it wrong.

That Hockney concedes this was as close as he came to Pop also highlights how resistant he was to the label being applied to his work at all. It's true that many of his contemporaries – especially Pauline Boty, Derek Boshier, Peter Phillips and the slightly older Peter Blake – were absolutely engaged in something that was easily labelled British Pop. But Hockney had a very different project. The seated figure in *Tea Painting in an Illusionistic Style* clearly has allusions to Bacon, but it was also an implicit attempt to knock the older man off; to take what Bacon had passed down in a new and clever direction. Up until this painting, Hockney's days at the RCA had been spent grappling with his forebears: with Alan Davie, with Picasso, with Jean Dubuffet and Bacon. But with *Tea Painting in an Illusionistic Style* he stepped over a line, from the burden of influence into a genuine originality of his own.

America was about to become hugely important to both Bates and Hockney, but that most British of drinks – tea – had advanced them down their respective transformative paths.

As the summer break of 1961 approached, Hockney, like Bates, found himself with unexpected money in his pocket. Unbeknown to him, one of the printmaking tutors had entered one of his prints into a competition. He won £100. He'd also had money from the sales of the works in 'Young Contemporaries' and the support of the art dealer John Kasmin. In addition, P&O, the cruise-line operator, had just built the SS *Canberra* and commissioned the RCA's faculty to decorate it. Hockney was in turn commissioned to paint murals in the 'teenagers' room' – a sort of hangout space for young people. It netted him another £100.

In the spring of 1961, Flying Tiger Airlines introduced $99 round-trip fares from London to New York. Apple remembers that it was Hockney who found out about these cut-price flights. Thrilled at the prospect, because he'd thought travelling to the US would cost far more, Hockney told Bates about the opportunity, and the pair booked tickets for 9 July 1961: Hockney's twenty-fourth birthday. Frank Bowling was on the same flight. Apple has always recalled that it was a student charter flight, connected to the London School of Economics. This is corroborated by one of *ARK*'s art editors and fellow RCA student Brian Haynes, who told Alex Seago in 1990 that '[a] whole gang of us went, including David Hockney'. It seems completely plausible that the LSE might have chartered entire cut-price Flying Tiger flights for students on their summer break.

For Hockney, the appeals of New York, professionally and personally, were obvious. Through Mark Berger, he'd learned of American gay culture, both through magazines and Berger's own accounts of it. New York's reputation as a gay scene would have been temptation enough. He planned to stay with Berger's family in Long Island (Berger was back Stateside by then too) and to visit New Orleans. There were also the museums, and the fact he already had an introduction, via Robert Erskine, the dealer who had awarded him the printmaking prize, to William Lieberman, curator at MoMA.

For Bates, the temptations were different. His own obsessions with American culture were threefold. First, there was the fashion. Apple was inclined towards the hipster particularities of drip-dry suits, impeccable Levi's, sneakers and Oxford shirts, rather than the grimier fashions of the Beats or the uptight Englishness of some of his peers. The second was his passion for, and knowledge of, the latest developments in Madison Avenue typography and design. His own advertising successes in his second year, in particular winning the Layton Prize, had confirmed, in his mind, not only that he was right to be fixated with Madison Avenue but also that he was good enough to foot it with the best creators there.

But the third draw for Bates was arguably the most important: New York was the world centre of contemporary jazz, the development of which he'd been following closely for years. The scene had been dramatically improving where he was, too: the first half of 1961 was a watershed period for contemporary jazz in London. The Soho clubs were thriving, with several American-influenced band leaders, including Tubby Hayes and Ronnie Scott, introducing the city to modernist jazz. Thelonious Monk played in the UK for the first time, at London's Royal Festival Hall on 29 April, followed by separate gigs in Hammersmith and Kilburn on 30 April and 7 May. Bates saw one of these last two concerts, writing to his friend Leon Lesnie in Auckland that he'd seen 'Monk, Delonius [*sic*], yesterday. Things are happening so fast, I can't keep abreast.'

In that same letter, Bates wrote that he'd taken a date to see *The Connection*, Jack Gelber's 1959 play, which was then having a West End run. The play had been a controversial smash back in New York, where it had been first staged by The Living Theatre – an avant-garde company that had also presented works by the likes of Frank O'Hara and Kenneth Koch. New York's daily press had hammered Gelber's play when it first opened. There were, though, glimpses of recognition for it. The *Village Voice* named it the best new off-Broadway play of the year. And Donald Malcolm wrote in the *New Yorker* that:

> The jazz group, whose presence alone would justify an evening at the Living Theatre, consists of Freddie Redd (piano), Jackie McLean (alto saxophone), Larry Ritchie (drums), and Michael Mattos (bass). How they contrive to play so well, so spontaneously, and yet in such perfect coordination with the demands of dramatic timing is a matter I can never hope to fathom.

This intersection between jazz and dramatic performance was both *The Connection*'s greatest conceit and its greatest breakthrough. The play is ostensibly about a group of junkies waiting for their 'connection' to show up: the mysterious and serene 'Cowboy,' played by the equally serene African-American actor Carl Lee.

The play immediately breaks the fourth wall, with Jim Dunn, the narrator, desperate to portray himself as Hip, addressing the audience directly, as though they're witness to a kind of Big Brother-like reality show rather than a conventional play: here are real junkies, he says, but of course, because narcotics are illegal, we won't be using real ones here in front of you tonight. The whole thing is set up to leave the audience wondering if, in fact, the actors were using real drugs throughout the performance. The link is an uncomfortable one: in many well-known cases, jazz and heroin went hand in hand in turn-of-the-decade New York. Heroin was such a feature of the jazz lifestyle that Bates evidently felt the need to tell Lesnie in a letter, 'I'm not taking junk.' This was despite the fact that *Naked Lunch* was his favourite book around this time.

The Connection is, on the whole, a bleak work, with shades of Beckett's *Waiting for Godot* as the players, both musical and theatrical, lie around waiting for Cowboy. But out of this drudge, two features of the play offered a bracing analysis of the times in which it was being staged: first, the language of Hip and, second, its ambiguous morality. The critic Kenneth Tynan wrote in his preface to the Faber & Faber edition of *The Connection* that:

> The play is not a defence of dope. Nor does it attack the wage-earning, clock-punching, home-making technique of survival; as one of the characters says, '... what's wrong with day jobs? Or being square? Man, I haven't anything against them. There are lousy hipsters and lousy squares.' ... The junkie seeks euphoria. The average citizen seeks happiness. How do these goals essentially differ? If the aim of life is pleasure, why is it more pleasurable to achieve it by injecting dollars into the bank account than by injecting dope into the

> blood-stream? If, on the other hand, the aim is spiritual enlightenment, how can we be sure that the insights provided by heroin (or mescalin, so eloquently hymned by Aldous Huxley) are less reliable than those supplied by religious mysticism? *The Connection* offers no answers; it simply states the problem, and implies the questions.

After its long run in New York, the play's cast upped sticks, at the invitation of London theatre impresario Michael White, for a season across the Atlantic – White's first independent West End production. For Bates, who evidently attended a performance in early May 1961, *The Connection* was a revelation with its singular combination of self-conscious performativity – the artifice of the set-up, the direct address to the audience somehow made compelling and believable – and pitch-perfect hipster language and world-class jazz performances. Its thrill for the young jazz obsessive was also about to be doubled, because that same month the film version of *The Connection* – the debut feature by director Shirley Clarke – premiered at the Cannes Film Festival.

Despite its New York setting, the state itself hadn't wanted to know about Clarke's film adaptation, the film licensing board denying it a licence on the grounds that it used profanity and showed drug use. In Europe and the UK, though, the film had a very different life. It was received rapturously at Cannes. And in early June – still a month before Hockney and Bates flew to New York – London's National Film Theatre screened it for three nights as part of a programme called 'Square Pegs'. It's likely that the UK's Obscene Publications Act, and the failed prosecution of *Chatterley* a year earlier, meant that Clarke's film had a much easier time in London than New York. *The Connection* would even get a general release later in the year, screening at The Academy Cinema on Oxford Street. The other films in the 'Square Pegs' programme were two made by Robert Frank: *The Sin of Jesus*, and, with Al Leslie, his 1959 Beat film *Pull My Daisy*, which was written and narrated by Jack Kerouac.

Clarke translated Gelber's play using the same cast and musicians that Bates saw in London. Her solution to the fourth-wall issue was to reshape the play as a fly-on-the-wall documentary, transforming the narrator Jim Dunn into an aspiring hipster filmmaker: a young guy whose fashion is perfectly on-point for the time, and perfectly consistent with Bates's own preferences — turned-up jeans, a drip-dry jacket, buttoned-up Oxford shirt and white sneakers.

As the film opens, Leach, the lead junkie, clutches a boil on the side of his neck. There's music: a few bluesy bars of Redd's piano. Leach grabs a tea towel before tucking it into his pants: a makeshift apron. He half-disappears behind a wall, and another man, Solly, bald with a moustache, emerges from the toilet, holding a newspaper. He looks self-consciously into the camera. Written all over his two-second glance are scepticism and invaded privacy – and being caught emerging from the toilet is the least of it. He walks to the piano and puts his hand on Redd's shoulder. Redd turns and also gives the camera a dismissive look.

Leach, still nursing the boil on his neck, reaches into the apartment's pot-belly stove and, inexplicably, pulls out a pineapple. He's hungry. Then he addresses the camera directly:

> Look here. I live comfortable. I'm no junkie bum. Just look at my pad, it's clean! Yeah, it's clean except for these creeps that come here and call themselves my friends. My friends, wow. Like, they come here with a little money, see. And then they expect me to use my hard-earned connections to furnish them with heroin, see. Then when I take just a little for myself, they cry and they scream, the bastards. [He shoves one of them, who's sleeping at the table.] Come on, man! They just wait here, making me nervous, sleeping. That's all they do is sleep.

Seconds after his monologue, we hear the director's voice, and get the briefest glimpse of Dunn in front of camera, before the door opens and two more musicians – Jackie McLean and Larry Ritchie – come in, immediately asking if Cowboy has been yet.

What follows is a kind of lazy closed-room claustrophobia, with occasional bursts of agitation. Dunn starts to worry and gives directions: he wants the junkies to act naturally, but he's concerned that junkies lying around, doing nothing except occasionally sniping at each other as their withdrawals get worse, isn't the material he was hoping for. It's clear to everyone including the junkies that this young wannabe who, despite his fashion sense, is the squarest man in the room, is using them to try to make a name for himself as a gritty urban filmmaker.

'I gave Cowboy enough money to keep you high for a week, right?' Dunn reveals, as his cameraman Burden keeps rolling. 'Now, I'm giving you what you want, you give me what I want, huh?' From then on, Dunn becomes more present in the film, manipulated and parodied by the junkies. Gradually, they conspire to 'turn him on': a peer-pressure situation which eventually leads to him shooting up with the group, while Burden captures it all on camera.

When Cowboy finally does show up, McLean is the first to be shuffled into the toilet for his fix. The musicians follow one after another, the remaining members maintaining the tune. Redd, once he's high, plays with his eyes closed, sweat running down his face. With Cowboy is an old woman, dressed like a sister of the Salvation Army, who clutches her Bible close as Burden introduces her to the junkies; slowly, she tries to save their souls, oblivious to what's unfolding around her. Cowboy, played by Carl Lee, is beautiful: a white shirt, white high-waisted pants, a kerchief knotted around his neck. He's their dealer but he's also the devil, silver-tongued, languid and utterly amoral, having invited his oblivious elderly angel – 'Amen to that, Brother Cowboy!', 'Amen Sister Salvation. Now excuse me a moment . . .' – for no obvious reason other than to bat her around like a cat with a half-dead bird.

It's Cowboy who finally convinces Dunn to get high. Dunn justifies it to himself as research, that 'there is something dirty about just peeking into people's lives'. To really understand his subject, he rationalises, he needs to join them. Cowboy opens the bathroom door; Dunn strips down to a t-shirt and walks in: another innocent soul dragged down into hell, even as a soldier of the Lord is standing there observing. That is, until Sister Salvation reveals her true self. She's a shakedown artist, and tries a sob-story on Cowboy about needing money for her own funeral. The film closes with Leach insisting he isn't high enough and demanding another fix. Cowboy relents: 'It's your life,' he says; and as Redd and his quartet play, Leach ties off and self-administers an overdose, while Cowboy clicks along to the music. The musicians pack up while Cowboy revives Leach. Just another day in New York City, 1961.

For Bates, the film version of *The Connection* was the quintessential expression of contemporary American avant-garde culture: not the expressionist drips of Jackson Pollock but the improvisations of McLean and Redd; not the griminess of Beat fashion but the hipster sharpness of Dunn and Cowboy; not the fevered stream-of-consciousness of Kerouac and Ginsberg but the ultra-cool language of swinging black musicians.

This black-white contrast between two of the defining artistic subcultures of contemporary New York at the time – Hip on the one hand, the Beats on the other – was highlighted by the National Film Theatre's 'Square Pegs' programme. Alongside *The Connection*, Robert Frank and Al Leslie's *Pull My Daisy* was also ostensibly a fly-on-the-wall film. But it took a completely different approach to New York's cultural underbelly – by focusing on the Beats. And its unlikely leading man would have an impact on both Hockney and Bates just a few months later: the American painter and Bronx native, Larry Rivers.

In *Pull My Daisy*'s opening frames, we hear the ethereal voice of Anita Ellis singing lyrics that were written in a kind of 'exquisite corpse' game by Allen Ginsberg, Kerouac and Neal Cassady, and set to music by David Amram:

> Pull my daisy
> tip my cup
> all my doors are open
> Cut my thoughts
> for coconuts
> all my eggs are broken

The camera pans through a Bowery loft, before fading to a bird's eye view of a dining table. It cuts, and there's a woman in a kimono opening the shutters of the loft's enormous windows. We hear Kerouac's voice for the first time:

> Early morning in the universe. The wife is gettin' up, openin' up the windows, in this loft that's in the Bowery in the Lower East Side New York. She's a painter and her husband is a railroad brakeman, and he's comin' home in a couple hours. . . . She has to get the kid up to go to school. Pablo. He says 'why I have to eat that stuff all over again, that Farina. I ain't gonna say I'm gonna live a hundred years, but I've been eatin' Farina for about a hundred years.'

There's an elaborate knock at the door. Pablo gets up from the table, and lets in Gregory Corso and Ginsberg carrying armfuls of booze. They make themselves at home and, despite the early hour, each crack open a beer, while Pablo's hard-working mum, played in her first screen role by the French actor Delphine Seyrig, tries to get him ready for school. The pair kill time talking poetry until the man of the house and their drinking pal, Milo, gets home from work. As he comes through the door, in his railway brakeman uniform, we see the unmistakeable profile of Larry Rivers. Just behind him, wearing a tight beanie with ear-flaps, is Peter Orlofsky.

While the trinity of poets – Ginsberg, Corso, Orlofsky – play themselves, everyone else is in character. Rivers, playing Milo, stands in for Neal Cassady; *Pull My Daisy* is loosely based on an event in Cassady's life. His wife, worried about Cassady's bohemian lifestyle, organised a dinner with their local clergyman. In Kerouac's version, the dinner becomes an absurdist set-piece. The 'bishop' – played by the young art dealer Richard Bellamy (who would become a crucial figure in the early success of Pop art in New York) – arrives with his sister, played by Sally Gross, and his mother, played by the painter Alice Neel.

The drunk poets harangue the bishop until the entire evening descends into farce. Amram, playing the character 'Mez McGillicuddy' – another hanger-on – starts to blow a French horn. Ginsberg grills the bishop on the question of what's holy. Rivers/Milo blasts away on a sax. The bishop makes his embarrassed departure, just as Pablo, who should be tucked up in bed, emerges to join the party. Milo's wife, understandably, is fed up and loses her temper. The poets and Amram/McGillicuddy get up to leave, and Milo/Rivers follows them ('She'll get over it').

Beyond the film's terrible sexism (Milo's wife is just tying him down; the bishop's mum is a bore; the bishop's sister is prim and uptight), it's an important document of just how intertwined the jazz (as expressed by Amram and Rivers), art (Bellamy, Neel, Frank, Leslie, Rivers) and poetry (Kerouac, Ginsberg, Corso, Orlofsky) scenes were in late-fifties New York. And Rivers was one of the most important links between all three.

So too was The Living Theatre. Established by Judith Malina and Julian Beck, it regularly staged events and experimental plays written by some of the great poets of the era. Rivers performed in several of the plays, including Kenneth Koch's *The Election* (in which he played Lyndon B. Johnson). And, according to Rivers, he very nearly starred in *The Connection*. 'After *The Connection* had been running for many months,' he wrote in his autobiography *What Did I Do?*,

> the lead junkie had to leave the production. I was offered his role. I guess my reputation as a sometime user of heroin and the fact that the character actually played the saxophone were behind Judith Malina's offer . . .
>
> But performing in *The Connection* would mean remaining in New York for the summer. My art and the lure of the Hamptons in the summer – sun and sea, the nearness to my sons, the pleasure of my regular pals – made me let the offer go.

It was this production of *The Connection* that Shirley Clarke saw and decided to adapt, and that Bates later saw in London. But for the lure of the Hamptons, both might have starred Rivers.

Those first two years at the RCA were a remarkable time for Bates and Hockney: a period in which both accelerated away from their peers, charged by their respective ambitions but also by the extraordinary cultural and artistic forces swirling around them. Picasso, Bacon and Abstract Expressionism were, in London, suddenly available to Hockney first-hand and at scale: forebears he would first grapple with, then push against. The confidence and intelligence of men like Kitaj, Berger and Berg also helped him along the path towards a highly personal content, which in turn gave him a figurative language he'd been craving.

For Bates, it's no overstatement to say that Richard Guyatt's vision in letting him roam free at the RCA changed his life forever. By becoming an 'art director', Bates was able to bridge the two seemingly separate worlds that had till then been holding his attention evenly: contemporary advertising and contemporary art. Unburdened by having to make things himself, he was able to speed up both the production and quality of his work, focusing first and foremost on the integrity of the ideas – the concepts – underpinning his output, whether a poster or an art work. And his deepening engagement with jazz and Hip culture was planting the seeds of a dramatic change.

In retrospect, it's easy to see that both men simply had to go to New York that summer: too many things were pointing them across the Atlantic. They were cashed up and ready for a change of scene. And now they had a plane to catch.

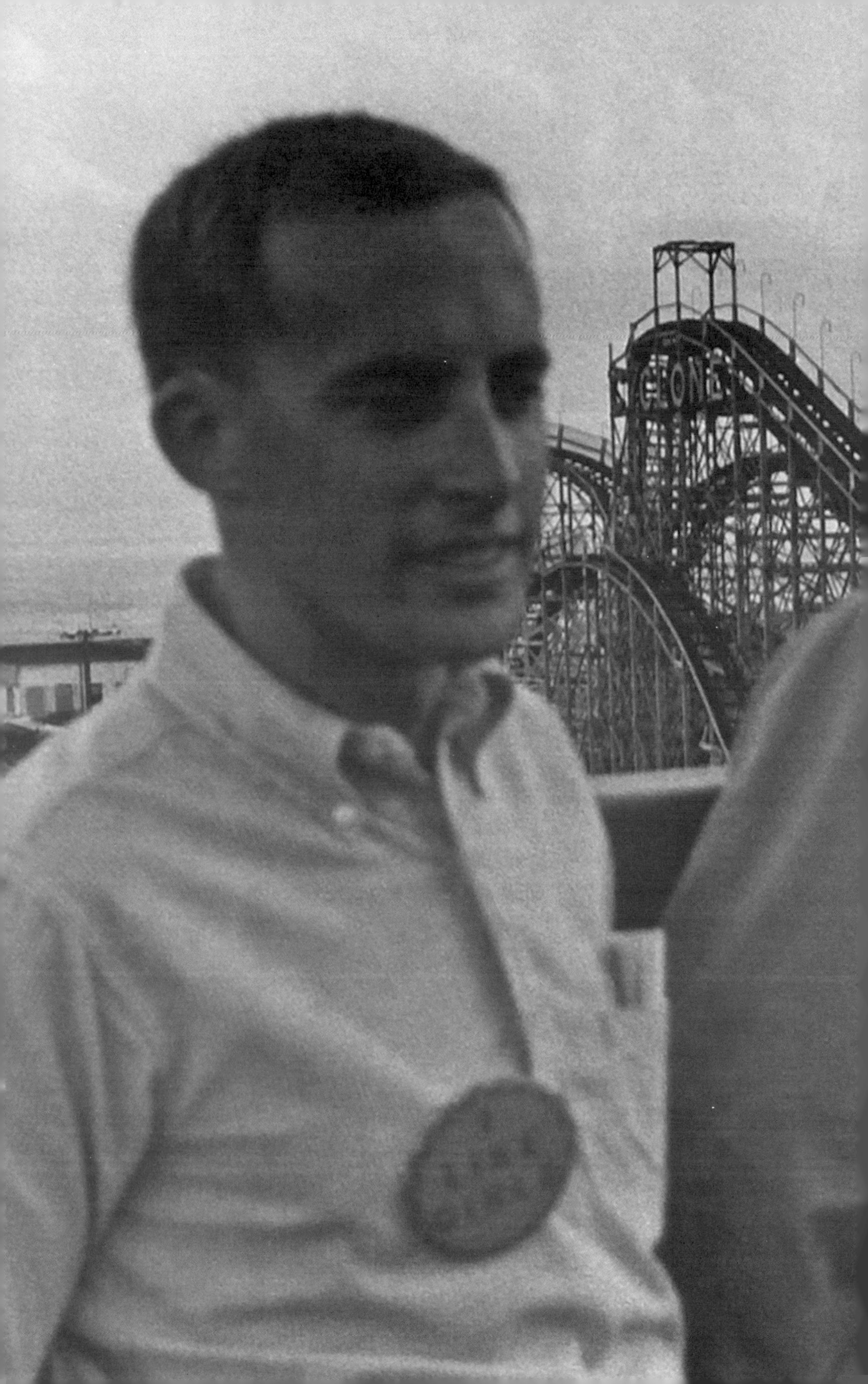

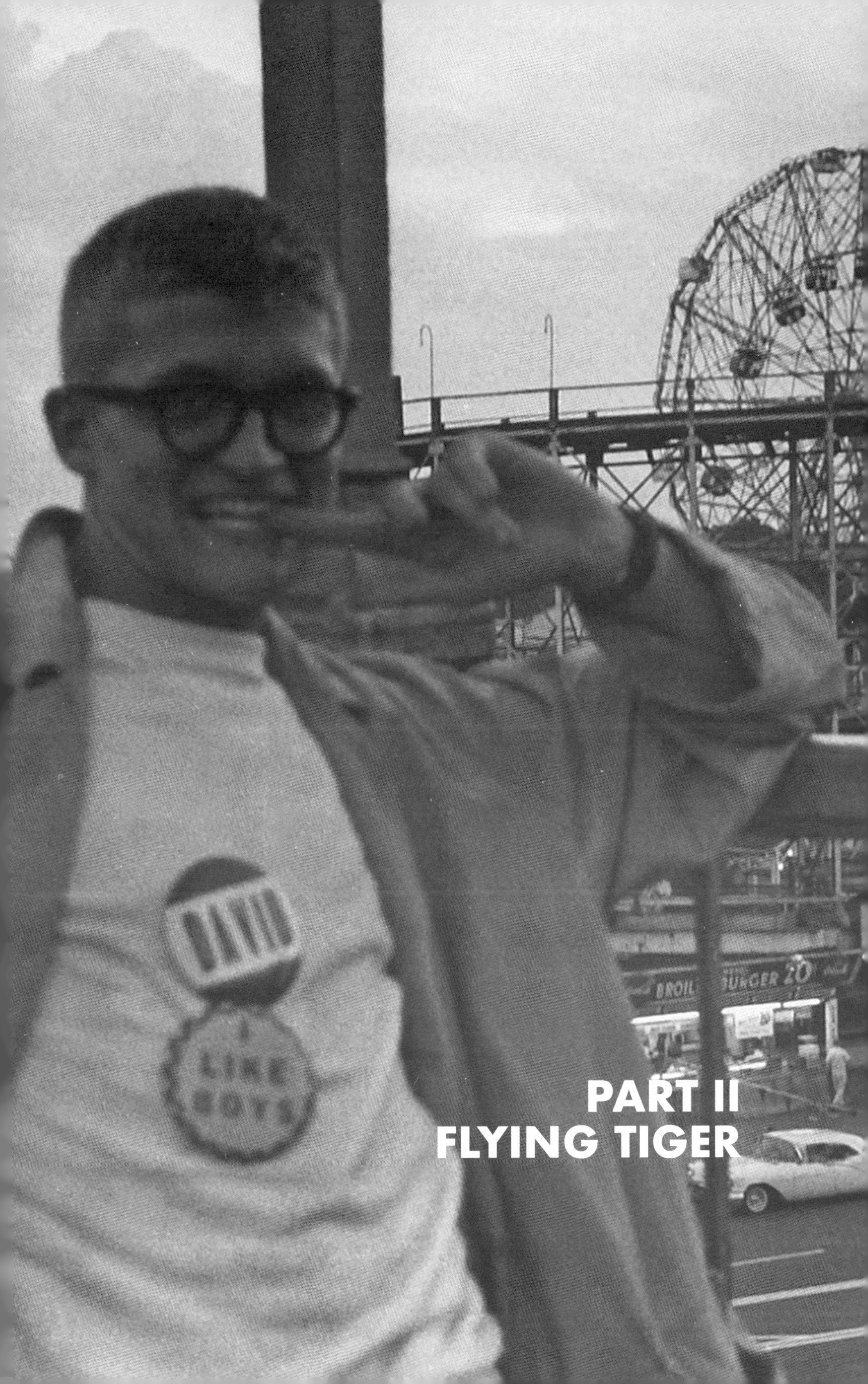

PART II
FLYING TIGER

Ideas. They brought around a plate and we spewed them out, patting our mouths dry with towel supplied. This done by chick who asked, 'So what else is there?' She looked sly and vaguely intelligent. 'I'll show you – quick into the fire escape, I suppose there is one' – 'Yeh, but it's occupied.' – 'Huh, at this time of day' – 'Yeh, well you gotta have luv, luv.' – 'Yeh. Later maybe.'

— BARRIE BATES, 1961

WHEN HOCKNEY AND BATES finally touched down at Newark Airport after their long trip, they were picked up by John Craddock, a young English aspiring filmmaker who'd moved to New York in 1959 and was studying in the Film Department at New York University (NYU). Apple says that Craddock was a friend of Bates's occasional girlfriend Joy Knightley. Knightley had written to Craddock asking if Bates could stay with him in Manhattan for a couple of weeks; it ended up being a couple of months.

Hockney, meanwhile, was due to stay with Mark Berger's father and stepmother in suburban Long Island (Craddock doesn't remember whether Hockney stayed that first night at his place before moving on to the Bergers). Berger, on exchange at the RCA for only a year, had already returned to the States and was actually in hospital with hepatitis when Bates and Hockney arrived, but Hockney moved into the Berger residence nonetheless. In Christopher Simon Sykes's telling, Berger's father – a pharmacist – liked Hockney well enough, but found him offbeat. His wife Helen, though, wasn't so impressed when the young artist dripped ink on her carpet. Eventually, the behaviour of Hockney and his friends would become too much for the Bergers senior, culminating in an altogether more significant moment in Hockney folklore than the carpet stain: the first time he bleached his hair.

But before that: Hockney's friendship with Berger became his vital entry point into New York's gay scene where, he felt, he could be much freer than in London, and where gay life was much more organised.

Berger also introduced him to Ferrill Amacker, whom Hockney would eventually move in with in Brooklyn Heights. Hockney described Amacker to Sykes as a 'bohemian' who had money so didn't have to work, and said they were occasional lovers. Hockney says that he was thrilled by the city, and that he and his friends 'revelled in a Bohemia that went on night and day'. Bates didn't share Hockney's enthusiasms for Amacker, though, which may be why the pair saw each other less during the second half of their stay in the States.

Hockney also had business to conduct in New York. Robert Erskine had suggested Hockney take some of his prints to show William Lieberman at MoMA. Lieberman acquired works including *Mirror, Mirror on the Wall* for MoMA's collection, and helped Hockney sell the rest of his editions, netting $200. Lieberman also arranged for Hockney to spend some time making new prints at the Pratt Institute. Whether Bates had followed Hockney's lead or acted independently, he also wrote in a letter to his friend Leon Lesnie in Auckland that MoMA had accepted some of his work on the same trip: a '[f]ew old posters and things'.

But this wasn't the only professional opportunity on the horizon for Bates. Over the previous year in London, he had attended weekly workshops run by Bob Gill, a gifted graphic designer who'd moved from New York to London in 1960 to take a position at the Charles Hobson Agency (it didn't last long: in April 1962 Gill co-founded the Fletcher/Forbes/Gill studio). Gill was part of an increasing traffic between the London and New York advertising worlds, and his workshops were a vital part of Bates's exposure to the best Madison Avenue work being done at the time. Apple remembers a lot of Americans participating in the workshops, and can't remember if it was Gill himself or another of them who gave him the letter of introduction that would lead to one of the most transformative periods of his early career: a month-long internship with one of the twentieth century's great commercial typographers, Herb Lubalin.

Already, then, the young men were starting to strike out on different paths: Hockney, the ambitious painter and printmaker embracing New York's gay scene; Bates the aspiring young art director keen to learn from the best of the best in an ambiguous business – mass communication.

In 1961, Herb Lubalin was part of the Madison Avenue powerhouse agency Sudler & Hennessey, which specialised in work for the pharmaceutical industry. He was also vice-president and creative director of the agency's commercial advertising arm, known as Sudler, Hennessey & Lubalin. According to biographer Adrian Shaughnessy, Lubalin was 'an ace talent spotter' who'd hired George Lois – who became arguably the greatest art director of the 1960s and 1970s – and Andy Warhol, who did occasional illustrations for the company in the late 1950s. (Years later, in 1975, Lubalin was commissioned to design the cover of Warhol's book, *The Philosophy of Andy Warhol*.)

Shaughnessy writes that while at Sudler & Hennessey, Lubalin developed his ideas about 'graphic expressionism' and 'word pictures': namely, that typography wasn't just a way to make a message more visually compelling but was itself a carrier of concepts and ideas. Lubalin once told *Idea Magazine* that: 'The American people react to ideas. We are a concept-conscious society', and in the late fifties and early sixties he was putting this to the test, through several projects that subsequently became iconic moments in the history of American design.

One of the clearest examples of his worldview came in an advertisement for Sudler & Hennessey's services: 'let's talk type', the ad reads, before its instruction to potential clients: 'let type talk'. In 1962, Lubalin worked on a campaign for CBS, one of Sudler & Hennessey's most important clients. 'What in the world is going on?' reads the copy, below overlapping, near-illegible headlines in different types – Lubalin's design standing as a metaphor for the fast pace of current events and the way CBS made sense of them for its audiences. Geopolitical issues were a common thread in Lubalin's work: in 1960, he was commissioned to create a sixteen-page spread for the Russian-language magazine *Amerika*, published by the US Department of State and distributed in the USSR. Civil rights were deeply important to Lubalin, too; in the mid-sixties he made ads for *Ebony Magazine*, some of which directly referenced racism against African-Americans. And he was opposed to the Vietnam War. In 1968, *Avant Garde Magazine*, which Lubalin art-directed, ran an anti-war poster competition. Billy Apple was among the winners. And one of the judges was Larry Rivers.

Avant Garde was a magazine project Lubalin worked on with the publisher Ralph Ginzburg; their third and final collaboration. The second was *Fact* – a kind of satirical take on mid-sixties current affairs. But the first was Ginzburg's most famous and controversial: *Eros* – a quarterly magazine of high-end erotica and sex-related articles, which lasted only four issues, in 1962. Most famous among them was Issue 3, which featured Bert Stern's nude images of Marilyn Monroe taken weeks before her death. That same issue included French erotic postcards; a long article about Samuel Roth, the pornographer whose case in the Supreme Court established the 'prurient interest' standard; a philological discussion between two language experts about why the English language has so few slang words for the clitoris; and a condensed version of *Fanny Hill*, the eighteenth-century book of erotica that, when published in its entirety in the US by Putnam in 1963, went all the way to the Supreme Court as another test of the *Roth* judgment (once again that hero of anti-obscenity litigation, Charles Rembar, led the defence).

If Issue 3 was the raciest of the four *Eros* publications, it was Issue 2 that caused the publication's eventual downfall, and the conviction of its publisher Ginzburg – ironically, under the very *Roth* case law he'd published an article about. Issue 2 opened with an article by Faye Emerson called 'We all Love Jack', about President John F. Kennedy's effect on women. 'First there were the "jumpers",' Emerson opened:

> It began with the primaries, when John F. Kennedy was fighting desperately for the nomination a lot of Americans thought he was too young, too Catholic, and too rich to deserve. His political advisers and the press, alert to any straw in the wind, began to notice an odd reaction in the crowds. An increasing number of young women seemed to be traveling by pogo sticks and when Mr. Kennedy approached, they bounced in the air like lady jumping jacks. They shrieked ecstatically, threw kisses and waved madly at their hero.

The short essay goes on to discuss 'Jack's' effect on women from all strata of society: teenage girls; the 'astonishing number of ladies in café society' who seemed to have had an intimate relationship with him at some point; and '"the touchers." These were for the most part respectable, mature women who, with incredible determination and stamina, fought their way close to Mr. Kennedy, patted him gently and retired dazed and happy.' A photo-essay, across several double-page spreads and laid out by Lubalin, followed Emerson's piece, showing women looking at Kennedy with expressions that were often comically overloaded with desire.

The article was a canny, and funny, early foray into a discussion of a president who wasn't just a leader but an image and an object: a figure the American public projected onto as much as followed. The Kennedy Administration didn't see the funny side, though; and Ginzburg's big problem was that JFK's little brother Robert was also the country's top lawyer, the Attorney-General of the United States.

Initially, the US government held back because Robert Kennedy was concerned that prosecuting Ginzburg would look like political interference. But when Issue 4 of *Eros* included images of a naked black man and white woman together, the prosecution began. The case went all the way to the Supreme Court. Rather than falling on the 'prurient interest' criteria, the judges emphasised Ginzburg's motivation: that his business model was to sell a publication on the grounds of titillation rather than artistic or journalistic merit. Ginzburg was convicted, in the end, of promoting himself – albeit classily – as a smut peddler, even if his publications weren't actually all that pornographic.

What Bates encountered in Lubalin in 1961, then, was a deep thinker and a social liberal who believed in civil and sexual rights, freedom of expression, and the conceptual potential of graphic design as a progressive social force. Bates, armed with his letter of introduction, showed Lubalin some of his RCA posters. And in Apple's words, the older designer gave him 'a hundred dollars and a corner office' for a month.

When I asked Apple what Bates had to do while he was in Lubalin's office, his answer was quick and straightforward: nothing. He wasn't required to work on specific briefs. Instead – much like the licence Richard Guyatt had granted him back at the RCA – he was free to roam. And that's what he did, soaking up as much as he could from some of the best technicians, copywriters and commercial artists in New York. Apple recalls two figures as being particularly important: the designer and, as Apple remembers him, sometime copywriter Ernie Smith, and the lettering artist John Pistilli, the man who made Lubalin's typographical designs a reality.

Without any specific projects, it would have been easy for Bates to come and go as he pleased. But Apple says he showed up every day, and that the most important thing he learned in Lubalin's office was that good ideas – and not just good-looking designs – were essential. A letter to Lesnie in Auckland that Apple thinks Ann Quin wrote for him once he was back in London confirms this. 'Time-table first day,' Quin/Bates writes,

> nine ackemma, strolled up the avenue, Madison (you know) and strolled into one of the taller sky-scrapers and caught an overnighter to the top floor. Fascinated, caught it down again. Then went up again to the thirteen – just above the basement and took up position behind a desk. Nine-fifteen, morning coffee. Ideas. They brought around a plate and we spewed them

> out, patting our mouths dry with towel supplied. This done by chick who asked, 'So what else is there?' She looked sly and vaguely intelligent. 'I'll show you – quick into the fire escape, I suppose there is one' – 'Yeh, but it's occupied.' – 'Huh, at this time of day' – 'Yeh, well you gotta have luv, luv.' – 'Yeh. Later maybe.' 'Bi.' – 'Bi. I'll bring around the plate again later and send someone to clean up your shoes.'

Apple remembers cigar smoke and shoe-shine boys, and the quote above plays directly into *Mad Men* tropes, all the way down to its implicit misogyny. But as much as Lubalin was one of advertising's heroes at the time, he was also one of its doubters, eventually leaving Sudler & Hennessey to set up an independent design studio because he felt the ad industry underestimated the intelligence of the American people. Bates wasn't oblivious to this himself: he was still having his own internal battles about whether advertising was the way forward for him. This was exacerbated, as Christina Barton has written, when Hockney visited him at Lubalin's offices and dashed off a drawing called *Madison Avenue. Lie$, Lie$, Lie$*, 1961, which portrays Bates in a drip-dry suit. The title's moralising dollar signs say everything about Hockney's attitude towards the men Bates was learning from.

Bates was well and truly familiar with how many of his peers felt about the advertising industry – that mass consumerism, while interesting subject matter, was also, in the end, the enemy of high culture. The 1951 book *The Mechanical Bride: Folklore of Industrial Man* by Canadian theorist Marshall McLuhan – his first great examination of America's advertising and pop-culture industries – had been circulating among the young RCA artists in London: Derek Boshier, for example, cites it as a big influence on his work at the time. In it, McLuhan framed mass consumerism – supported by the mass communication of Hollywood and Madison Avenue – as a kind of organised violence against critical thinking. '[I]t has long been plain', he wrote,

> that the executives of production and selling have been thinking in military terms, smashing public resistance with carefully planned barrages followed by shock troops of salesmen to mop up the pockets. It will take more than a change of vocabulary to eradicate this lethal aspect of know-how, for it is not easily separated from its origins or its uses. The public may smile at the suggestion that it need be perturbed at being the target for a barrage of cornflakes or light bulbs. But this industrial ammunition has the character of exploding in the brain cortex and making its impact on the emotional structure of all society.

Boshier literalised McLuhan's ideas in paintings like *Special K*, 1961, which included the distinctive Kellogg's 'K' logo. The painting featured prominently in Ken Russell's 1962 film about four young British Pop artists, *Pop Goes the Easel*. As we watch Boshier sit down at his table and hear the artist's own voiceover, it's clear he's channelling McLuhan: 'I'm very interested in the whole set-up of the American influence in this country,' he says,

> I'm interested in the, sort of, infiltration, of the American way of life. And I think it's through advertising and advertising techniques that this infiltration has come through. I think the Englishman probably starts with America at the breakfast table, starting with the cornflake packets, which are American in design, American in packaging, and American in the whole set-up: the giveaway gifts, the 'something-for-nothing' technique.

As if to hammer home the McLuhan-esque message, the 'giveaway' Boshier pulls from the cereal box on his table is a toy missile.

Boshier's stance here is one of critique. In a 2013 interview, he made clear that rather than celebrating American consumer culture, he was deeply wary of its encroachments on British life. Chris Stephens has described the paintings Boshier made while at the RCA as an 'extraordinary body of work' that examined 'the contrasts between the rising hegemony of the United States and the declining imperial power of Britain, and that between corporate strategies and the apparently increasingly homogenized individual'. The defining visual embodiment of that 'homogenized individual' in Boshier's paintings from 1961 and 1962 was a falling, or 'fallen', man – who had in fact originated in an RCA painting assignment. The students had been required to respond to an historical work; Boshier chose William Blake's *Simoniac Pope* from Blake's illustrations for Dante's *The Divine Comedy*.

Across a number of paintings, Boshier used this figure to channel his interest not just in McLuhan's analysis of mass communication but also in Vance Packard's ideas in the 1957 bestseller *The Hidden Persuaders*, which had exposed how American ad men used 'motivational research' to manipulate the needs and subliminal desires of consumers. The title of Boshier's *So Ad Men Become Depth Men*, 1962, for example, is taken directly from the title of a chapter in Packard's book. In the painting itself, a mouth is squeezed between the handles of a pair of toothbrushes to which giant tubes are applying toothpaste. Falling towards the bottom right of the painting is a succession of male figures, which gradually disappear, replaced by handguns – another reference to the advertising industry's 'weaponisation' of consumer desire. In *The Identi-Kit Man*, 1962, similarly aggressive toothbrushes scrub away at Boshier's male figure, whose arms and legs morph into toothpaste, all within the silhouette of a jigsaw piece – which, in Stephens' words, refers to 'the fragmentation of identity', a threat to the self from advertising's psychological warfare. The head of Boshier's 'identi-kit man' has snapped away from his body in an echo of the earlier 1961 work, *Man Playing Snooker and Thinking of Other Things*, in which a schematic male head has its cranium compartmentalised into visualisations of contemporary crises, including the hydrogen bomb and postcolonial troubles in the Congo (Frank Bowling also made work about the situation in Congo in the same year: his *Martyrdom of Patrice Lumumba*), as well as references to that ubiquitous popular American publication *Mad Magazine*.

Bates's position, by contrast, was more complicated, because as much as he understood the debates about mass communication, he'd also been drawn into its beating heart, Madison Avenue. Creative directors and specialist typographers like Lubalin were also at the sharp end of the theories that McLuhan was, in 1961, formulating as his book *The Gutenberg Galaxy: The Making of Typographic Man*, which he would publish the following year. In it, McLuhan argued that the invention of the Gutenberg press, and in particular moveable, reproducible type, represented a profound shift in the way Western societies thought and were organised. This change, he argued, moved Western civilisations from oral to visual cultures: language and image, in other words, were inextricably linked. 'As the literal or "the letter" later became identified with light *on* rather than light *through* the text,' he wrote,

> there was also the equivalent stress on 'point of view' or the *fixed* position of the reader: 'from where I am sitting.' Such a visual stress was quite impossible before print stepped up the visual intensity of the written page to the point of entire uniformity and repeatability. This uniformity and repeatability of typography, quite alien to manuscript culture, is the necessary preliminary to unified or pictorial space and 'perspective'.

Designers like Lubalin and Bates, who were both equally obsessed with typography's function as a conceptual and visual form – as carrier of message *and* image – were the modern inheritors of this print/visual revolution: 'Gutenberg Men' who corralled the technologies of reproducible type and mass communication to sway the masses.

The additional complexity, when deciding how best to critique mid-century advertising's social and conceptual effects, was that the work being produced on Madison Avenue was, very often, astoundingly good. Apple remembers the work of this era with remarkable accuracy, given nearly sixty years have passed. In particular, he remembers that his host John Craddock had a stack of *New Yorker* magazines in his apartment, which Bates would flick through to look at the advertisements. Over that summer, the *New Yorker* included some of the classic campaigns of the era, including full-page ads for American Airlines, Kodak, Schweppes, Revlon, Coca-Cola, Gordon's Gin and Cutty Sark Whisky.

There were though, for Bates, two standout campaigns from that period. One of them is regarded as perhaps the greatest print ad campaign of all time: Doyle Dane Bernbach's work for Volkswagen. DDB began working with the German car manufacturer in 1959, and developed the iconic 'Think Small' campaign which made the VW Beetle's greatest weakness in the American automobile market – its tininess compared to American cars – its greatest strength. Small meant affordable. Small meant easier to park. Small meant cheaper insurance. Variations on the hugely successful concept came thick and fast, including one with 'Lemon.' as its strapline, followed by an explanation of VW's rigorous factory controls. The *New Yorker* ran others that summer. 'Why does this station wagon look like a bus?' one full-pager asked, making a virtue of the VW van's snub nose. 'Impossible.' was another, an ad that went on to explain that, because VWs were cooled by air rather than water, it was impossible for them to overheat. 'You might get all steamed up,' the copy read, 'but not your Volkswagen.'

One of the great innovations of the VW ads was their stark, clean layouts, which were developed by the art director Helmut Krone (who Bates met that summer). Unlike most American car ads, which were filled with smiling suburban families driving down freeways or standing next to their oversize cars and oversize houses, there were seldom ever people in Krone's VW ads. They were essentially studio portraits of the cars – minimally presented objects against blank backgrounds. The ad copy also turned the logic of American auto on its head. This was the height of the conceptual advertising that figures like Bill Bernbach, Krone and Lubalin were spearheading at the time.

So, too, was the Wolfschmidt vodka campaign, developed by arguably the most influential agency of the era, Papert Koenig Lois. (Julian Koenig had also worked on the original Volkswagen campaign before leaving DDB; and George Lois had worked at Sudler & Hennessey with Lubalin.) That Apple was able to place his encounter with the Wolfschmidt ads to that summer in New York illustrates just how much they impacted him – and, given his own eventual transformation, they might well have planted an idea that there was something inherently American about fresh produce.

The most famous of the Wolfschmidt ads were a pair. In the first, a bottle of the vodka stands next to a tomato. 'You're some tomato,' the bottle says. 'We could make beautiful Bloody Marys together. I'm different from those other fellows.' 'I like you, Wolfschmidt,' the tomato replies. 'You've got taste.' The second ad in the pair depends entirely on the success of the first. This time, a Wolfschmidt bottle, horizontal, nudges its neck towards an orange. 'You sweet doll,' the bottle says, 'I appreciate you. I've got taste. I'll bring out your inner orange. I'll make you famous. Roll over here and kiss me.' But the orange isn't having any of it. 'Who was that tomato I saw you with last week?' it asks.

PKL were also behind a well-known television campaign for Xerox in 1960, in which a chimpanzee called Sam makes photocopies for his boss, showing how simple the machine is to operate (in early 1965 one of the first exhibitions Apple made after moving permanently to New York was called 'Apples to Xerox'). That same year, PKL also made print ads for Coldene. On a completely black ground there are two statements: 'John, is that Billy coughing?' one asks. 'Get up and give him some Coldene' comes the reply – which, despite its sexist tone, was a brilliant way to represent a married couple lying in bed in the middle of the night, hearing their kid coughing: a breakthrough in using text as image.

Just like DDB's Volkswagen ads, there was no extraneous detail in much of PKL's work – no smiling models, no atmospheric setting, just a stark ground where idea, image and message come together seamlessly. Campaigns like these leave no doubt that in the hands of Bernbach, Lois, Lubalin, Krone and a small group of other Madison Avenue revolutionaries, advertising became an art form in its own right. It might have been, in Hockney's eyes, 'Lie$, Lie$, Lie$', but it was subliminal and conceptual thinking of the first order, as culture-shaping as any of the art or literature then being made. And, for a month at least, Bates got to stand at the coal-face.

In one of those same 1961 *New Yorkers* Bates flicked through at Craddock's apartment was a review for a book about America's jazz scene, just published: Nat Hentoff's *The Jazz Life*. Hentoff, at that time a columnist for the *Village Voice*, was a jazz-world insider: not just a writer but also the former New York editor of *Down Beat*; a friend of several of the leading musicians of the day; and briefly the director of Candid Records, a label that released albums by Charles Mingus, among others.

The Jazz Life is an on-the-ground account of what the New York grind was really like for professional musicians. For most, except for the very small handful at the top of the game like Miles Davis, it was pretty terrible. Hentoff described poor pay, racial discrimination both ways (including the reluctance of some black musicians to hire white players), long hours, unscrupulous club owners and even worse booking agents, alcohol and drug dependency, and the constant sense that, even if you 'make it', your fan base can move on from you in a heartbeat, forever chasing the next hot thing.

But Hentoff also showed that jazz, as a truly American art form, was in the midst of a revolution, which he described as a 'changing intellectual climate' led by some of the great pioneers then active in the New York scene – premier among them the likes of Davis, John Coltrane and Ornette Coleman. Rather than simply referring to this shift as 'hard bop', Hentoff suggested that the main characteristic of the new jazz, which had emerged in the 1950s, was that it was 'an object in itself, a non-functional music in the sense that it is no longer designed for dancing or background listening', and that this, despite its comparative toughness, was attracting a sizeable audience.

Central to this revolution, he argued, was the club scene rather than the recording studio. Although albums were important both for profile and income, it was in the clubs where musicians really hammered things out – and that discerning audiences understood this too. 'In more and more clubs,' he wrote, 'the audience expects the experimenting and "stretching" out to be done during working hours for *them*, and not later for musicians only. As Miles Davis, Thelonious Monk and Ornette Coleman have proved, it has become "commercial" (in the denotative sense of that word) to be as uncompromising in public as one wants to be.'

Bates had already established, through the RCA's Jazz Society, his reputation as the college's most obsessed jazz fan. New York's jazz scene – which Cannonball Adderley described to Hentoff as 'like a world governing body of jazz' – was as much a draw for the young artist as Madison Avenue had been. This was also the main point of connection between him and his host Craddock, who was then aspiring to make 'a really great jazz film'. Craddock says that when he first arrived in New York in 1959, he kept notes on everyone he saw perform in the clubs.

Apple recalls that, very early during his stay, Craddock took Bates to see the Miles Davis Quintet, and that pretty much every night after work, Bates would hit the jazz clubs, either with Craddock or on his own. Throughout July alone, Bates would have had the opportunity to see Eric Dolphy and then Coleman at the Five Spot; Coltrane and Art Blakey at the Village Gate; Buddy Rich at Birdland; and Monk at the Jazz Gallery. In a letter to Lesnie, Bates also described having a run-in with one of the biggest acts in town. 'Saw every one who's any one in music,' he wrote. 'Had a drink at Vanguard with a doll and was interrupted by Chico Hamilton. "Blow buddy, blow, she's mine."'

In *The Jazz Life*, Hentoff makes an important point about New York's club scene around the late fifties and start of the sixties. 'Much has been written about the "inner democracy of jazz",' he wrote,

> insofar as the alleged absence of racial prejudice among musicians is concerned [something Hentoff disputes later in the book]; but actually, much of what the music has done to blur and, in many cases, erase racial lines has happened within its audiences. . . . What jazz has created . . . is one of the very few areas in American life where whites and Negroes, otherwise residentially segregated, have been able to form relatively casual friendships.

New York was, at the time, a comparatively liberal city. But as Hentoff points out, black musicians who had relationships with white women still risked assault, or worse, when they went out in public. Inside the clubs, there was often a different respect, although Hentoff tells the story of one club owner who stopped booking Charles Mingus after pressure from Greenwich Village cops, because of the number of mixed couples his gigs were attracting. 'That guy encourages miscegenation,' the cops told the owner.

The spring and summer of 1961 also saw the first Freedom Rides, as busloads of activists from the north travelled to southern states to test new anti-segregation laws. The 1954 Supreme Court ruling in *Brown v Board of Education* had started the dismantling of Jim Crow. Rosa Parks's action in 1957 had led to the Montgomery bus boycotts. That same year, Little Rock Central High School became the subject of world focus as the National Guard was ordered in to make sure the school integrated. And in February 1960 four black students initiated sit-ins in Greensboro, North Carolina, occupying seats at a whites-only lunch counter. Over the next two years, sit-ins would develop into a national civil rights strategy.

Jazz was – is – an overwhelmingly black art form, and inevitably it became closely associated with the civil rights movement throughout the sixties, via figures like Mingus, Archie Shepp, Coltrane and Nina Simone. Hentoff, too, was involved in the civil rights movement, and as a columnist wrote about political issues just as much as jazz. In 1960, the drummer and band leader Max Roach made this connection crystal-clear with *We Insist! Max Roach's Freedom Now Suite*, released by Candid and with liner notes by Hentoff. The album's cover was an obvious reference to the Greensboro sit-ins, as Roach, along with two other black men, sit at a lunch counter, with a white server over Roach's shoulder. The record itself was entirely focused on black rights, from the legacies of slavery and inequality in America to apartheid in South Africa. Among its featured musicians was the Nigerian percussionist Babatunde Olatunji. In late July 1961 Bates would have been able to see Olatunji perform in New York at Birdland, and then later in the summer at the Village Gate with Coltrane.

It's little wonder Bates was out at the clubs most nights, and that he told Lesnie he'd seen 'every one who's any one'. Jazz in New York in 1961 was, in the words of Hentoff, 'beginning what should be its most daringly exploratory decade'. He was right: that September, Coleman released his groundbreaking album *Free Jazz*; Coltrane would release *A Love Supreme* in 1965; and Davis would close out that decade with *In A Silent Way*, 1969, and *Bitches Brew*, 1970. Bates had seen all of them during a vital incubation and experimental period, from which they'd go on to create some of the most important music of the twentieth century. To hear performers of such quality play every night was a huge leap from his excitement, just a couple of months earlier, at having had the chance to catch a set by Monk, or watch Freddie Redd and Jackie McLean in the stage version of *The Connection*.

Seeing those performers live and so intimately also developed Bates's understanding of, as Hentoff puts it, jazz's 'object-ness': the idea that it was a stand-alone art form of ideas rather than an entertainment. In that sense, it wasn't so far from the conceptual work he was seeing during the day from Lubalin, Ernie Smith and John Pistilli at Sudler & Hennessey (Lubalin had also made a design and typography portfolio in 1960, called 'Come Home to Jazz!'). Bates had put himself in a position to witness some of the great breakthroughs in arguably the two most influential art forms of America's mid-century: jazz music and advertising. Perhaps it's no surprise, then, that when he arrived back in London later that year, he began to consider himself an 'Ideas Man.'

The New York trip was formative for Hockney too, though in very different ways. The success of the prints he'd made at the RCA, via the support of William Lieberman, was an early clue that graphic work would come to play an essential part in his output, and in his mythology. Nowhere is this clearer than in his first major body of work, 'A Rake's Progress', 1961–63, which was based on drawings he made and experiences he had over that summer in 1961. Building on earlier paintings like *We Two Boys Together Clinging*, in which Hockney himself is a masqueraded presence represented through a numerical code, here he dialled things up so that he became his work's central protagonist: a conscious performance of self that cast the artist as subject and object.

'A Rake's Progress' is made up of sixteen etchings that tell the story of a young innocent – Hockney – losing himself in the pleasures and dangers of gay New York. But the series is also Hockney trying to get a thoroughly British art-historical monkey off his back: William Hogarth's eighteenth-century series *The Rake's Progress*, about a young man who receives an inheritance and proceeds to spend, drink and fuck it all away before ending up in debtors' prison and, after he loses his mind, Bedlam. Both series, more than two centuries apart, are moralising tales about the dangers of money, temptation and vice. But as Marco Livingstone points out, Hockney's was also a 'warning to himself as well as to others of the loss of identity which occurs when one bows to external pressures. The destruction of innocence and individuality, we are reminded, is not simply a matter of personal morality. Also at issue is the corruption and debasement of art.'

That moralising tone in his drawing for Bates – lies, lies, lies – was clearly part of a wider concern Hockney had about art's commodification and the impact of advertising and consumerism on society, but also about his own potential to get lost in the attractions and promises of American life. As was often the case during this period, there was a literary bent to his hero's journey: a Tate Gallery Report from 1972 states that the young artist had already read the works of Theodore Dreiser, whose novel *An American Tragedy* from 1925 tells the story of a young man's moral and sexual downfall when he moves to the big smoke.

The first plate of 'A Rake's Progress', *The Arrival*, is a scene-setter in which we see Hockney, carrying a case, arriving in the metropolis. The words 'Flying Tyger' shoot out from behind him, referencing the plane he and Bates had travelled on. But it's also as though Hockney himself is part of the plane, like his feet have touched down and now it's time to continue on foot (this effect of words conveying motion is something he also includes in *Flight into Italy – Swiss Landscape*, 1962, 'thats [*sic*] Switzerland that was' shooting out from behind Michael Kullman's Mini van). In the distance is a skyscraper, a portentous visual shorthand for the city about to unfold in front of him (Hockney says that part of the thrill of New York was the tallness of its architecture, compared to the UK and Europe). Next to that is a dark portal similar to the mirror in the earlier *Mirror, Mirror on the Wall*: a threshold through which the young man is about to pass. *The Arrival* also sets the tone for the way Hockney presents himself throughout the series – a stark young man whose face is a bare outline of his humanity: glasses, close-cropped hair, and an expressionless mouth, a single horizontal slit that never opens. True to the cautionary shape of his story, this is a man to whom things are done: a product of external forces rather than the determiner of his own journey.

The second plate, *Receiving the Inheritance*, drives this home. Hockney sits at a table with an art collector, an arch-capitalist with bald head, goatee beard and bow-tie. The collector holds a bill of sale for Hockney's etching *Myself and My Heroes*, which is lying face-up on the table. The bill says $20, but next to the man's mouth is a different price, $18.

The Hockney figure sits impassive, staring straight ahead and seemingly naked, with a speckle of chest hair (like the photo of him and Bates on the beach together): a limbless torso acquiescing wordlessly to the ten percent discount.

Receiving the Inheritance is also the plate that sets the rake's demise in train. It's a direct reference to the first plate of Hogarth's series, in which the protagonist Tom Rakewell, having just received his inheritance from his father's estate, is being measured up for new clothes while he pays off a young woman he no longer wants to marry. Rakewell's new-found wealth leads to the themes of Hogarth's second plate, his entry into London high society. Similarly, for Hockney, his third and fourth plates capture his own engagement with the upper echelons of American society: first, *Meeting the Good People (Washington)*; and second, *The Gospel Singing (Good People) Madison Square Garden*, a reference to Hockney hearing the black gospel singer Mahalia Jackson perform. Like some of the jazz musicians Bates was seeing live, Jackson was one of the great performers of her generation and an important figure in the civil rights movement. Hockney once again casts himself here as passive, with arms folded and legs crossed. In a way similar to *Tea Painting in an Illusionistic Style*, he presents himself as a seated figure inside a box, a comparatively tiny form inside the stage Jackson is standing on as she belts out 'Hallelujah'.

After Rakewell has his high-society moment, Hogarth starts his rake's descent, the third plate in the series a pub orgy in which a thoroughly wasted Rakewell enjoys the entertainments of London prostitutes. Hockney's debauch, across a succession of plates, is less obviously sexual, and more loaded with a kind of sullen longing. In *The Start of the Spending Spree and the Door Opening for a Blonde*, we see the Hockney figure, naked again but for that chest hair, with a huge bottle of Lady Clairol hair bleach on top of his head. In front of him is a door – again, like the mirrors and portals in other works, a compositional divide that also acts as a threshold – beyond which is a radiant sun and palm trees:

the promise of new American beginnings. The idea that doors would open for him with his new, golden look was taken from the pop culture message that blonde women were the sensual ideal, a trope cemented by the incredible cultural force of Marilyn Monroe's image at the time, but also imprinted on the American psyche by Clairol's blonde campaigns of the late fifties and early sixties. The breakthrough campaign had been 'Does she . . . or doesn't she?', written by one of the few women copywriters at the top of the Madison Avenue game, Shirley Polykoff, of Foote, Cone & Belding. Polykoff went on to develop Clairol's 'Is it true blondes have more fun?' ads – the campaign that led Hockney to bleach his hair in the first place.

Hockney then replaces Hogarth's pub orgy with two scenes. The first is *The Seven Stone Weakling*, in which his rake stands under a tree in Central Park, passively watching fit men jog by. The second is *The Drinking Scene*, in which we see our hero from behind, standing at a New York gay bar, a taller man putting his arm around his shoulder. In the bottom right corner are two more men, facing out, one with his hand on the other's shoulder, a couple of tears rolling down his cheek. In the next plate, Hockney explicitly refers to Hogarth again. *Marries an Old Maid* mirrors Hogarth's *The Marriage*, in which Rakewell, now broke, marries an old woman for her money, all the while eyeing up her young maid during the ceremony. Hockney's marriage takes place in another of his doorway-portals, which could just as easily be a dark space for a clandestine sexual encounter.

From here, Hockney's rake begins to lose his identity even more quickly: he's witness to an arrest in *Viewing a Prison Scene* in which two male arms, one naked and one besuited, are handcuffed together. It's at this point that the rake himself becomes a sculptural object – a torso with no arms or legs, like the remnants of a classical statue. In the distance is the outline of another man, with a prison number written across his chest, a harbinger of the rake's eventual fate. In *Death in Harlem*, his physical detachment from his surrounds becomes even more pronounced as a dead figure lies in a bed while Hockney – a bust printed in red – floats freely.

In *The Wallet Begins to Empty*, Hockney has assumed his full form again as he's cast out by his old maid and the art collector. For the first time in the story we see real emotion from him as he stomps down a staircase, shoulders hunched and head dropped, dejected, the spike of the Washington Monument standing alongside his ostracisers. He sinks into drink in *Disintegration*, his head breaking free from his body. In *Cast Aside*, his bust form has become the size of a trinket, thrown by a giant hand into the mouth of a monster. In *Meeting the Other People*, he encounters a man at the bottom of a long staircase wearing a t-shirt that says 'I swing with WABC' (a reference to a popular radio station that played Top 40 pop songs in New York); the man has a wire running up to his ear and musical notes emanate from a transistor radio in his back pocket. It's the prelude to the rake's final downfall, in the last plate of the series, *Bedlam*. The institution's name is scrawled in red on a blank wall faced by five men, all wearing the same 'I swing with WABC' t-shirt, all with transistor radios, all with that same wire running up to their ears. The only way to identify our rake is by a tiny arrow above his head. Having passed through that threshold in *The Arrival*, and having sunk deep into the fabric of the American metropolis, his disappearance is complete.

The implication here is that conformity is a form of madness, and that popular culture is the cause of this loss of self. There are echoes here again of McLuhan in *The Mechanical Bride*:

> The ordinary person senses the greatness of the odds against him even without thought or analysis, and he adapts his attitudes unconsciously. A huge passivity has settled on industrial society. For people carried about in mechanical vehicles, earning their living by waiting on machines, listening much of the waking day to canned music, watching packaged movie entertainment and capsulated news, for such people it would require an

> exceptional degree of awareness and an especial heroism of effort to be anything but supine consumers of processed goods.

Hockney was clearly aspiring to that 'especial heroism of effort', making work that showed his deep desire to resist the processed, canned nature of contemporary culture. But 'A Rake's Progress' also seemed to signal a new approach to self in his work: an understanding that an identity could be both a subject and an object, something internal and lived but also performed and externalised. There had been hints of this thinking in works like *Mirror, Mirror on the Wall*. But 'A Rake's Progress' gave those instincts a new scope and scale.

It's difficult to overestimate just how important 'A Rake's Progress' became in establishing Hockney's public persona and his status as one of the foremost artists of his generation. When he returned to London for the 1961/62 year, he'd planned to make a series of eight prints based on his trip to New York. Robin Darwin, though, encouraged him to think bigger, and to expand it to over twenty so it could be printed by the RCA's Lion & Unicorn Press. Hockney settled on sixteen, but wouldn't finish them until 1963, after a second trip to New York. He then sold the publishing rights to Paul Cornwall-Jones of Editions Alecto for £5,000 (paid over three years): an absolutely monstrous sum for the time, and for an artist who'd graduated only the year before. In 1961, Hockney had been excited to have a few hundred quid in his pocket for his trip to New York. After he sold 'A Rake's Progress', he was loaded. It was this money that carried him, eventually, to California – the land of palm trees and sunsets and swimming pools and beautiful men and art collectors he intuited in his New York prints, and which eventually became synonymous with his best paintings.

The last straw for Mark Berger's parents, when it came to their house guest Hockney, is also one of the most significant moments in the artist's early story. Hockney's biographer Peter Webb tells it like this:

> One evening, Mark and he [Hockney] were watching television in the house with Barry [*sic*] Bates from the Royal College, who was also visiting New York, and Ferrill Amacker, a friend of Mark's from New Orleans. They were all a little drunk when an advertisement for Lady Clairol hair colouring came on the screen: 'Blondes have more fun. Doors open for a blonde.' Hockney announced that if that were so, he was going to dye his hair. The others all agreed to do likewise and they went out to buy some Lady Clairol from the drugstore. They set to work immediately, and by the time Mark's father returned home, all four were blonde. He was furious, and said he was not having such behaviour in his house.

In Christopher Simon Sykes's later biography, Bates is absent from the scene. But there are contemporaneous documents that support his presence. Bates's girlfriend Ann Quin, writing as him in late 1961 or early 1962, makes a clear reference to Hockney in an untitled fragment. 'Called round at 2 a.m. to say goodbye before going to Paris,' she has Bates say, 'guess he was in love with me at one time. Went round together in New York, until he shacked up with this guy [Amacker, in Brooklyn Heights]. Yeh we went blonde together, dyed it overnight at some party so they told me.' And in the letter to Leon Lesnie from the same period that Quin likely also wrote, he/she writes, 'Accidentally bleached my hair at a party one night, so I found out (doors open for blondes) this boy insisted on running his fingers through my hair.' Apple thinks this likely happened in the second half of their trip, after he'd finished up at Sudler & Hennessey.

It's clear that the transformation had nowhere near as much significance for Bates as it did for his friend; the bleached hair was an essential aspect of the transformed Hockney who returned to London, and the RCA, for his final year in September 1961. With the money he'd made from selling his prints via Lieberman, Hockney had also bought an American suit, and he'd taken up cigar smoking, as evidenced by the photos of him and Bates together at Coney Island.

These were youthful affectations, but they were also symptomatic of a new way of thinking about self: from that moment on, David Hockney was 'David Hockney', as much a public manifestation of an artistic identity as a real person. This is not at all to suggest that he became somehow insincere. But it is to suggest that his change, and his maintenance of it for years – particularly the blonde hair – demonstrated that he was more aware than most of his contemporaries that artists needed to be known, and seen, and heard: defined not just through their work but in relation to the world.

Aside from the perceived sexual allure of blonde hair, which was played upon – and preyed upon – by Clairol and its brilliant copywriter Polykoff, bleaching one's hair is a very particular process: a stripping out of what was there before, rather than an adding in – a kind of 'fresh start'. Its appeal, then, to so many American women might not just have been its fashionability but its thoroughly existential American-ness: the prospect of shaking off one's past and becoming someone new. Certainly for Hockney, and later on for Bates, it represented just that.

It also seems relevant that, over the course of the summer, the major exhibition at MoMA was the largest survey to date of Futurism, a radical art movement born in Italy in the early twentieth century. It crashed into the world with a manifesto written by the poet Filippo Tommaso Marinetti: a wild and proto-fascist veneration of machines, technology and individualism that called for an erasure of the art-historical past, and a new art that embraced the accelerated times and the industrial forces causing this speed. In his catalogue essay for the show, Joshua C. Taylor wrote:

> Like many of their fellows elsewhere, the Italian Futurists were fighting the estrangement from the world, the lonely isolation of the individual that was not only the inheritance of the artist but a common threat to modern man. They rejected firmly the temptation to brood over man's plight, sentimentalizing over his helplessness in the way fashionable at the turn of the century. They turned against the Lombard tradition that encouraged a crepuscular sadness to invade the works of even the most methodical divisionists. With Nietzschean arrogance they despised the weak and the timid, the thoughtful or hesitant, and wished to feel themselves rash, audacious, and capable of infinite accomplishment. They wanted their art to restore to man a sense of daring, an assertive will rather than submissive acceptance, to break through the insulating shell of self by sheer force if need be.

It's easy to see how Bates, who'd already expressed enthusiasm for Futurism's conceptual cousin Dada, would have been attracted to this proposition (soon, he'd be producing his own manifestos with Quin). His love for the technologies of his own time, particularly in the printing and advertising worlds; his desire to transcend his New Zealand roots and become a major international figure; and his interest in individual acceleration, rather than collective wellbeing, also made Futurism a natural fit.

In just a couple of months, Hockney and Bates had encountered exactly the kinds of cultural experimentation and freedoms they'd hoped for when they paid for their cut-price plane tickets to New York. For Bates, the conceptual thinking he was part of on Madison Avenue during the day was complemented by the musical revolution he saw night after night in the city's jazz clubs. For Hockney, the successes of the Lieberman sales, combined with his embrace of New York's gay bars and cruising spots with Berger and Amacker, gave him a new opportunity to be himself, and, eventually, to manipulate and perform that self in his work and in his daily life. Both returned to London for their final year as 'changed men'. 'I arrived back looking like Kennedy,' Bates wrote to Lesnie, 'except I had a hat on, chewed gum and called everyone buddy (or darling).' Hockney's new blonde hair and his cigar habit were talking points at the RCA too.

The hair bleaching had been a point of connection between the two men, but it was also arguably the last meaningful one. Both were beginning to manifest new ideas of what an artist could be, but in opposite ways: Bates now relentlessly driven by ideas and looking towards new technologies and the future; Hockney more interested in grappling with, and conquering, the shadows of art history.

These differences of approach were cemented by the very first works each of them made when they returned to the RCA. Hockney made *A Grand Procession of Dignitaries in the Semi-Egyptian Style*, 1961, his biggest painting to date at around two metres by three, partly because 'people were already grabbing places where they were going to paint the whole year. I'd got that big stretcher and I thought, I can grab a bigger area to paint on it, so I'll do it first; it's a good reason for painting this picture, it means I get more space. Selfish, I know.'

There was, of course, more to the work than that; it was based on a C. P. Cavafy poem called 'Waiting for the Barbarians' which, Livingstone suggests, attracted Hockney for its 'wry comment on human nature: our tendency to inflate our self-image by contrasting ourselves with those we deem inferior, and the ease with which we can invent false motives for our actions and then delude ourselves into believing them.'

Bates, meanwhile, returned to his poster designs. At Sudler & Hennessey he'd got into a conversation one day with Ernie Smith. Smith asked Bates what he was working on, and the young man told him that as soon as he got back to London he had to produce a poster for the RCA's Film Society screening of Federico Fellini's *I Vitelloni*, 1953. The film is about a group of unemployed chancers in their twenties, drifting through a summer and refusing to grow up. On the spot, Smith came up with the headline for Bates's poster: 'PSST!! Hey you, Spiv!' It was a perfect play on the film's plot, but also on Bates's prospective art student audience. Smith quickly came up with the rest of the poster text:

> The lights are low at the JCR, our brothers are there. Why not join us and them in breakin' the joint apart? Fred Fellini's chief buster, buster. You take your cue from him. Okay, not a word to Joe. See you Thursday, 7.30, outside.

In London, Bates printed Smith's words, white on plain black paper, with no images or extraneous detail. It embodied everything he'd picked up from Lubalin, Smith and their colleagues, and the wider revolution in advertising's treatment of image and text: a marriage of language, idea and target audience, stripped down to its essentials. Bates would soon be deploying exactly the same tactics in his art.

Hockney and Bates stayed close after the New York trip. In October, they travelled together to the wedding of printmaking student Michael Adams in Cornwall. It was there that Ron Fuller, the student who'd given Hockney so much technical know-how on making etchings, photographed them together – Hockney wearing Adams' Union Jack waistcoat, Bates sharply dressed alongside him. Bates played jazz that night on the church's bells, channelling the music he'd heard in New York. The pair huddled together that night on the stone floor of a lean-to attached to the Rose Cottage on the Heligan Estate.

What they didn't know was that the New York they'd just left was about to come to them, in the form of Larry Rivers – regarded, at the time, as one of America's most significant contemporary painters, and a key figure in the post-Abstract Expressionist 'New York School'. His arrival at the RCA in November 1961 would have a profound effect on Bates, and present an unexpected writing opportunity for his new girlfriend, Ann Quin.

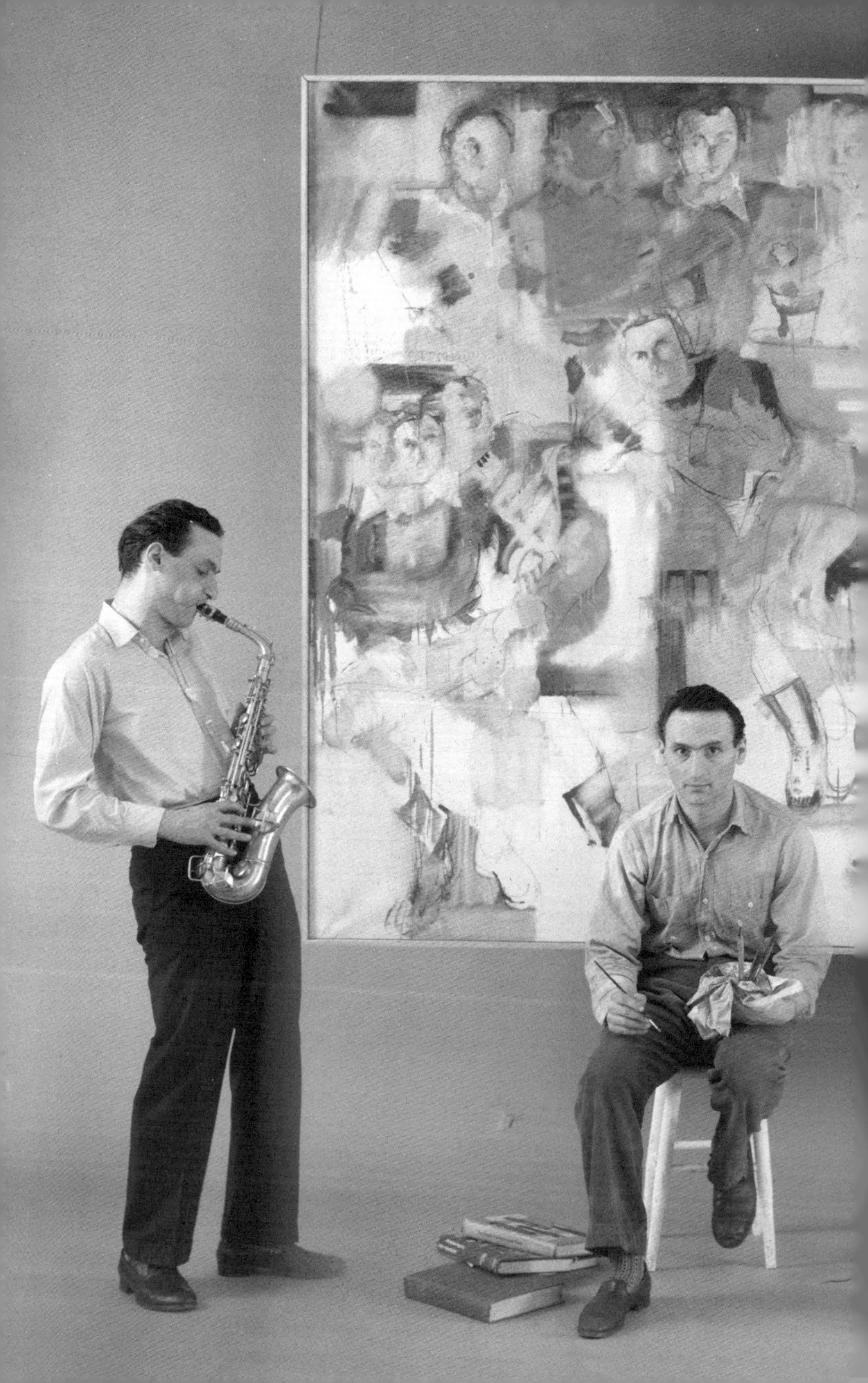

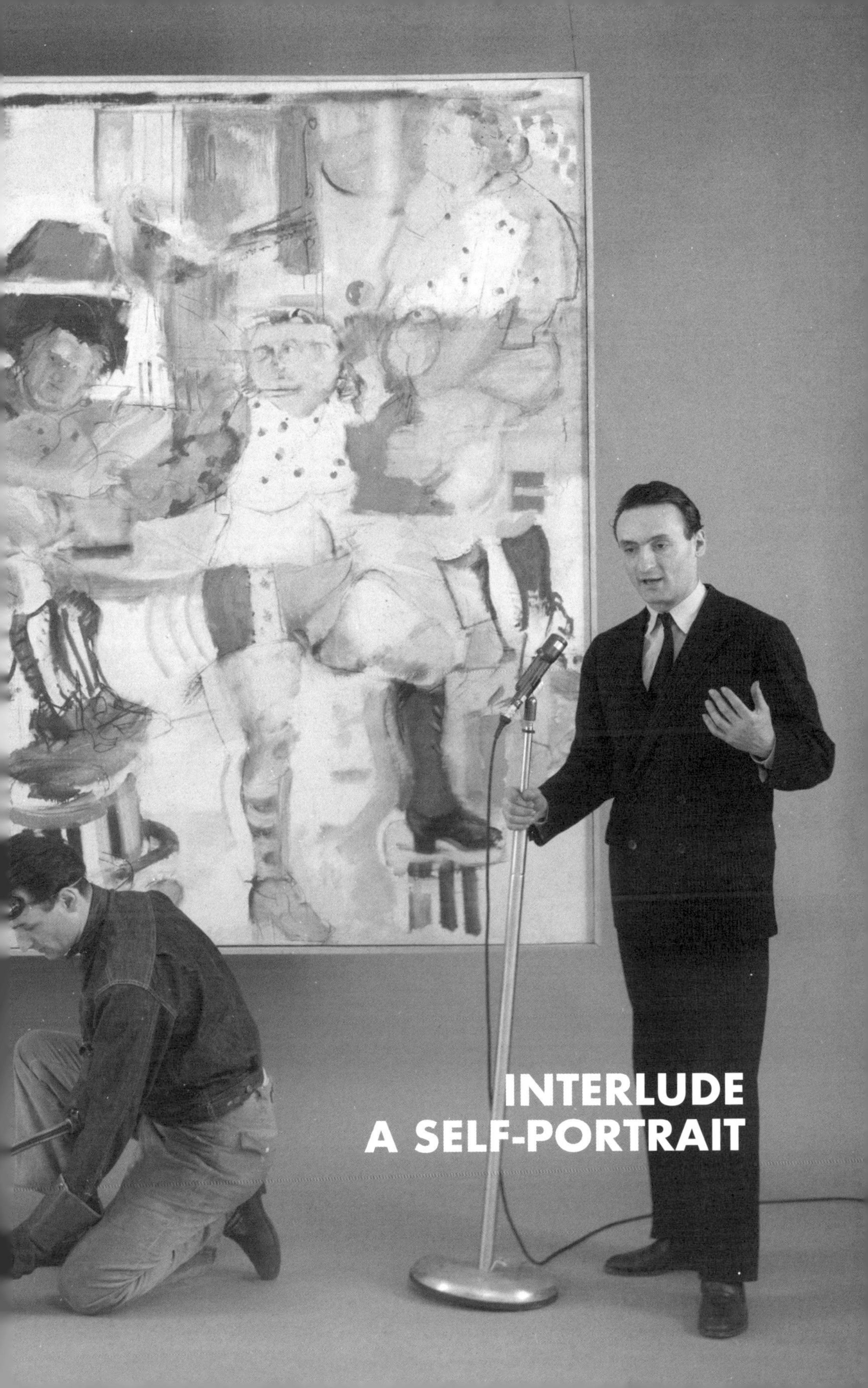

INTERLUDE
A SELF-PORTRAIT

There are four elements that ultimately determine quality and meaning in painting . . . one, the colour you choose and how much; two, where you put it; three, in what manner. The fourth is outside of you, and in its ambiguity lies the nagging sensation of never really knowing that will follow you as long as the need to identify with painting exists, and that is life. Life, however dimensional you make the word: the physical world comprehended through the senses; one part of it nature, another man-made; culture – define it any way you wish – the social institutions, exposure to art, erroneous notions mixed with some accurate ones of history, the private struggle with semantics and meaning; Mother, Father, Uncle Dave, the size of your infant crib; everything, but everything as it moves through the individual, depositing mountainous amounts of material, adding and destroying and organizing on new bases as it passes through, creating associations, memory, and passion, and all those uncontrollable elements embodied either in yourself or the observer of a painting, that finally transform the obvious physical appearances into sensations and 'spiritual' significance.

— LARRY RIVERS, NOVEMBER 1961

'REVLON! The greatest name in cosmetics presents the one, two, four, eight, sixteen, thirty-two, sixty-four – yes, the 64,000 Dollar Question!'

So begins one of America's most iconic game shows, which ran on CBS between 1955 and 1958. A forerunner to *Who Wants to Be a Millionaire?*, *The $64,000 Question* had contestants answer questions for money, then invited them to risk their winnings on a shot to double up on the next round, all the way to $64,000. As with its modern counter-part, the tension and the difficulty increased the more money there was at stake: the sudden jump from $16,000 to $32,000 was huge by 1950s standards, as was the gut-churning risk of plummeting back to nothing.

It was one of the most popular television programmes of its time, and gave birth to a spinoff: *The $64,000 Challenge*, in which a contestant who'd won at least $8,000 on the original show would go up against someone in their own area of expertise in a kind of winner-takes-all showdown. The artist Larry Rivers received a call from the show's producers, asking him to be a challenger – on the topic of modern art. He appeared on the show in early 1957.

Rivers claimed in his 1992 autobiography that the show's producers had got his name from MoMA, where his close friend and occasional lover, the poet Frank O'Hara, was working (Rivers quipped that Franz Kline and Philip Guston had also been on the list). He accepted, and began to study hard for the shows. Once he was on screen, he became an instant hit: a tall, charismatic man who broke America's primetime mould with his big nose, his thick New York accent and ribald anecdotes about having his mother-in-law pose nude for a painting. At one point, when the show's host Ralph Story asked Rivers how his art dealer, Tibor de Nagy, came up with the prices for his paintings, Rivers replied, 'It's hard to decide exactly what they're worth. I mean, what anything is worth on a certain day. For instance, what are you worth?' The audience laughed. Story, for a moment, looked lost for words, then quickly shot back, 'Actually, Larry, there's a shortage of stupid emcees, so I command a big price.' For all of the fifties, Rivers had been part of New York's bohemian set, from the jazz clubs to the poets' and painters' lofts. Now he was in America's living rooms, cracking jokes and answering questions about the history of modern art.

The 'champion' Rivers was pitted against was in fact the successful jockey Billy Pearson. Though horses had made him well known, Pearson's knowledge of art history was also impressive – he'd already won thousands in prize money. As well as Rivers, Pearson was challenged by Charles Duveen – a member of the influential Duveen dynasty of art dealers – whom he dispatched at the $4,000 level. Rivers, by contrast, was a much tougher opponent. Both men cruised through the first rounds. Rivers almost stumbled at the $16,000 level, after answering that an Alexander Archipenko sculpture was made from 'metal' (semantics: made from bronze, it was technically metal, and he was let through). Both men got through the $32,000 round too. Then there was a week of suspense while they went home and prepared for the final $64,000 round. If his opponent failed and Rivers succeeded, the artist would be $64,000 better off, and vice versa. If they both got it right, they'd split the cash.

As Rivers tells it, O'Hara arranged for him to have access to MoMA's library so he could study during the week between shows. The librarian, who recognised Rivers, quietly told him that the panel who came up with the questions had also used the library, and that he happened to have the notes they'd left behind. Written on the notes were the following week's questions and answers. 'He showed them to me,' Rivers wrote, 'and said the world was a commercial place and artists were the only pure people left in this society.' And the topic of the questions-to-come? Pierre Bonnard: Rivers' hero, and the painter to whom New York's most powerful art critic, Clement Greenberg, had compared him favourably in 1949 when Rivers had his first solo exhibition. In other words, Rivers cheated – and nailed the $64,000 question. But Pearson nailed it too. They received $32,000 each.

Rivers was asked to appear again the following year, and didn't fare as well. He had, though, become a celebrity. On 20 October 1958, *Life* ran a feature about him, with the headline 'Wonder Boy and his Many Sides'. The opening double-spread shows Rivers in front of one of his paintings, in four guises: blowing a saxophone; on a stool holding paintbrushes with a few art history tomes stacked messily at his feet; welding a lump of steel, with safety goggles on his forehead (he'd begun making sculptures); and finally in a black suit, his hair oiled back, holding a mic stand.

The *Life* spread was the early peak of Rivers' fame: held up, at thirty-five, as a whizz-kid polymath. The even spacing between the portraits suggested that all four identities were equally valid; there was no sense of one being the 'real' Rivers and the others being performed or fictional identities. 'The paintings, made up of countless fragmentary images of people and objects, seem as many-sided as the painter himself,' the feature writer noted. '"But I think," says Rivers, "in my life and my art there's a central Larry Rivers running through everything."'

Three years later, Rivers would stand in a lecture hall in the Victoria & Albert Museum, in front of the RCA's most talented intake, and unpack who that central Larry Rivers might be. And for one student in particular – Barrie Bates – it would be transformative.

Rivers was born Yitzroch Loiza Grossberg in the Bronx in 1923 to first-generation Jewish immigrant parents. He was eleven years younger than Jackson Pollock and almost two decades younger than Willem de Kooning, the two painters who cast such long shadows across post-war American art and against whom Rivers would spend so much of his early career kicking.

Rivers didn't take up painting seriously until after the end of the war, when he began studying with Hans Hofmann in New York. He had been – and for several years continued to be – a professional jazz musician: a sax player who, in his own words, was a solid if unspectacular hornblower whose greatest claim to fame as a musician was that he went to the Juilliard School for a while with Miles Davis.

Rivers' status in American art history has suffered two fates in recent years. The first is that, after the death of his ally and lover Frank O'Hara in 1966, his historical significance quickly started to fade and has stayed dim, eclipsed by the increasing emphasis placed on his contemporaries Jasper Johns and Robert Rauschenberg, and by Andy Warhol's immense cultural impact. The second is that he became something of a toxic asset after the *New York Times* and *Vanity Fair* in 2010 picked up the story of the split in the Rivers family over what should happen with videos he made of his adolescent daughters in the late seventies and early eighties, which were edited into a single work called *Growing*. In it, there are points at which the girls are shown nude, and are interviewed by their father about their developing bodies. One of Rivers' daughters, Emma, said she'd been pressured into being filmed, and had demanded that *Growing* be removed from Rivers' archive, which was in the process of being sold to the Fales Library at New York University (where it now resides). The video has stayed with the Larry Rivers Foundation.

Sex and drugs were staples in Rivers' 1940s and 1950s life just as much as music and painting, as his remarkable book (co-written with Arnold Weinstein) *What Did I Do? The Unauthorized Autobiography* tells in often excruciating detail. Like many of his generation, Rivers married and had kids young, before realising what a terrible idea that was. As a nascent sexual revolution started to unfold around him, he found himself in New York's art galleries and jazz clubs and literary parties, sleeping with everyone he could, and spending more and more time away from home.

He was on the road, playing for a band that had an extended residency over a Maine summer, when he first met the painter Jane Freilicher, the wife of a bandmate. Rivers was impressed as he watched her paint, and became curious. She and her husband Jack encouraged him to give it a try; from then on, every afternoon, the three would get together and paint. 'The weather was pleasant and the afternoons vanished,' Rivers wrote:

> It's hard to think we suddenly discontinued gossiping, but the gossip was sprinkled with art, literature, and politics. I liked those spices. After a week or two I began thinking that art was on a 'higher level' than jazz. The blue romance that haloed jazz was still strong. Jazz reached into the past through songs with touching chord changes and simple words. I was still thrilled to walk into jazz spaces, where I could freely enjoy the faces, personalities, and speech patterns of young men and women, black and white. I had been caught up in this romance with jazz, blues, drugs, and night.
>
> Now I began to have pleasure in the daylight, painting in the afternoons there in green Maine.

Other women artists were instrumental in Rivers' early development. Nell Blaine, who had a serious reputation in the New York art scene, was a graduate of Hofmann's school, and became the conduit through which Rivers met key figures like de Kooning and Greenberg. Jenni Quilter describes Blaine as 'a formidable force in the downtown painting world in the 1940s and '50s', with her apartment acting as a kind of hub for the group that would become known as the New York School until she contracted polio on a trip to Mykonos, Greece, in 1959. Blaine had encouraged Freilicher and Rivers to study with Hofmann, advice they both followed in 1947. Grace Hartigan was also an essential figure within the scene, profiled in *Life* in 1957, and the only woman included in 'The New American Painting' in 1958–59 – perhaps because of the curatorial involvement of her close friend O'Hara, with whom she'd collaborated on her painting series 'Oranges: 12 Pastorals', in 1952.

Known for her incredible wit, Freilicher acted as the scene's glue: over many years, she was the vital and much-loved link between the poetry worlds of O'Hara, John Ashbery, Kenneth Koch, Barbara Guest and James Schuyler, and the painters of their generation. According to Eric Brown, '[n]ot only did she forge close relationships with the poets, she also served as their creative muse.' Frank O'Hara's 'Jane' poems were just one example of this. Quilter writes that Freilicher '[inspired] unparalleled devotion among her friends, particularly the poets'. O'Hara's biographer Brad Gooch also describes her as an important figure in O'Hara's New York life. 'A pretty twenty-six-year-old painter,' he writes, 'with dark hair and a misleadingly serious and preoccupied demeanor, Freilicher had a campy wit and a brainy zest for literature in the vein of Ivy Compton-Burnett that made her a natural focus of O'Hara's enthusiasm.' Rivers evidently adored her too; the pair had an occasional affair through to the early 1950s (her marriage to Jack Freilicher was dissolved in the late forties, and in 1957 she married Joe Hazan).

In 1949, just a few years after Rivers had started painting, New York's pre-eminent art critic Clement Greenberg put him on the map. Reviewing the young artist's first gallery show at Jane Street Gallery (a kind of artist-run co-operative), Greenberg compared him favourably to Bonnard. This was pretty much the last polite encounter the two men would ever have; in later years, Greenberg, the great arbiter and defender of Abstract Expressionism, wrote Rivers off as a hack. Rivers' closeness with that other great (though less credited) assessor of contemporary American art in New York at the time, O'Hara, proved far more significant, and fruitful: an intellectual connection that led to them collaborating on work, and a tempestuous sexual relationship (which overlapped with their mutual obsessions with Freilicher). When O'Hara died after being struck by a jeep on Fire Island in 1966, Rivers delivered a dreadful eulogy at his funeral, describing in graphic detail how O'Hara's body had looked in the hospital after the smash that killed him.

Of all the characters who pass through *What Did I Do?*, O'Hara is the one Rivers seems to struggle with most: at times wanting to poke fun, as he does so relentlessly at others; sometimes wanting to venerate; sometimes wanting to downplay the intensity of their connection. It is absolutely clear, however, that the two men felt deeply for each other, and that O'Hara was vital in establishing Rivers' artistic credentials. Hartigan told Gooch that she believed Rivers was never as good an artist or person as he was 'when Frank was running herd on him'. Ashbery believed O'Hara was genuinely in love with Rivers; and Koch told Gooch that '[a] lot of [O'Hara's] very unhappy, wretched, miserable poems about unsatisfied love I think were about Larry.'

The pair met at a party thrown by Ashbery in 1950 (which Freilicher was present at too). O'Hara hadn't yet moved to New York – that would happen the following year – but was visiting over the Christmas break from Ann Arbor, Michigan. According to Gooch, both were already aware of each other's work. They hit it off, snuck behind a curtain and made out. 'I liked his Ivy League dirty white sneakers, he liked my hands full of paint,' Rivers wrote:

> He was a charming madman, a whoosh of air sometimes warm and pleasant, sometimes so gusty you closed your eyes and brushed back the hair it disarranged. He was thin and about five seven. He walked on his toes, stretched his neck, and angled his head, all to add an inch or two to his height. I never walked the same after I met him. Through a moist pair of lips like Cupid's bow, he smoked and spoke with enthusiasm about the virtues of a thousand subjects. His days, no matter what he was up to, were

> divided almost equally between getting over what he drank the night before and drinking toward the same pleasant haze. When he was sober he was careful, objective, more a listener than a speaker. He always had something to add to anything I said. Anything. It was comforting being understood; until then I had the suspicion that I was a court primitive with privileges among the highly civilized.

This warm portrait is immediately contrasted when Rivers describes what a destructive drunk O'Hara could be. This push and pull continues, with Rivers then suggesting that they'd each influenced the other's work.

Rivers is far harsher, however, about their sexual relationship. A consistent and unattractive theme of his memoir is his suggestion that, in his gay encounters, he was almost always doing the other party a favour. With O'Hara, he writes, '[a]n affectionate grope at the door sent him optimistically on his toes off to dinner to one, two, or three of the four hundred people who, like myself, considered him their best friend. He was a professional fan.' And later: 'Sex with Frank . . . was not very thrilling.' He gave Gooch a more graphic account of their sex life, and his ambivalence about it, in 1989. Rivers does, however, show at least a modicum of self-awareness in his autobiography when he reproduces the blasé letter O'Hara sent in reply to his own letter of July 1953 calling off their sexual relationship. O'Hara tells Rivers he is 'very sweet but very stupid', and that if he was 'busier about other things than trying to imagine my feelings you might stop complicating one of the simplest and least troublesome little affairs you've ever had.'

This intimate connection between these two heavyweights of the New York scene had direct aesthetic consequences for both of them. The clearest and most famous example of this comes via the painting that established Rivers as a serious player in post-war American art, 1953's *Washington Crossing the Delaware*.

As its title suggests, Rivers' masterpiece was possibly the most unfashionable thing he could have set his mind to in the New York art world of de Kooning, Pollock and Greenberg: a history painting. At the time of its making, Rivers had just read *War and Peace*. He wanted to match its ambition in paint, and with an American subject. 'How did I actually picture the crossing?' Rivers asked. 'I knew it took place in the last days of December. I saw the moment as nerve-racking and anxious. I couldn't see getting into a very chilly river around Christmastime with thoughts of death and discomfort as an occasion for hand-on-chest heroics.'

Rivers' model for the figure of Washington was Jacques-Louis David's *The Emperor Napoleon in His Study at the Tuileries*, 1812: a camp moment in the history of neoclassicism in which the little French despot tucks his right hand into his waistcoat and wears a pair of high-waisted, tight white pants that leave no doubt that Napoleon hung to the left. Rivers' Washington has the same white pants, if not the same degree of anatomical revelation.

In her 2006 PhD dissertation 'Larry Rivers and Frank O'Hara: Reframing Male Sexualities', Dong-Yeon Koh suggests that Rivers' use of the white pants could be interpreted as a kind of code: in New York's gay scene of the 1950s, tight trousers were a uniform and a signal for young gay men. Koh also cites several O'Hara poems that make reference to tight or white pants. It's a completely plausible interpretation, not only because Rivers and O'Hara were so close, but also because in 1964 Rivers made another painting using the same Napoleonic source, this time called *The Greatest Homosexual*.

Other than its large dimensions, *Delaware* was the antithesis of what Greenberg held dearest in painting: it was figurative; it was tinged with irony; and, unlike Pollock's drips, de Kooning's garish *Women*, or Rothko's deadly serious floating boxes, it was seriously camp. It was also a ballsy statement in the era of McCarthyism, when many of the groups Rivers was himself closest to – Jews, communists, artists, gays, poets, musicians – were regularly targeted as 'un-American' threats to societal order. *Delaware*, by contrast with the works of the Abstract Expressionists, had more than a whiff of socialist realism about it, not just in its heroic subject matter but also in its original Tolstoyan inspiration.

The apotheosis of Rivers' *Delaware* came with its acquisition by MoMA in 1955 (the same year O'Hara began working in the International Program there): confirmation for Rivers that he'd finally achieved something in paint and that the world was beginning to take him seriously as an artist. The painting also became the subject of one of O'Hara's poems, 'On Seeing Larry Rivers' *Washington Crossing the Delaware* at the Museum of Modern Art', which opens with a reference to those trousers: 'Now that our hero has come back to us / in his white pants and we know his nose / trembling like a flag under fire, / we see the calm cold river is supporting / our forces, the beautiful history.'

Rivers' prominence – in the art world because of *Delaware*, in the wider public consciousness because of *The $64,000 Challenge* – had a third strand: he was one of the most significant links between what were emerging as the three most important cultural forms of America's post-war avant-garde, all of which were being advanced and refined in New York: contemporary painting (the worlds of Pollock and Rothko starting slowly to fade, replaced by Rivers, Hartigan, Johns, Rauschenberg and a handful of other painters); the new American literature, in the hands of Ashbery, Schuyler, Guest, Koch, James Merrill, O'Hara and the emergent figures of the Beats; and the incredible advances in jazz in the hands of Monk, Davis, Coltrane, Coleman and others. Rivers himself began organising events that brought many of these forces together, producing evenings in which some of New York's new young poets and jazz musicians performed at the Five Spot. His own versatility as a performer was given a different platform in 1959, when he was cast to play Milo (the fictional Neal Cassady) in Robert Frank and Al Leslie's *Pull My Daisy*.

The art dealer John Bernard Myers was also an essential connecting force in the scene at the time. As the director of Tibor de Nagy Gallery,

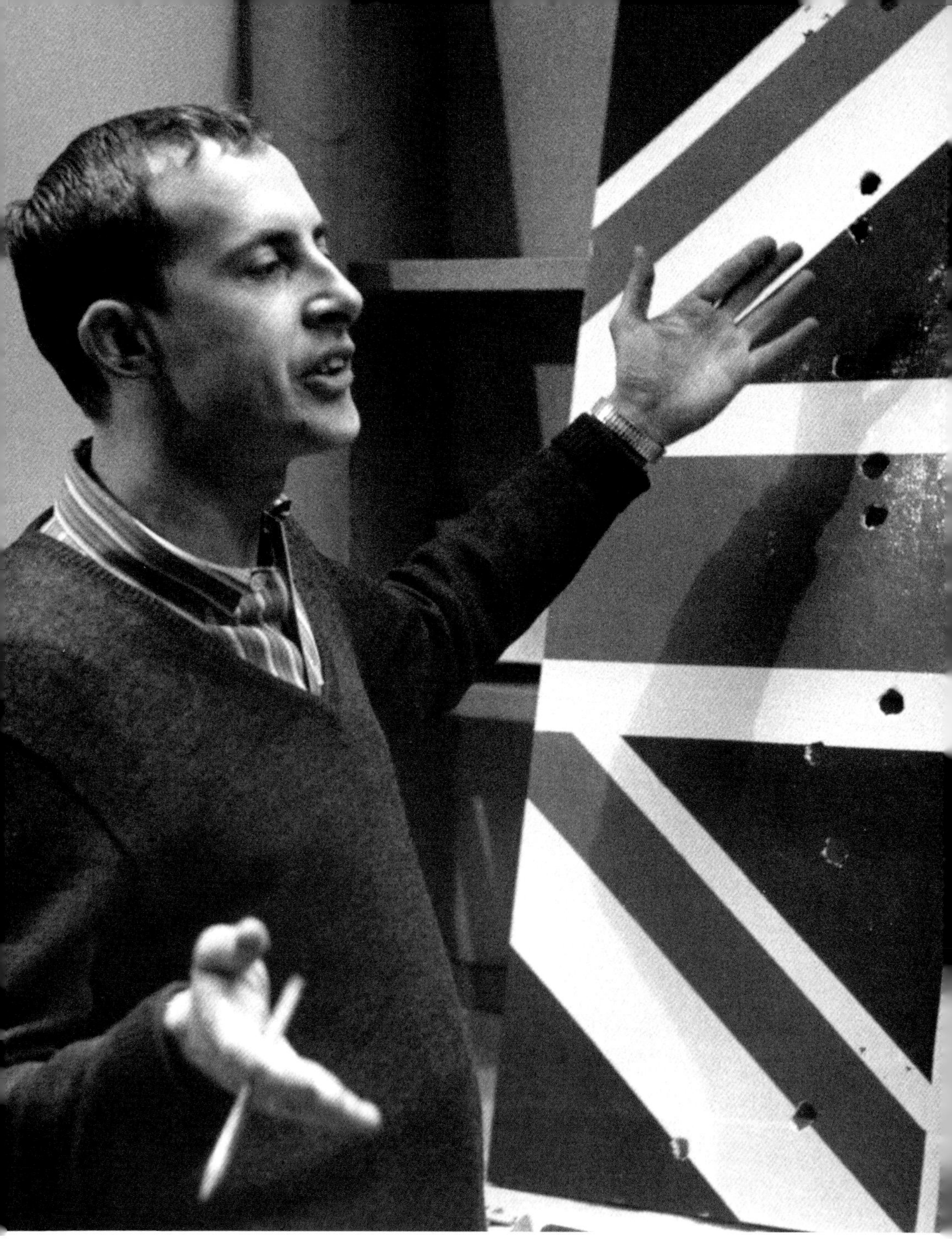

1 Barrie Bates with his work *B.E.A. Flight Over East Berlin*, 1961, at the Royal College of Art, London, 1961, photo: Frank Apthorp

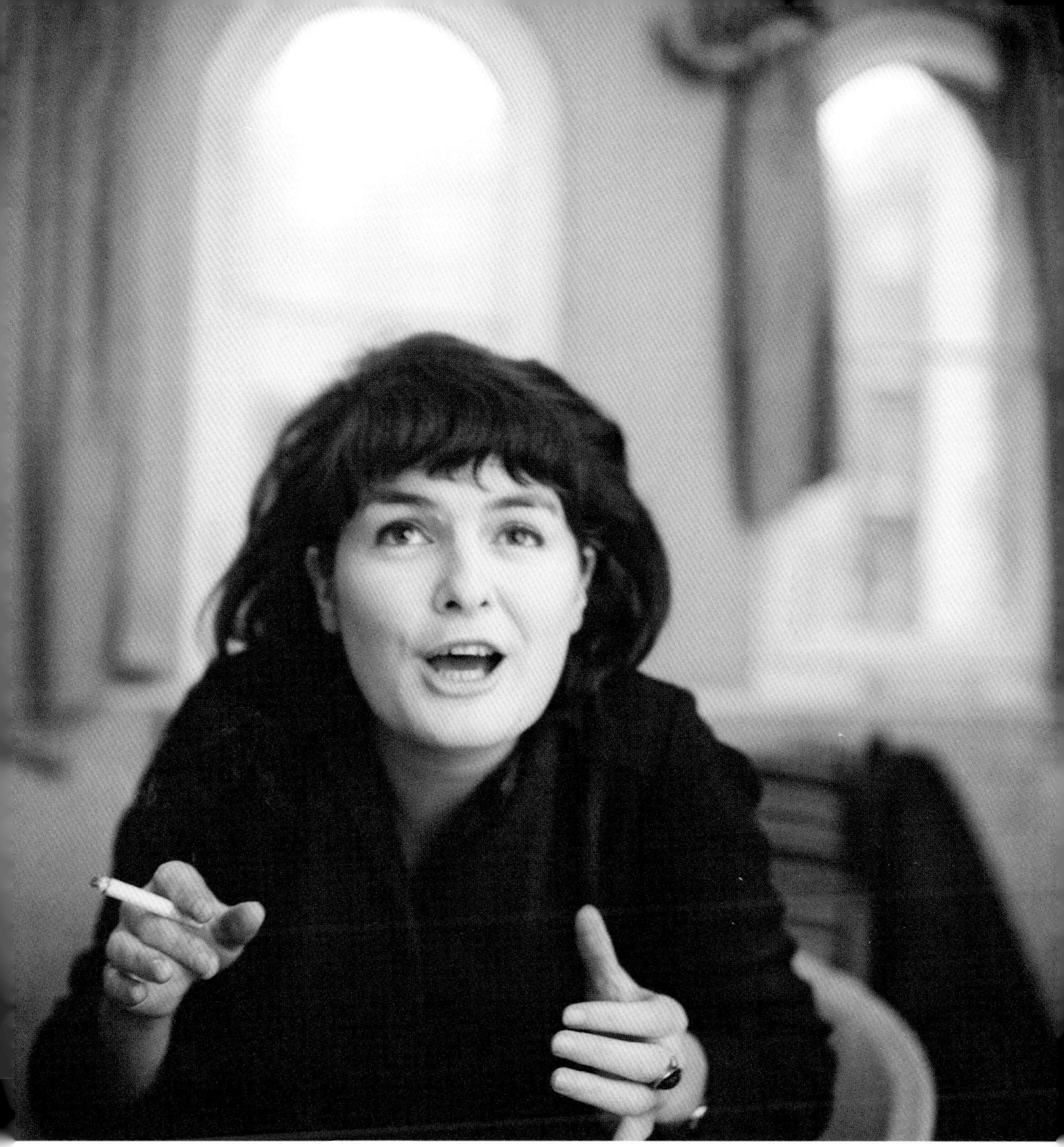

2 Ann Quin, c. 1968, photo: Oswald Jones

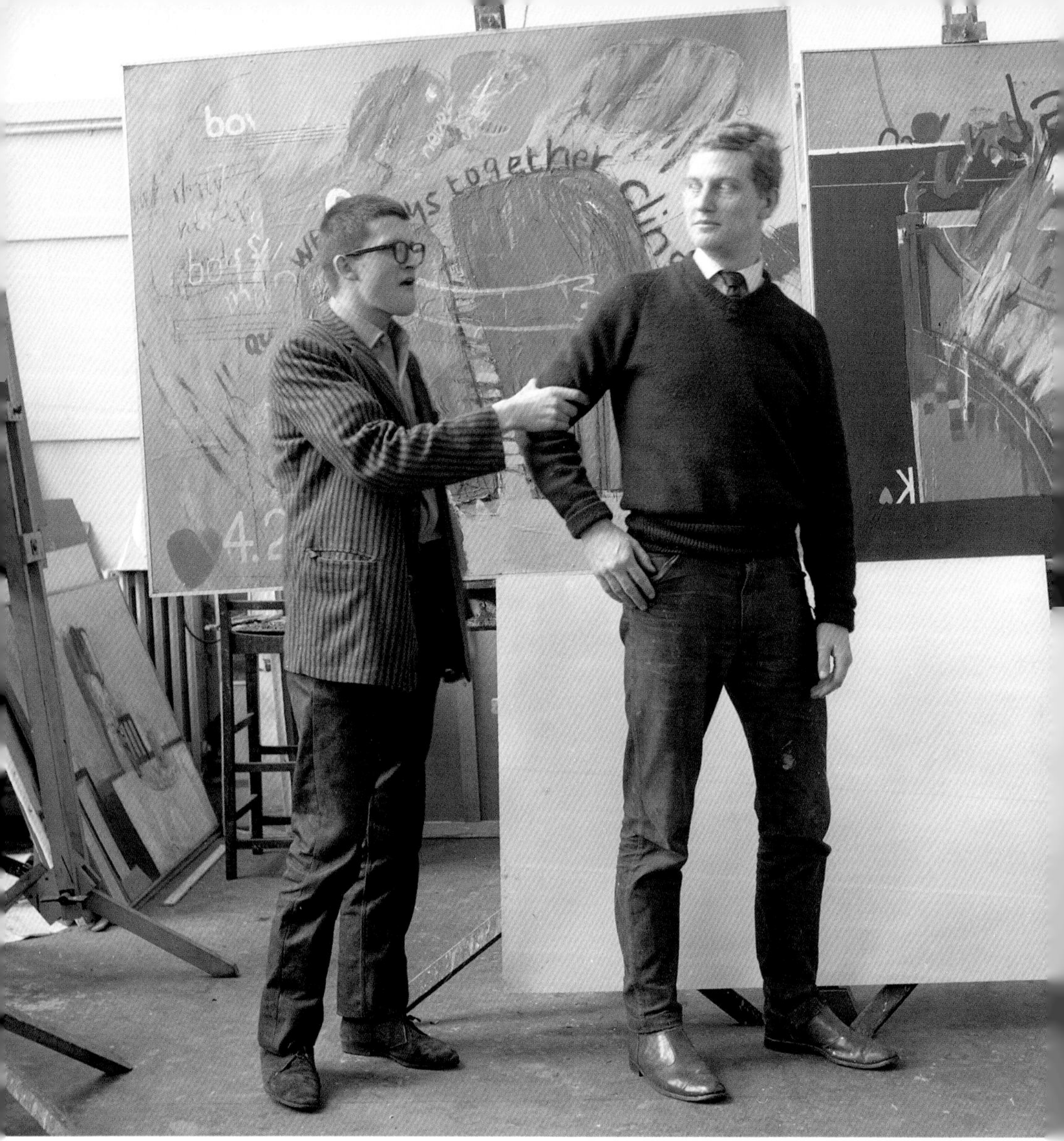

3 David Hockney and Derek Boshier
at the Royal College of Art, London, 1961,
photo: Geoffrey Raymond Reeve

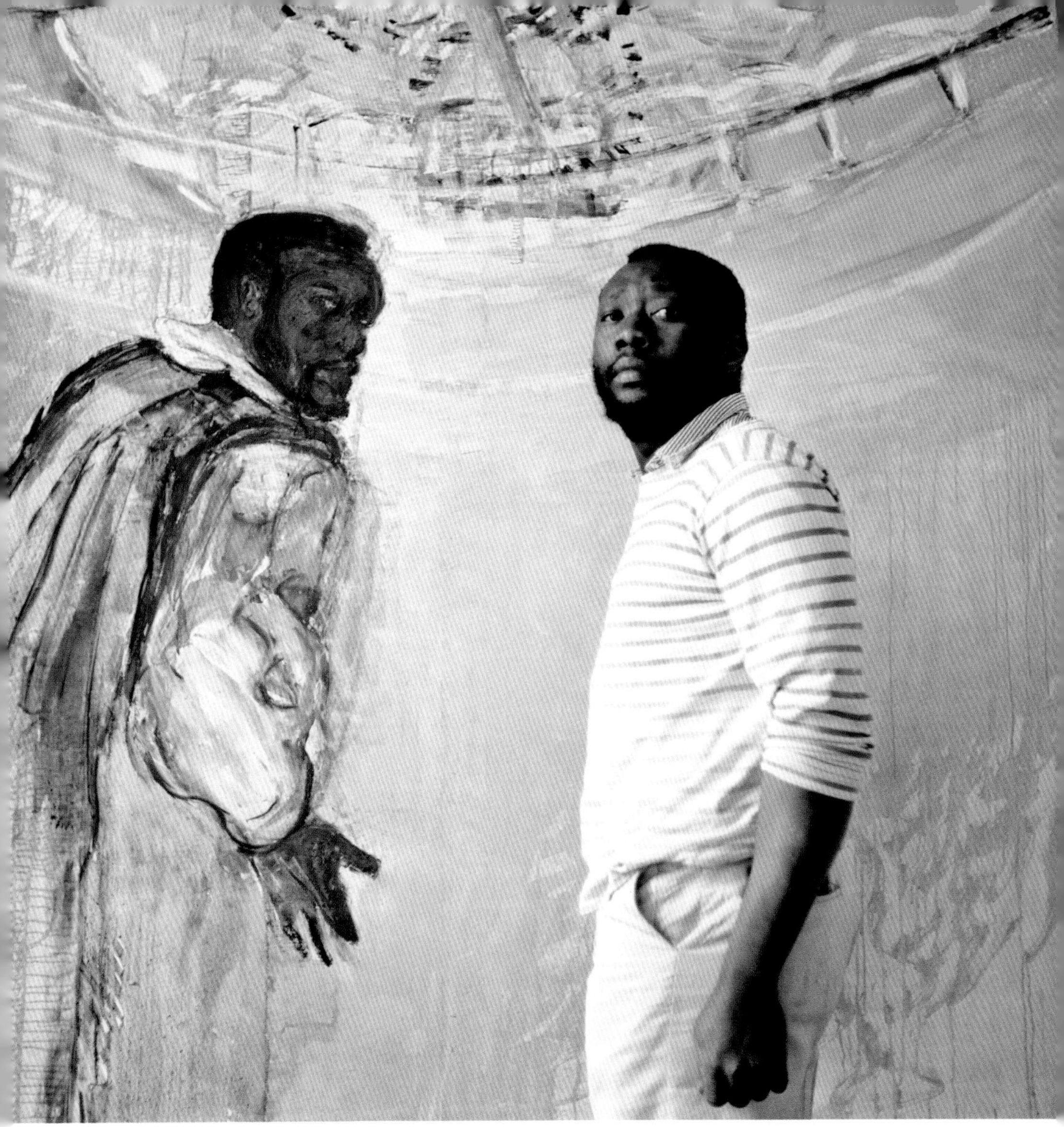

4 Frank Bowling, c. 1965, with his *Self-Portrait as Othello*, 1962, photo: Tony Evans/Timelapse Library Ltd

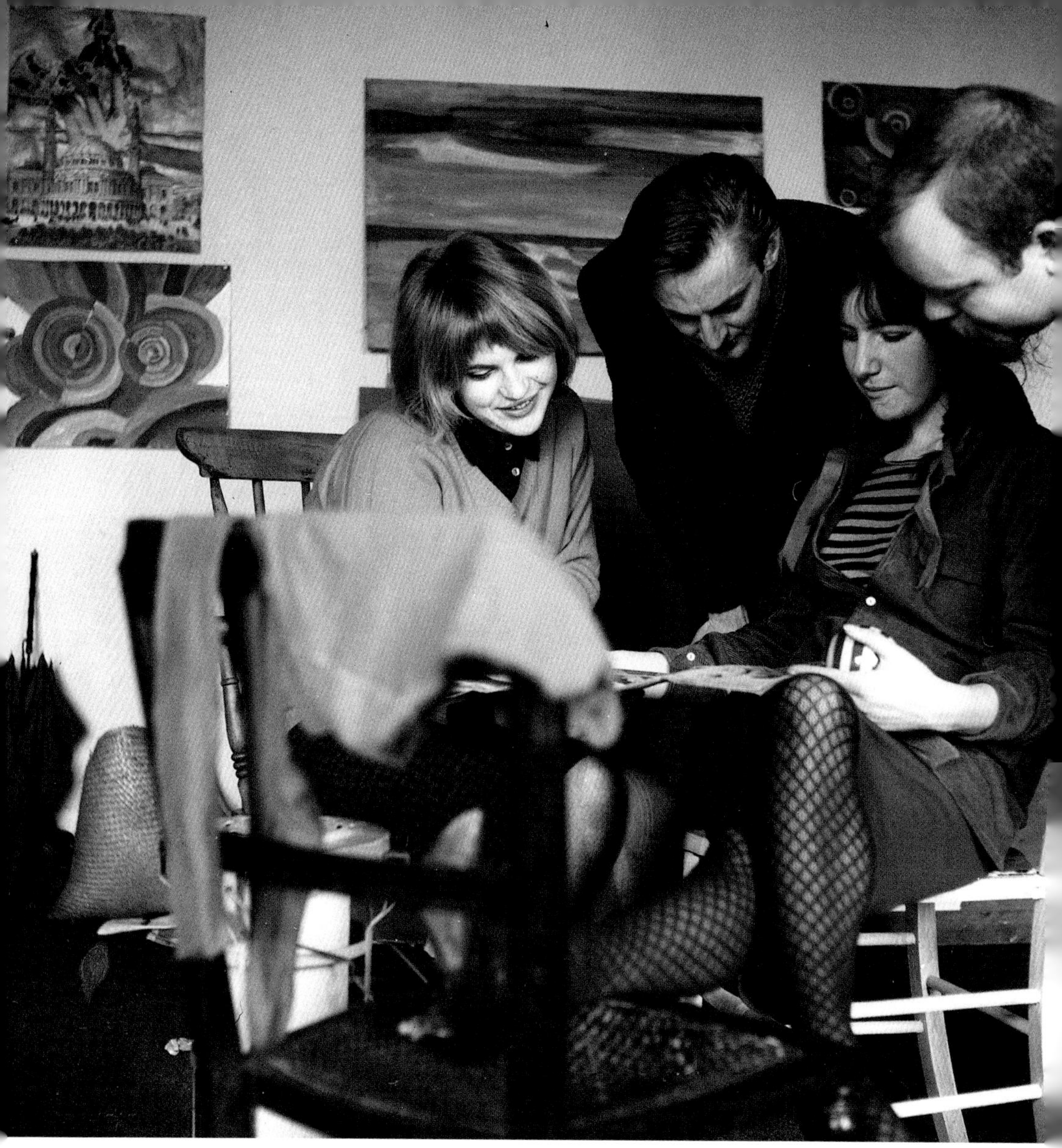

5 Pauline Boty (far left), Anthony Macley, Natalie Gibson and Peter Blake (far right), 1961, photo: Geoffrey Raymond Reeve

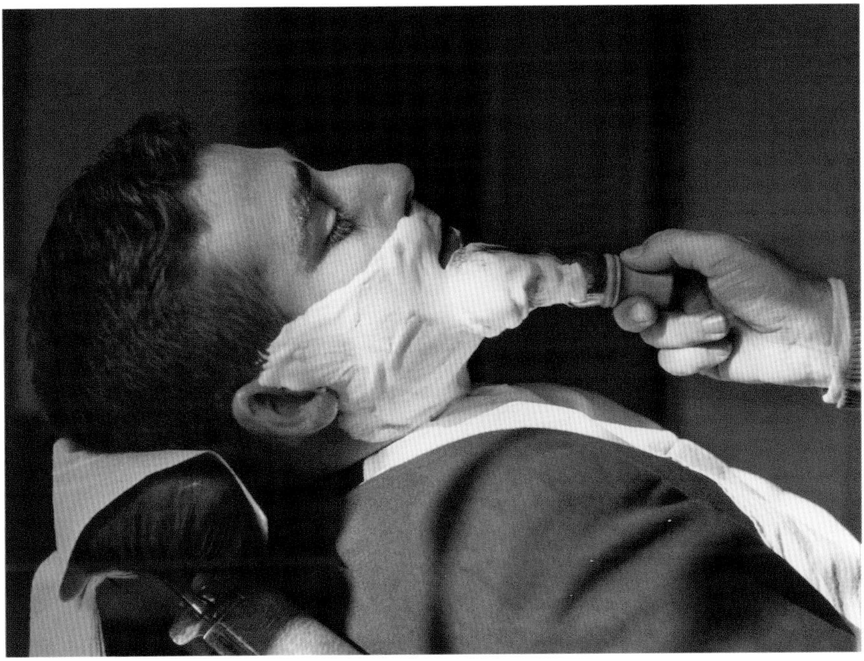

6 Billy Apple, *Art Declared Found Activity (Lathering, Alicante Spain, April 1960)*, 1960 (made while still Barrie Bates)

OVERLEAF **7** Billy Apple, *Drunk (Earls Court Road, London, Winter 1960)*, 1960 (made while still Barrie Bates)

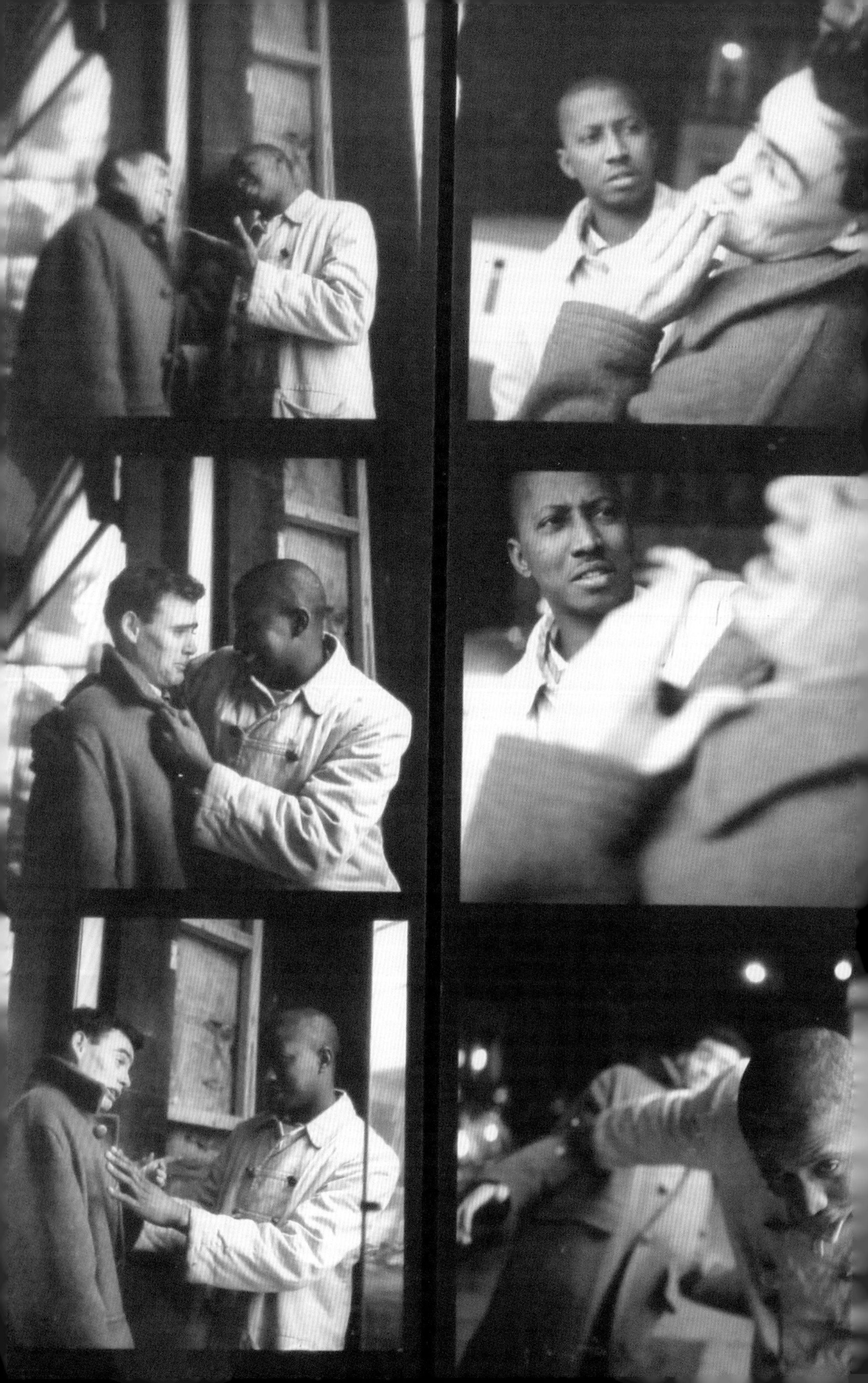

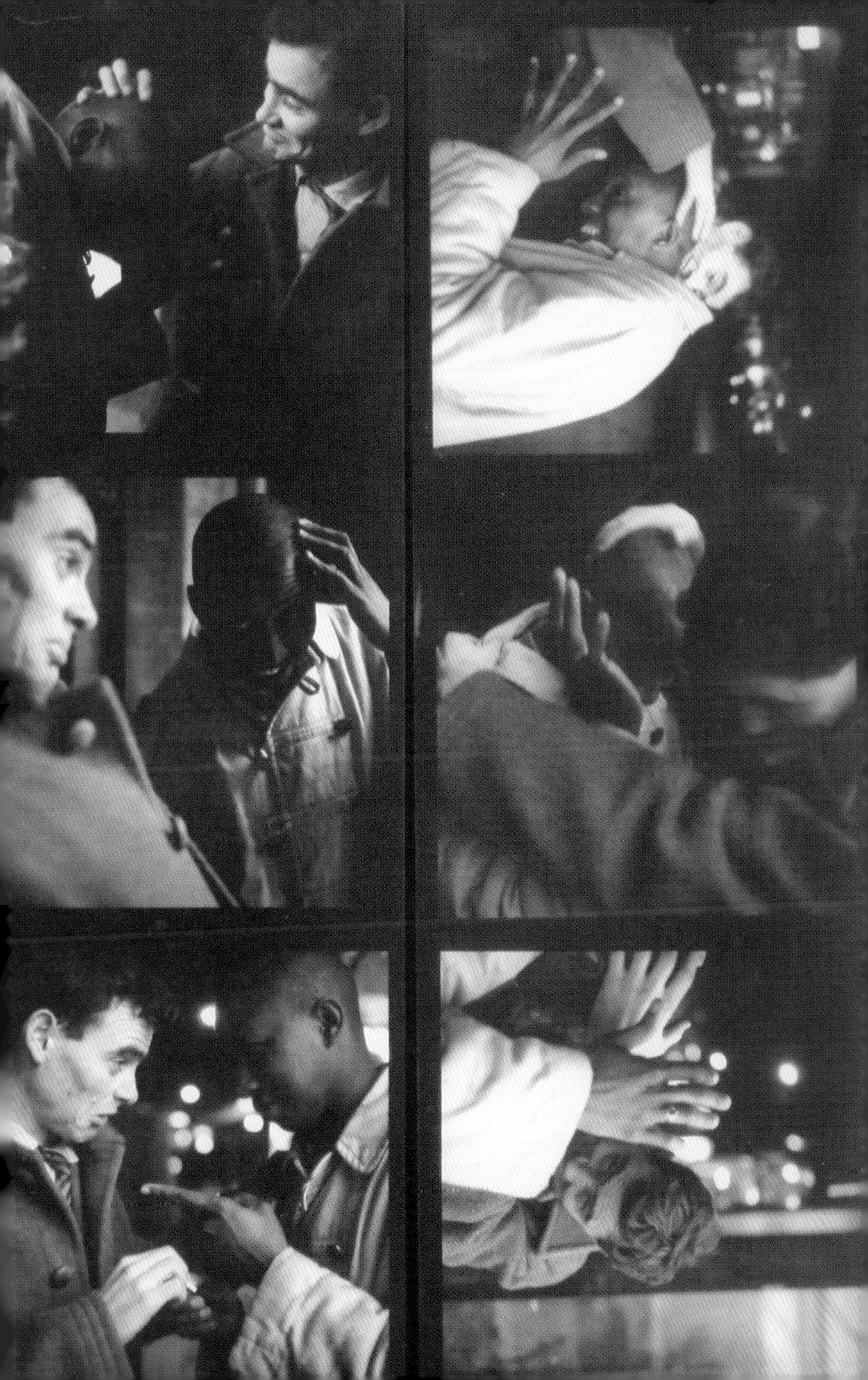

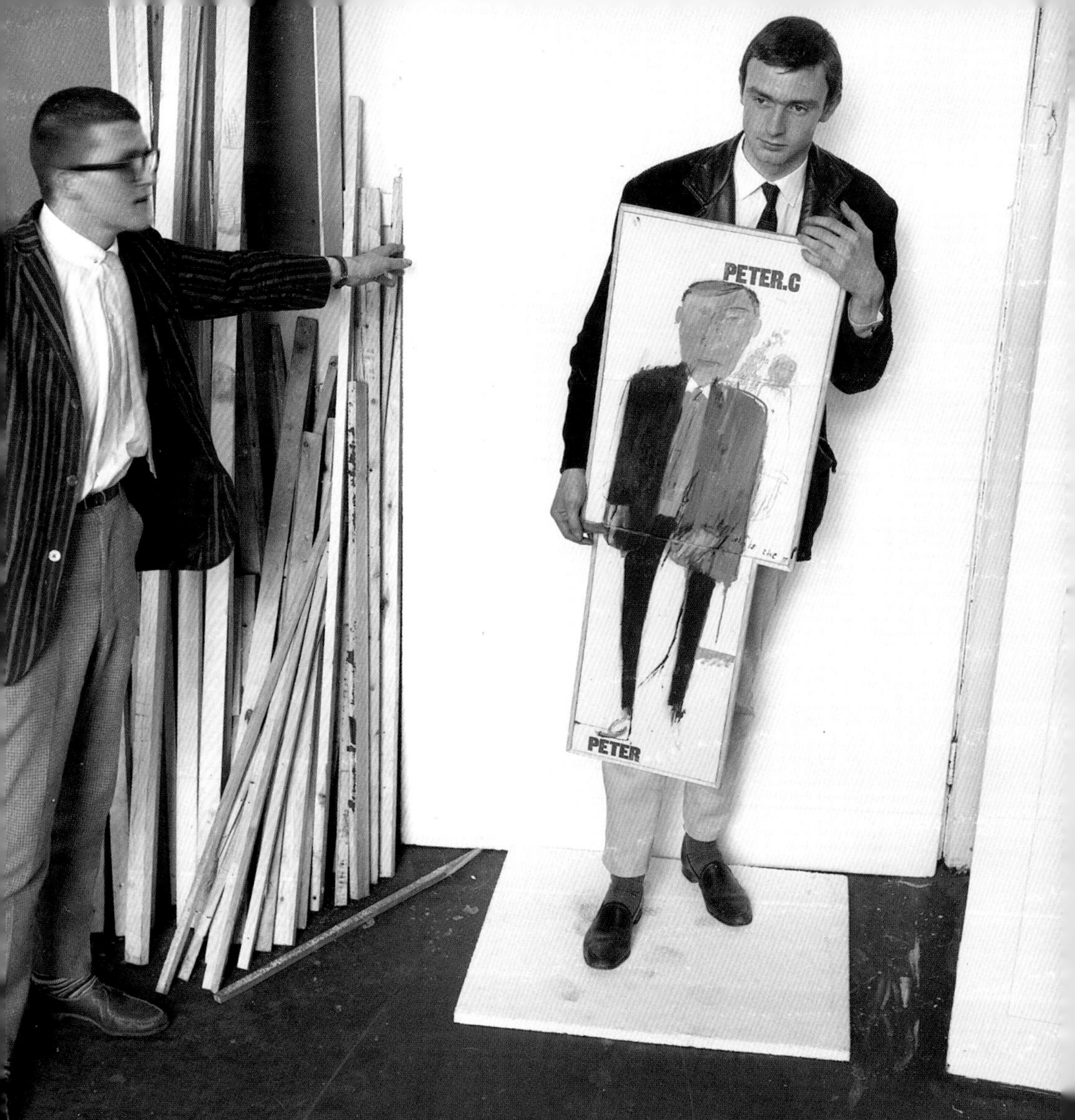

8 David Hockney and Peter Crutch
with Hockney's *Peter.C*, 1961,
photo: Geoffrey Raymond Reeve

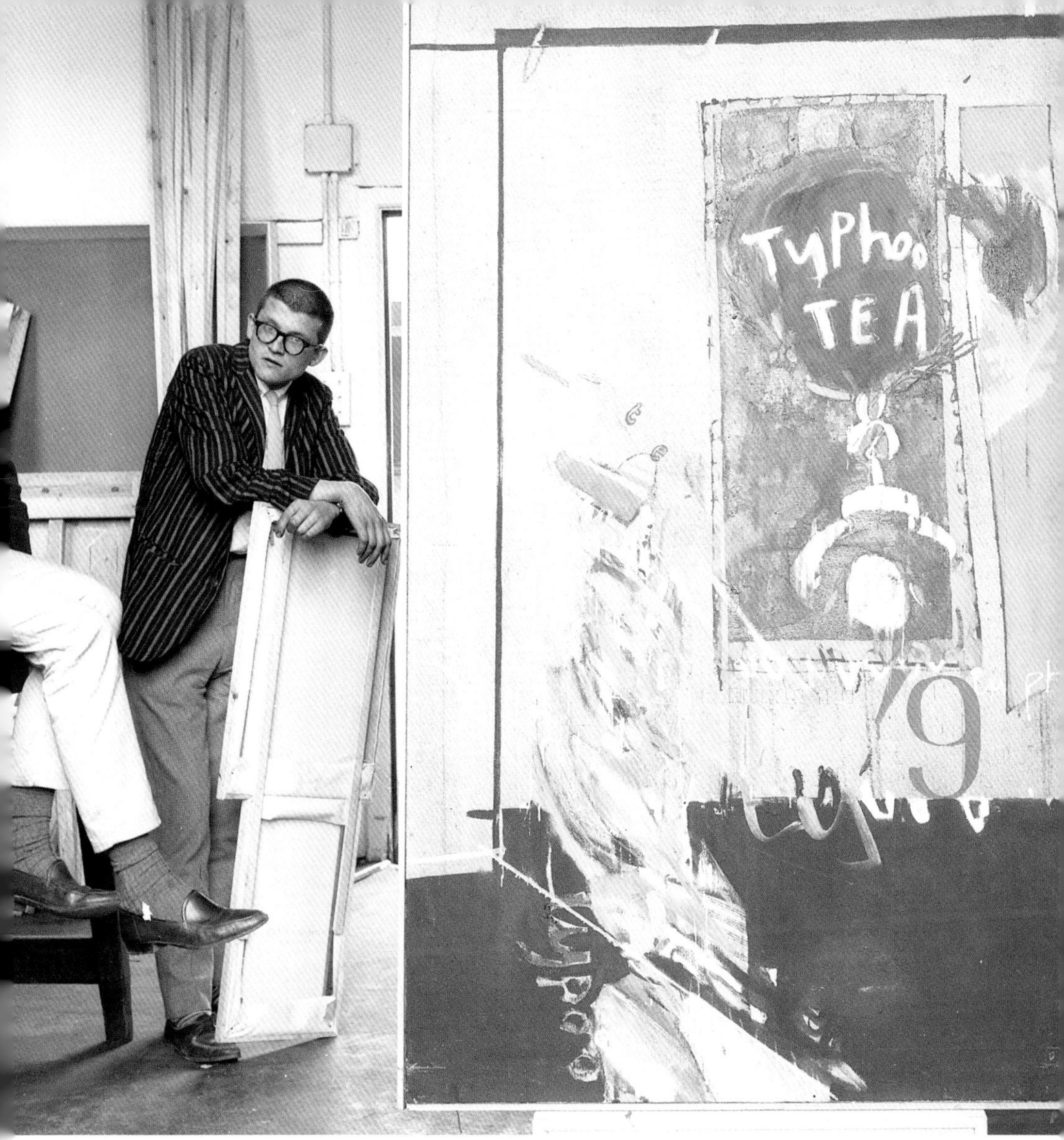

9 David Hockney and Peter Crutch with Hockney's *The Second Tea Painting*, 1961, photo: Geoffrey Raymond Reeve

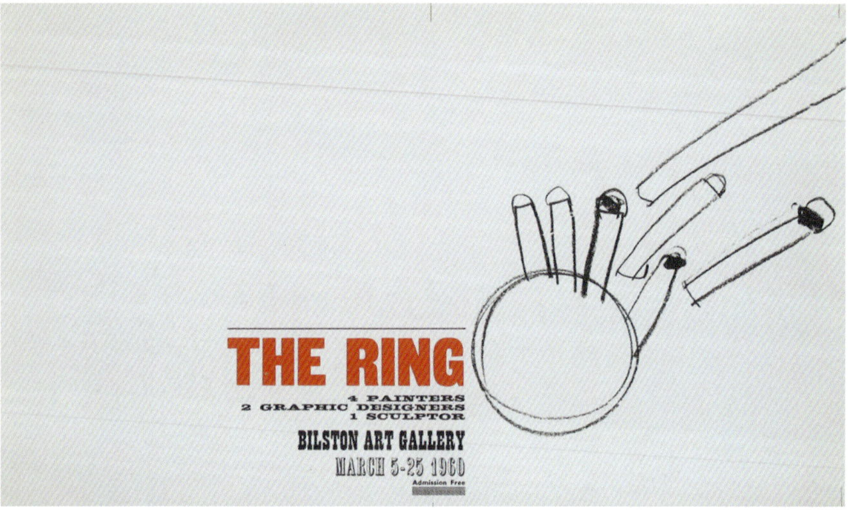

10 Billy Apple, exhibition poster for 'The Ring' at Bilston Art Gallery, 1960 (made while still Barrie Bates)

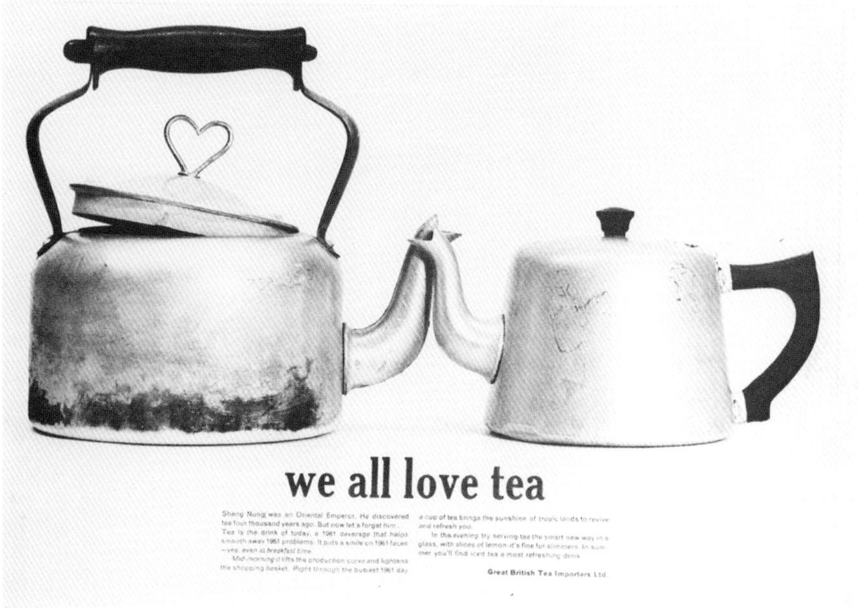

11 Billy Apple, 'we all love tea', award-winning design campaign, 1961 (made while still Barrie Bates)

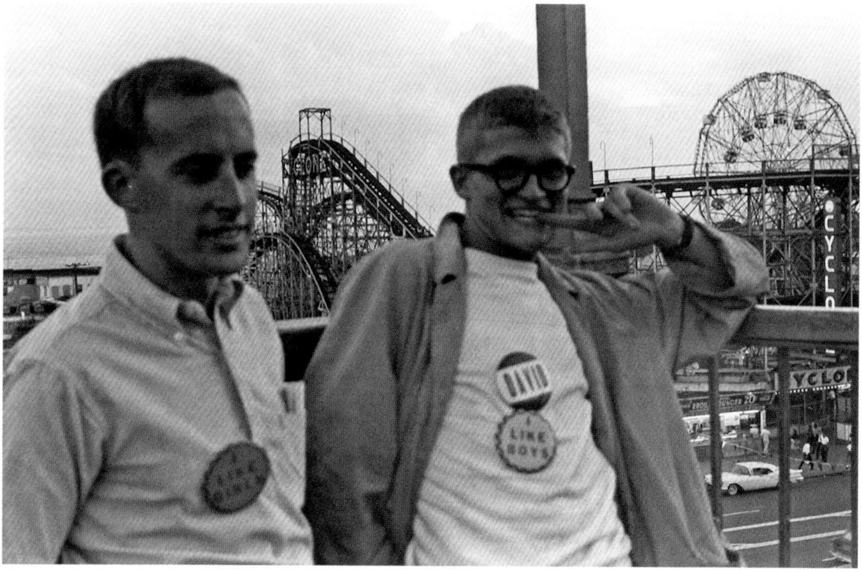

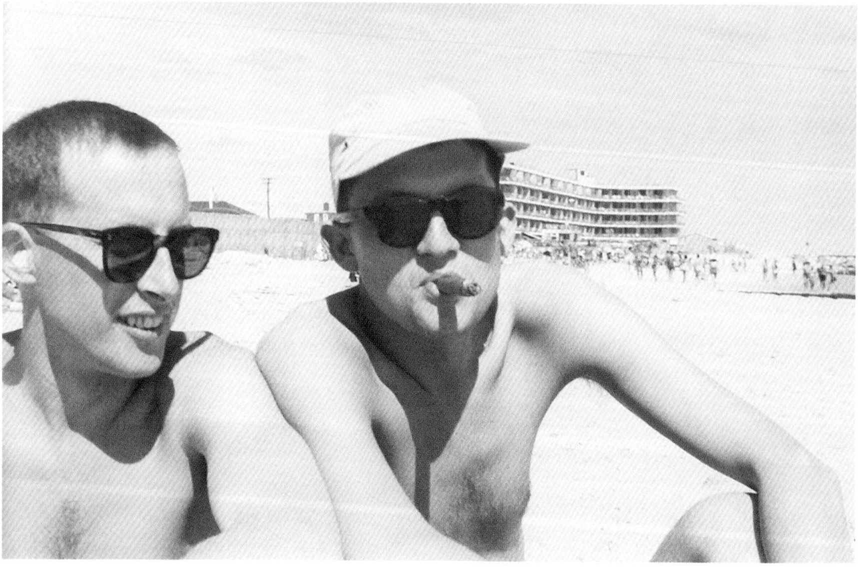

12–15 Barrie Bates and David Hockney, New York, summer 1961, photographer unknown

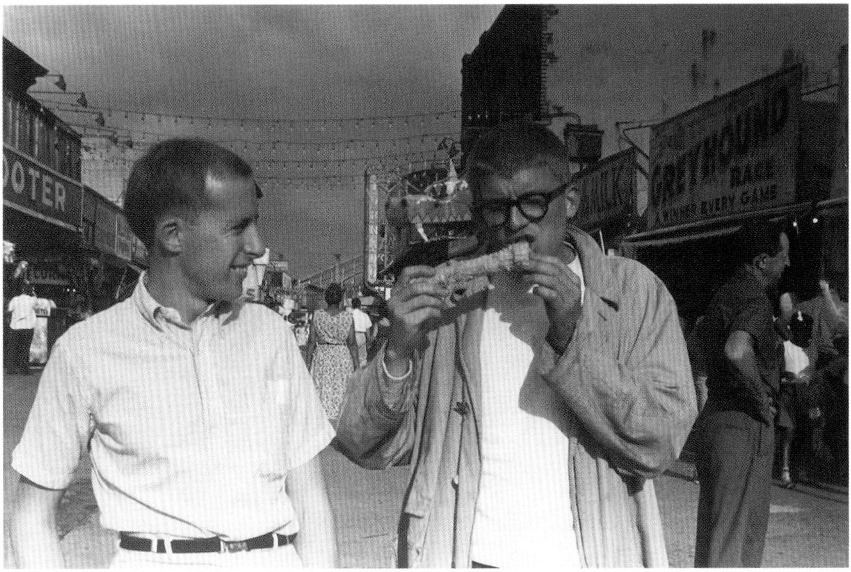
GREYHOUND
RACE
A WINNER EVERY GAME

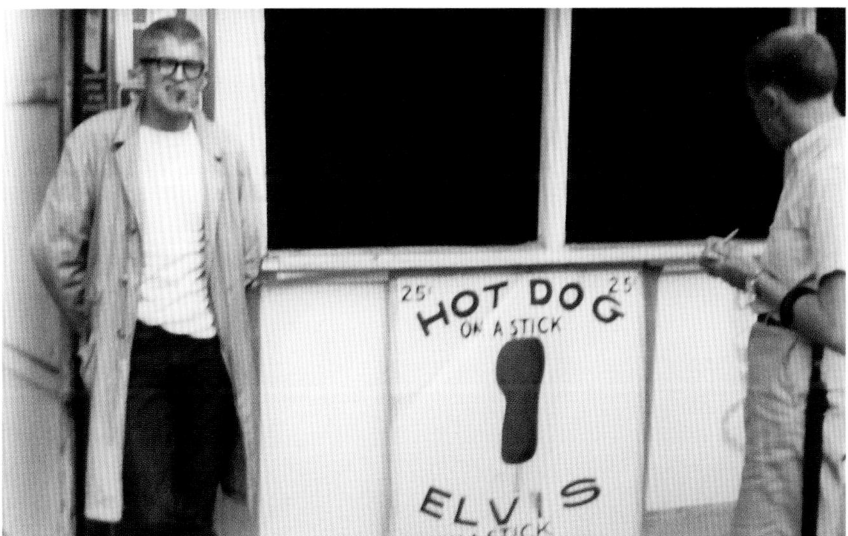
25¢ HOT DOG 25¢
ON A STICK
ELVIS
ON A STICK

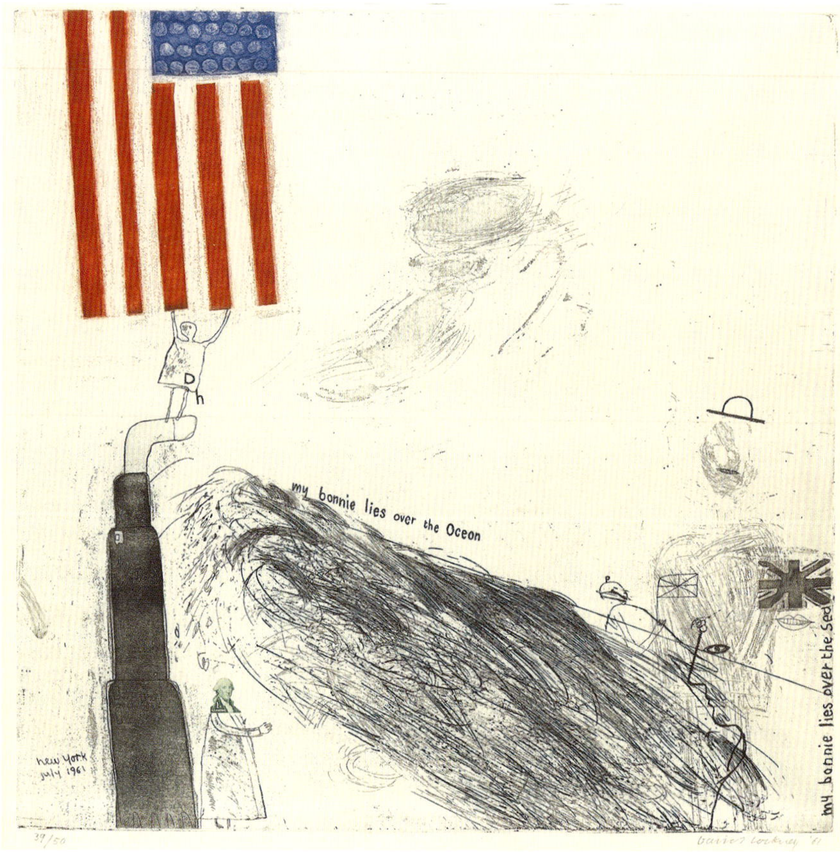

16 David Hockney, *My Bonnie Lies Over the Ocean*, 1961–62

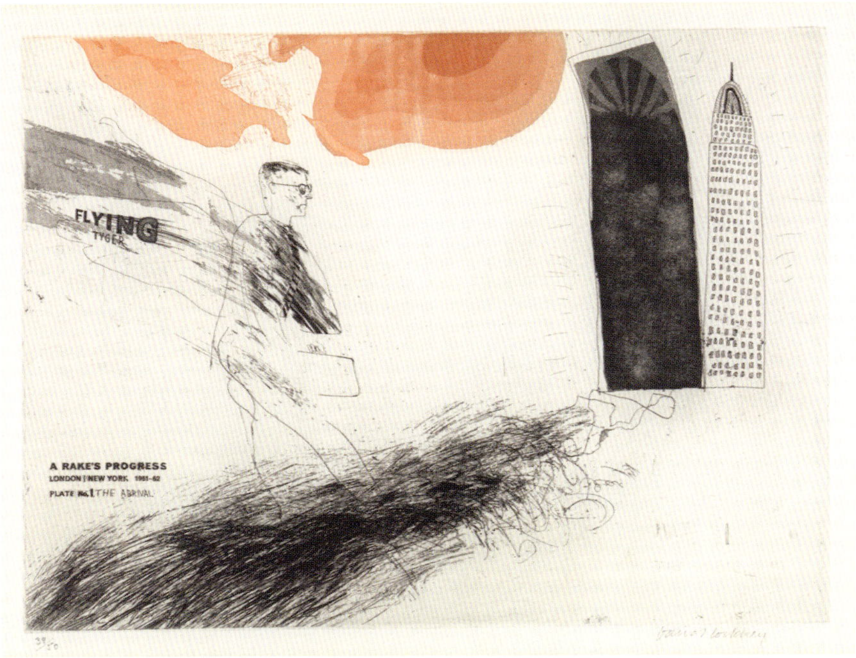

17 David Hockney, *The Arrival* from 'A Rake's Progress', 1961–63

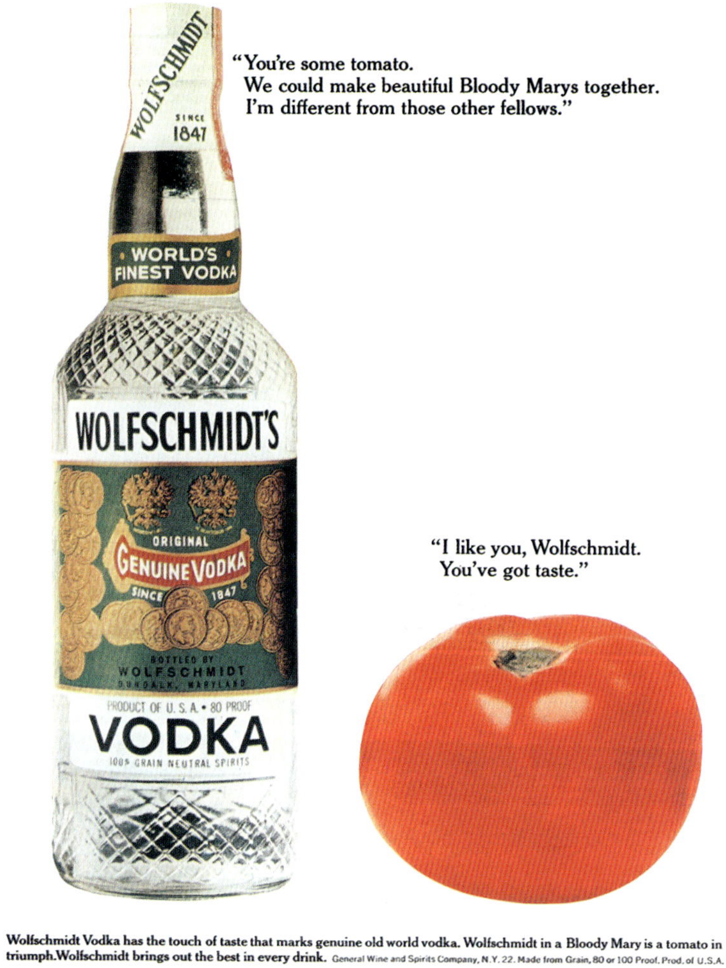

18—19 Wolfschmidt vodka campaign from 1960, by the agency Papert Koenig Lois, art-directed by George Lois

"You sweet doll, I appreciate you. I've got taste.
I'll bring out the real orange in you. I'll make you famous.
Kiss me."

"Who was that tomato
I saw you with last week?"

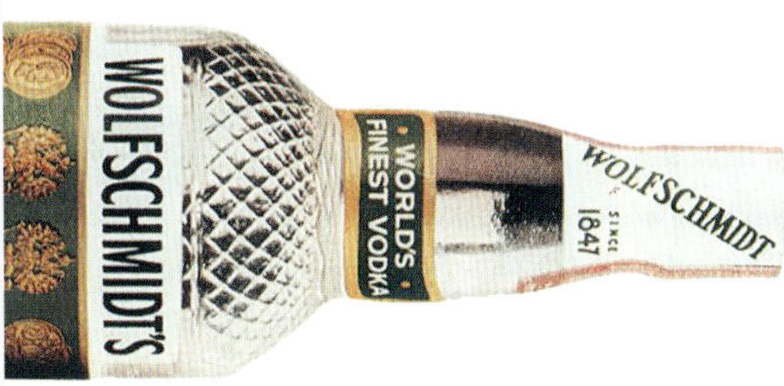

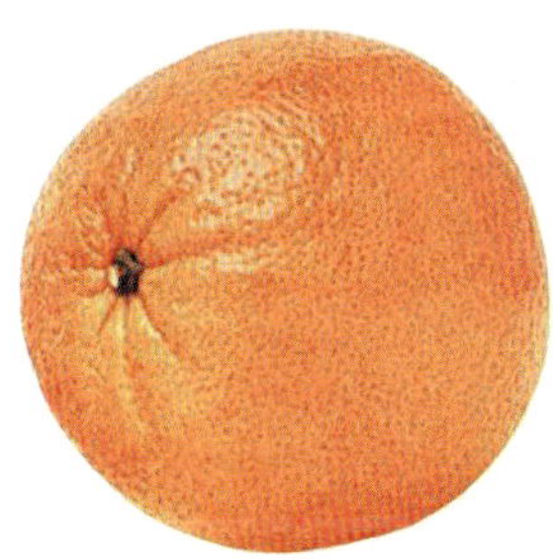

Wolfschmidt Vodka has the touch of taste that marks genuine old world vodka. Wolfschmidt in a Screwdriver is an orange at its best. Wolfschmidt brings out the best in every drink. General Wine and Spirits Company, New York 22, N.Y. Made from Grain, 80 or 100 Proof. Product of U.S.A.

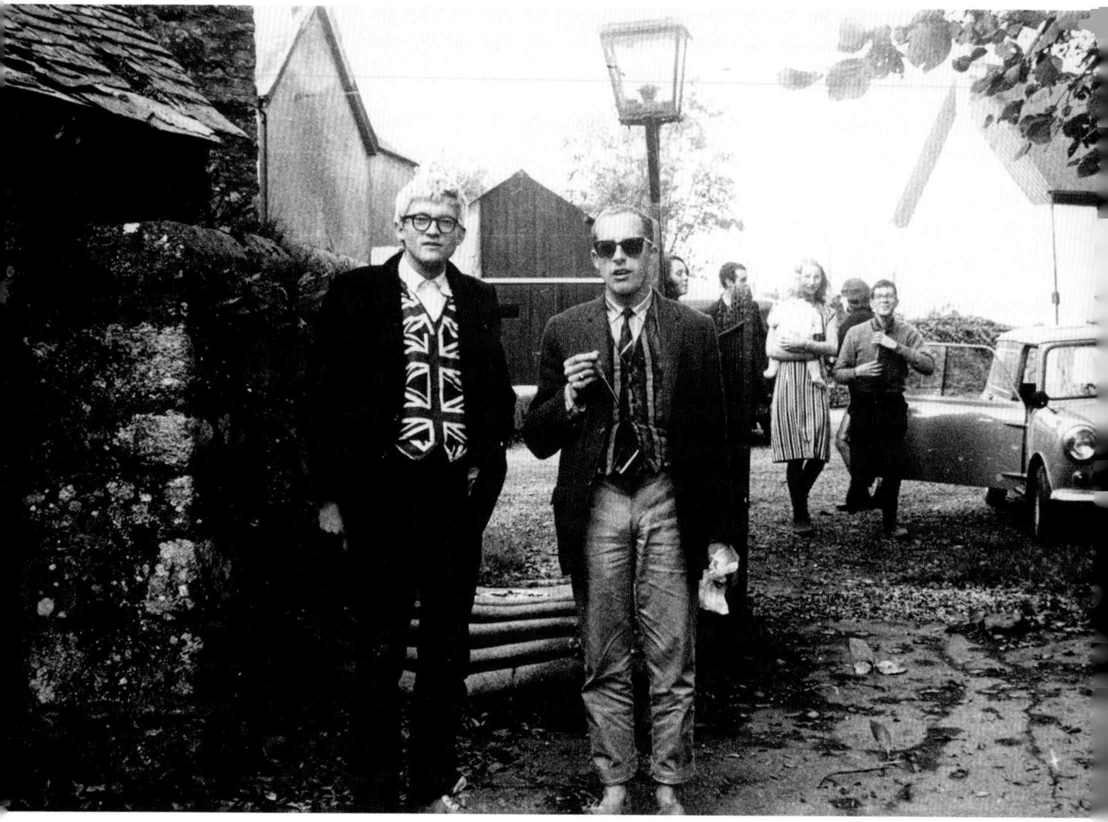

20–21 David Hockney and Barrie Bates in Cornwall, October 1961, photo: Ron Fuller

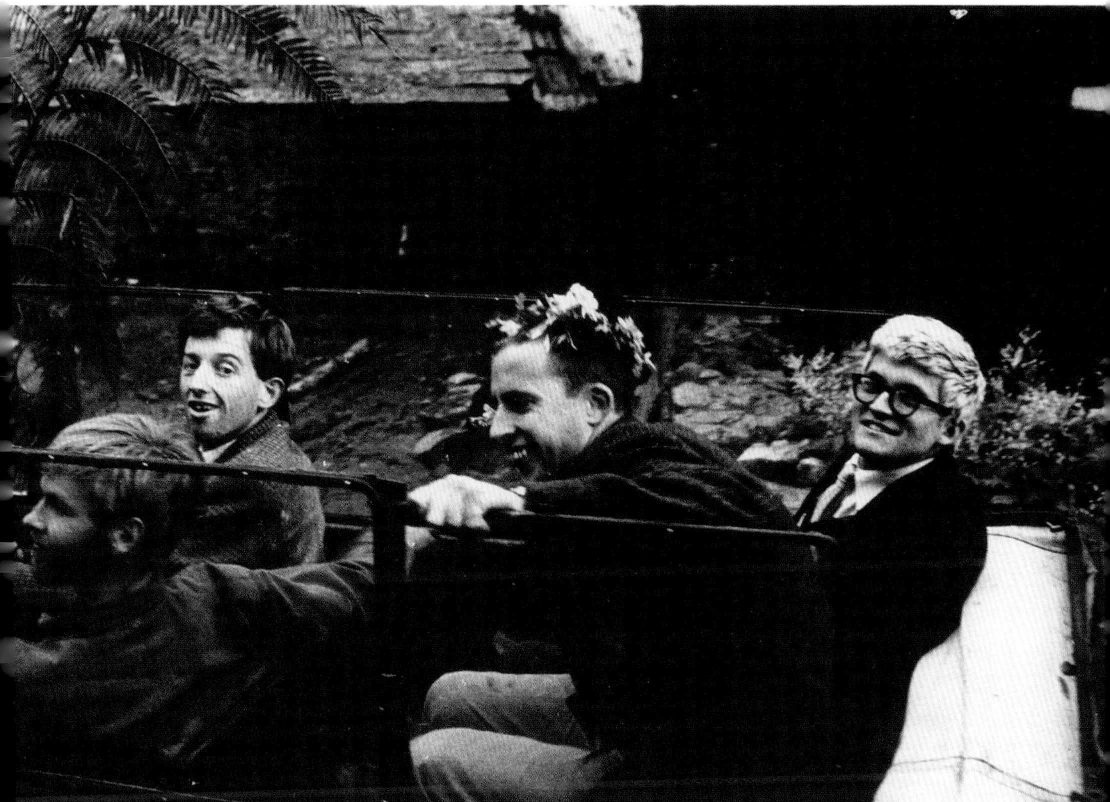

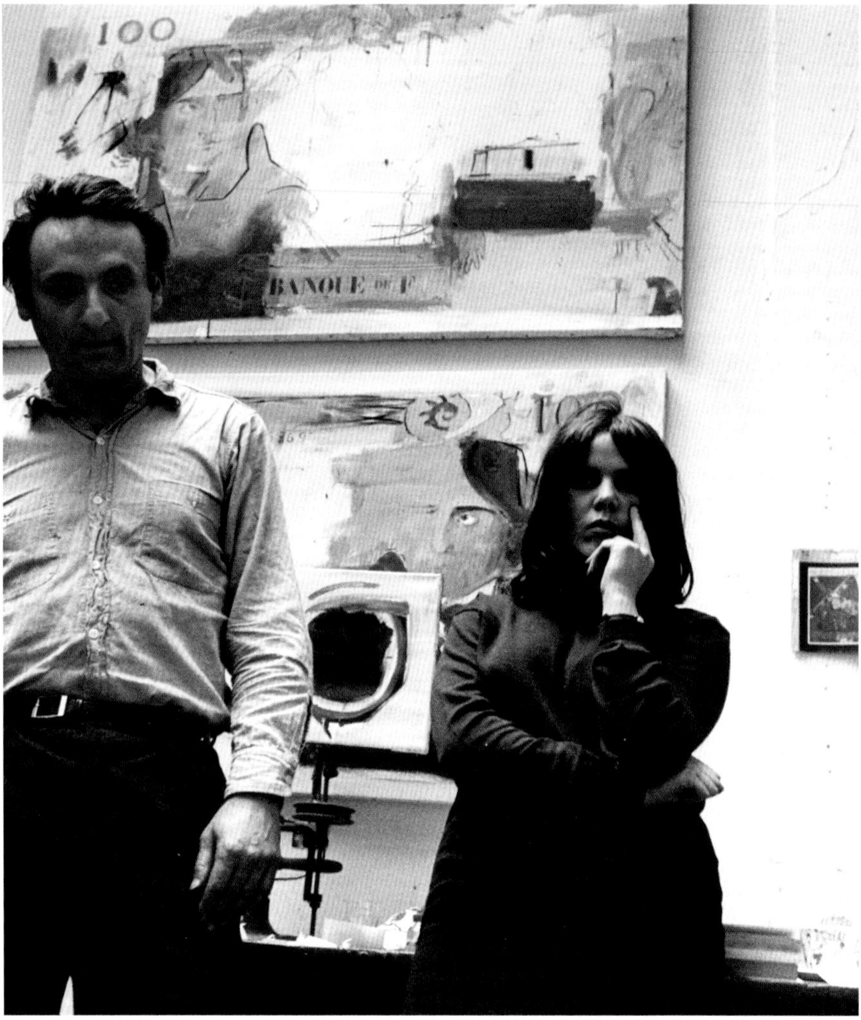

22 Larry and Clarice Rivers in Rivers' studio, 11 Impasse Ronsin, Paris, 1962, photo: Shunk-Kender

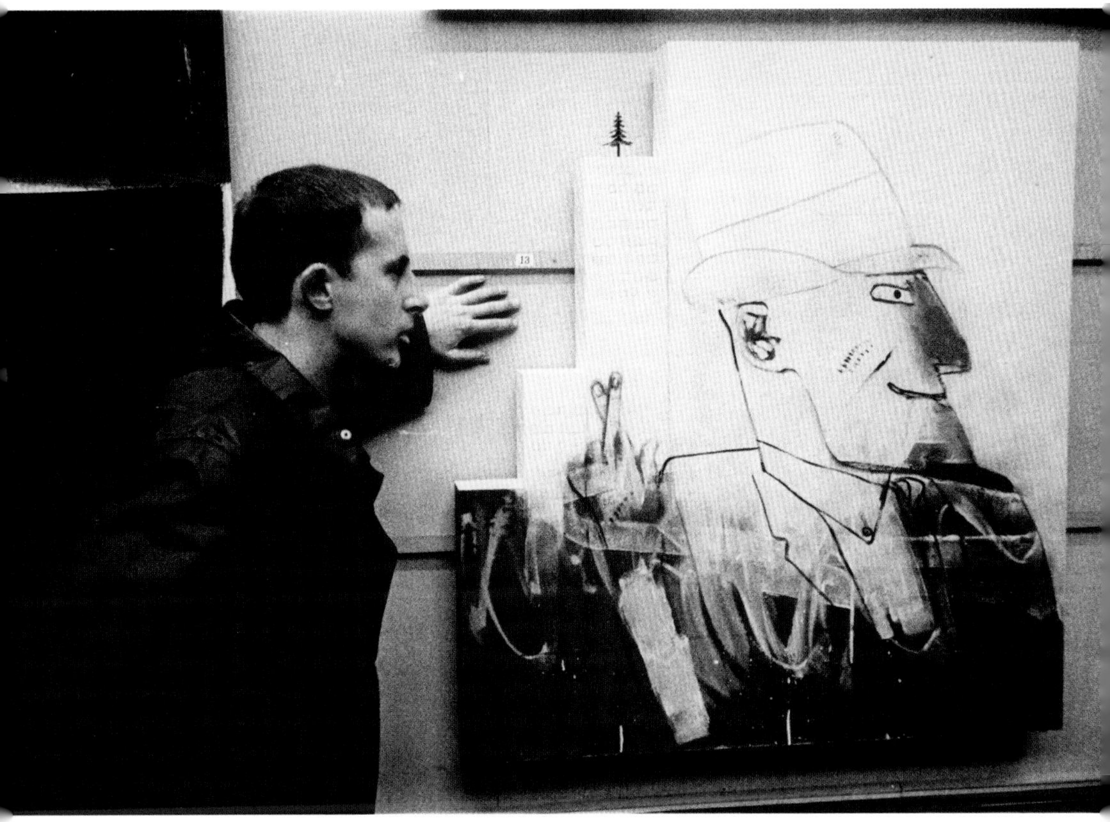

23 Barrie Bates with his work at 'Young Contemporaries 1962', February 1962, photographer unknown

OVERLEAF **24—25** Barrie Bates at 'Young Contemporaries 1962', February 1962, with works by him and David Hockney, photographer unknown

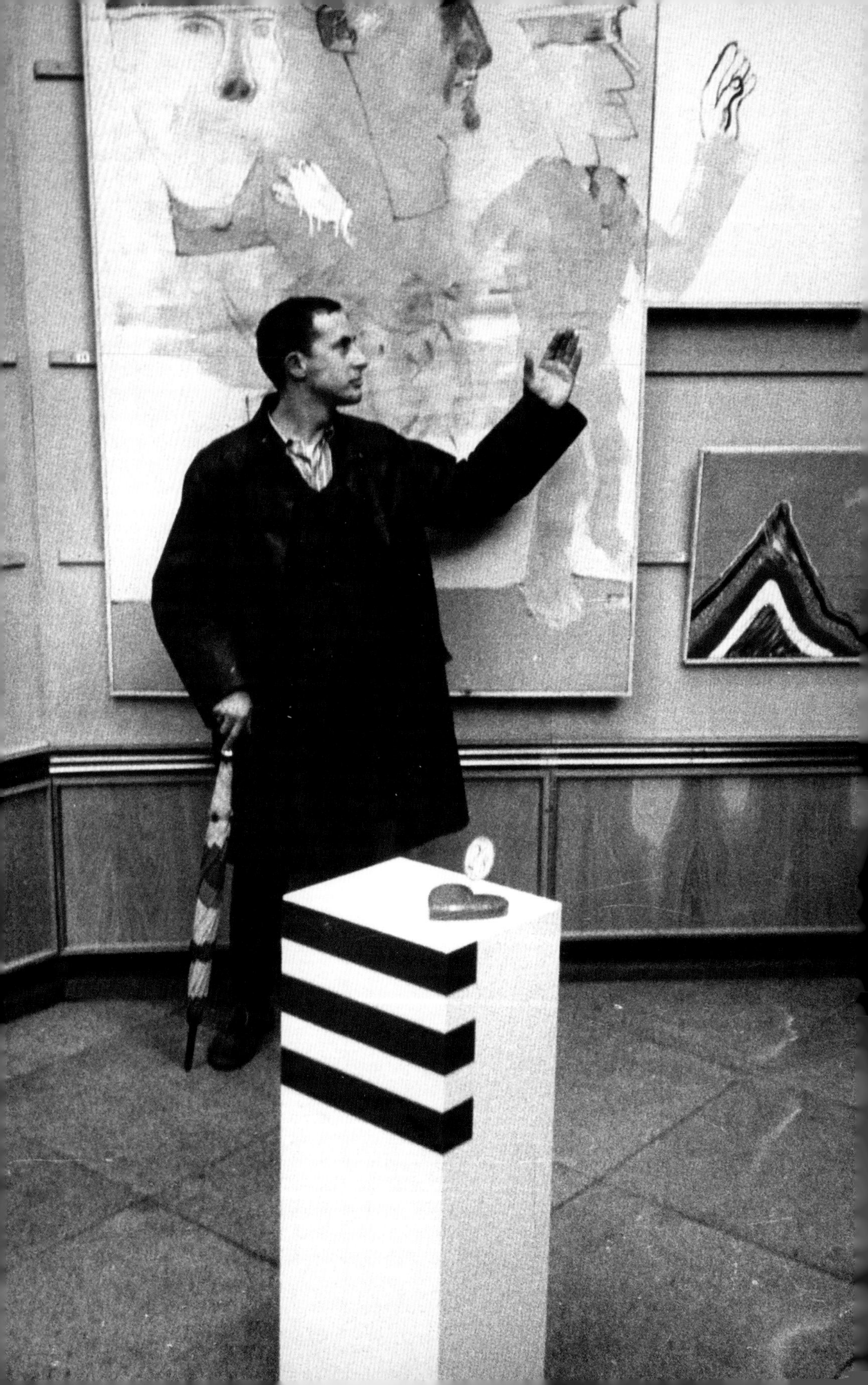

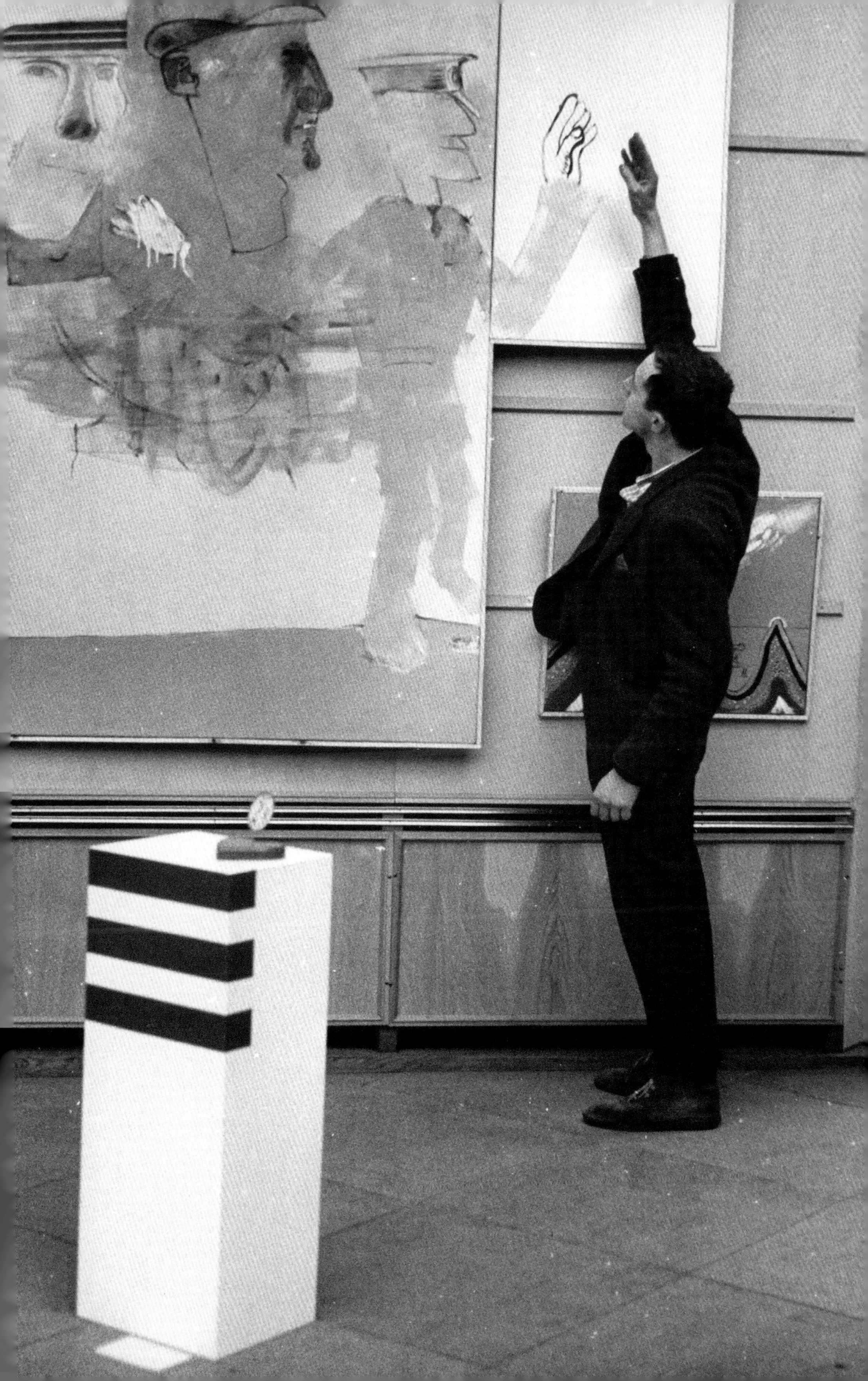

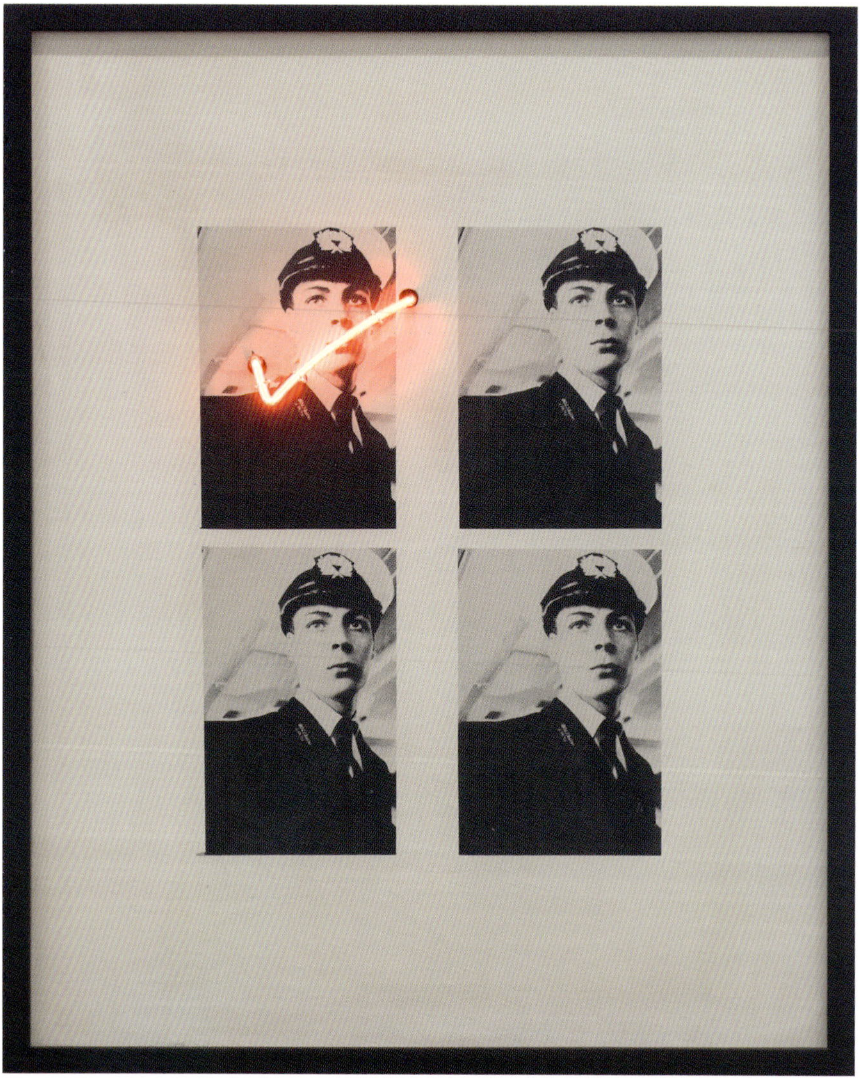

26 Billy Apple, *Relation of Aesthetic Choice to Life Activity (Function of the Subject)*, 1961–62 (made while still Barrie Bates)

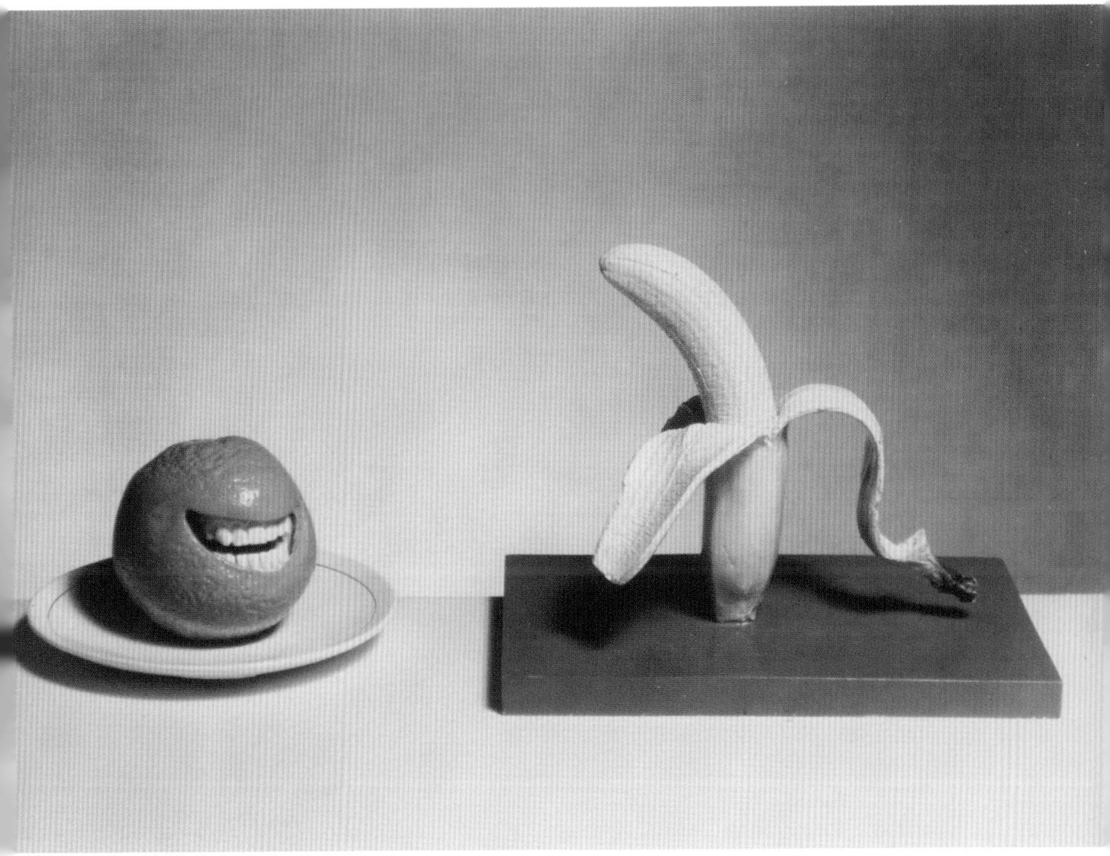

27 Billy Apple, *Smile, Slim, We're Having Our Photo Taken*, 1962 (made while still Barrie Bates)

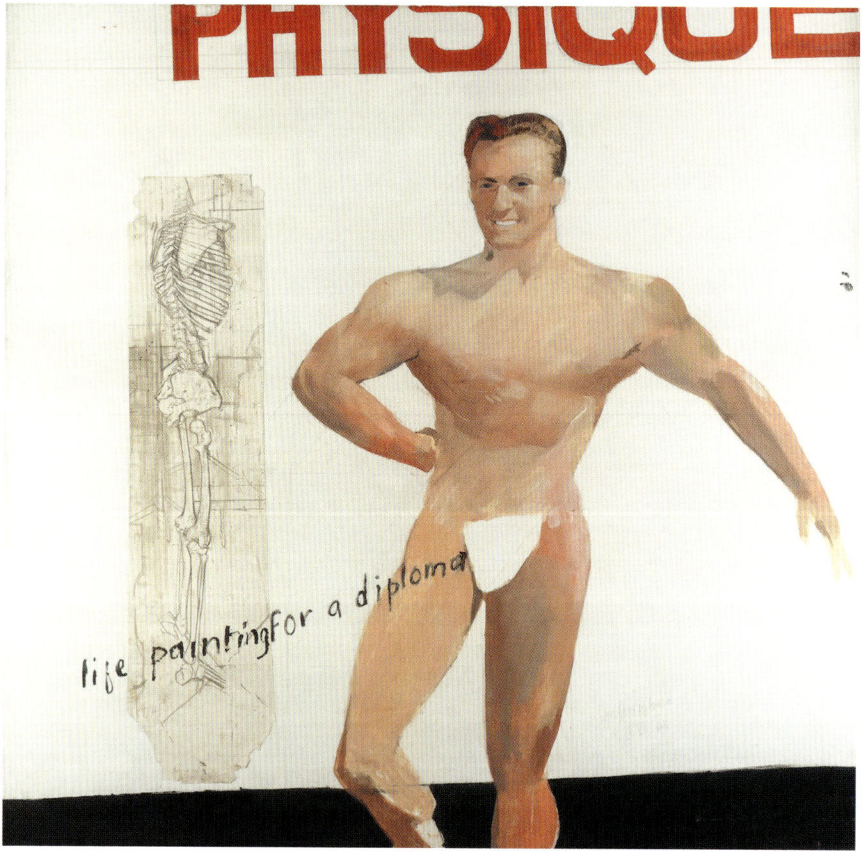

28 David Hockney, *Life Painting for a Diploma*, 1962

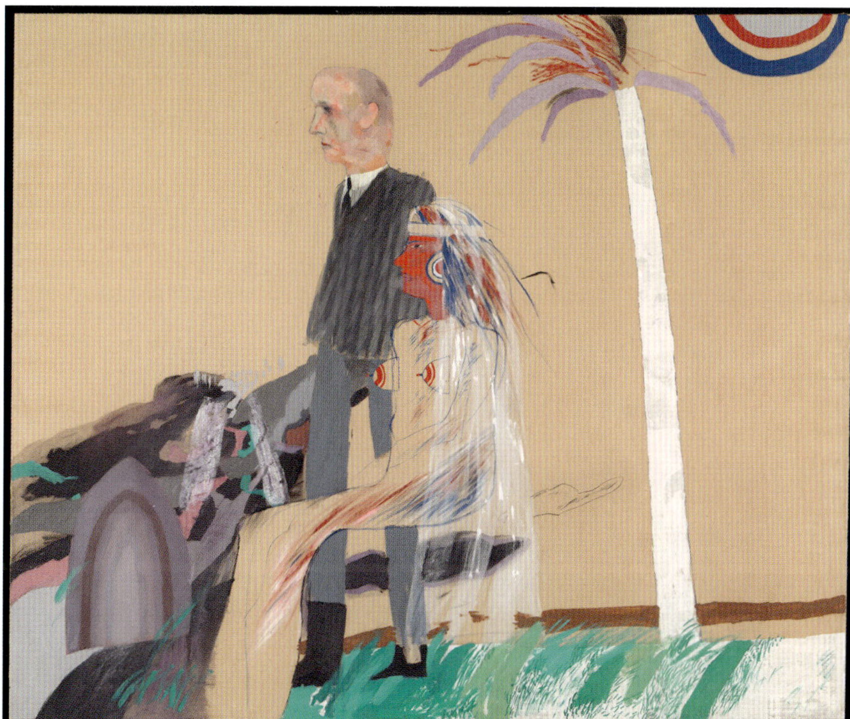

29 David Hockney, *The First Marriage (A Marriage of Styles I)*, 1962

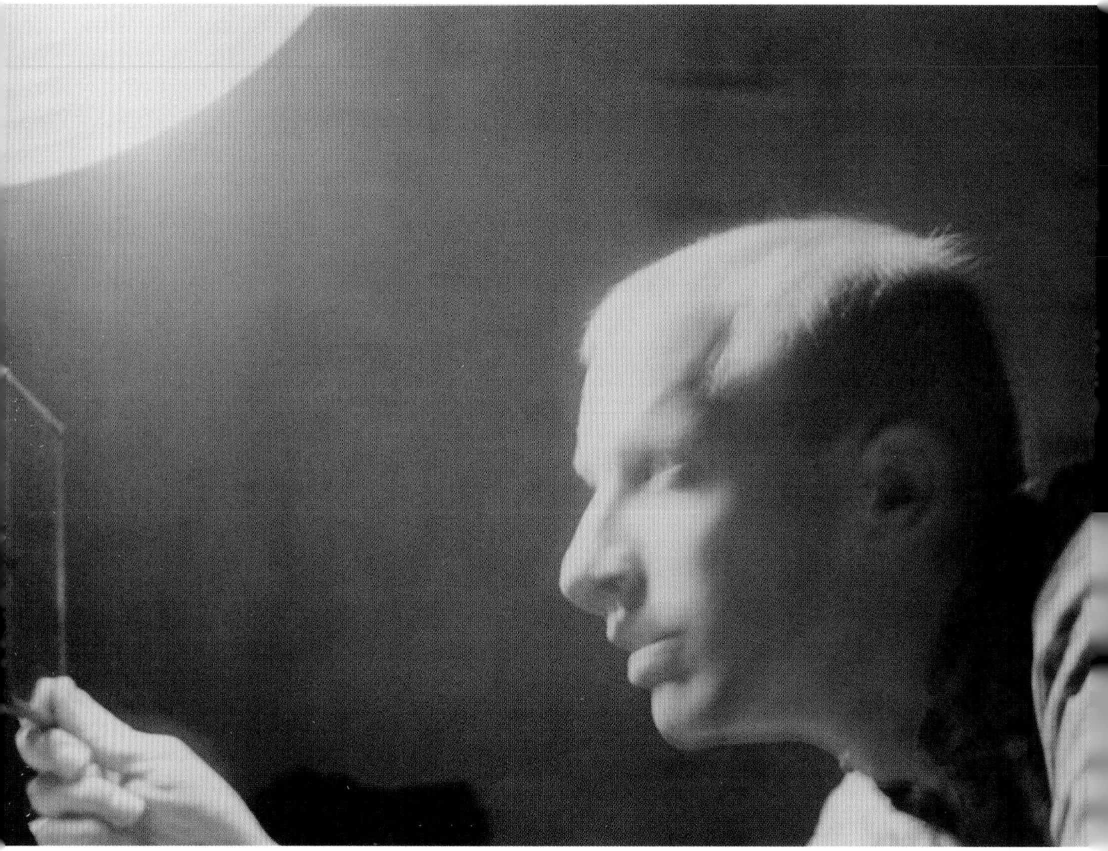

30 Billy Apple, *Billy Apple Bleaching with Lady Clairol Instant Crème Whip, November 1962*, 1962

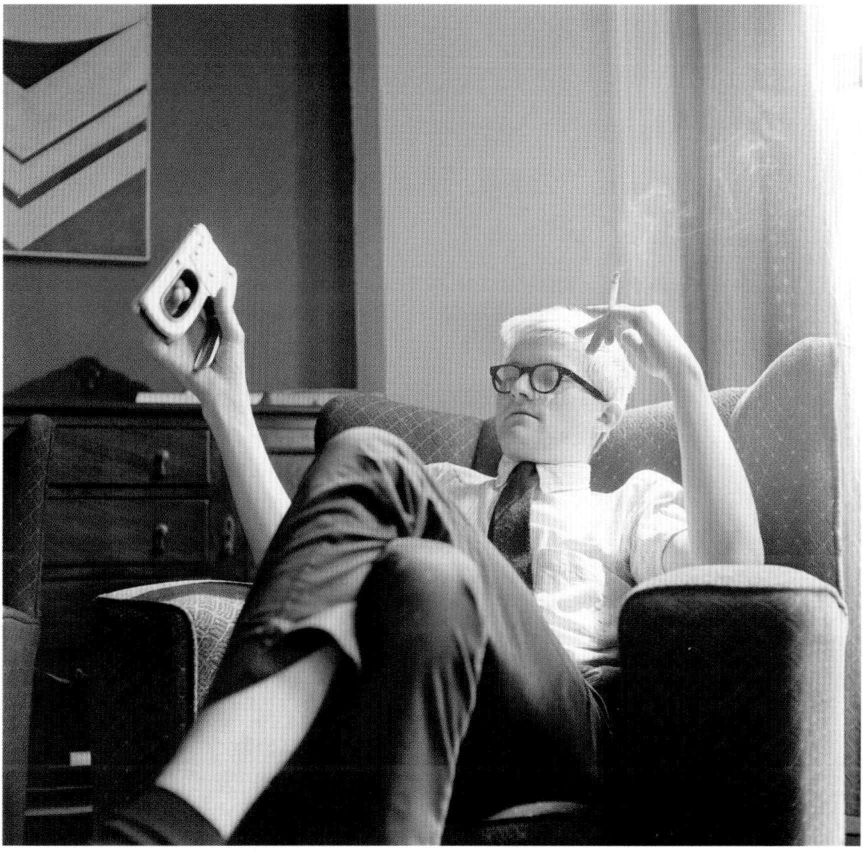

31 David Hockney, 1963,
photo: Tony Evans

which opened in 1950, Myers fostered the early careers of Rivers, Freilicher and Hartigan, as well as Leslie, Helen Frankenthaler and Fairfield Porter. It was Myers' deliberate strategy to back the younger New York generation emerging in the shadows of the older Abstract Expressionists. Alongside this, he consciously supported O'Hara, Ashbery and others, publishing their poetry and criticism, and setting up collaborations on editions and publications with the gallery's painters. In 1953, Myers also co-founded the Artists' Theatre with Herbert Machiz, staging works by the New York School poets, often with stage sets by artists, including Rivers. James Merrill – son of banking powerhouse Charles Merrill – supported the Artists' Theatre to the tune of thousands of dollars. According to Rivers, Myers also convinced Merrill to put up a $2,500 deposit so Rivers could buy a house in Southampton, Long Island. Merrill's biographer Langdon Hammer writes that Merrill gave Rivers the money in 1953. Rivers lived in the house with his sons for four years, until they moved to Greenwich Village.

But, as was so often the case with Rivers, sex made things complicated. Myers was gay and evidently in love with Rivers, and turned him into Tibor de Nagy's flagship artist (Myers' obsession with Rivers also led to rivalry with O'Hara). 'Rivers basked in the attention,' Gooch contends, 'using the opportunity to exchange sexual favors to hustle his own career advancement as well as to indulge in the thrill of breaking the homosexual taboo'.

After Rivers called things off, Myers continued to represent him, but at the end of 1962 Rivers signed an exclusive contract with Marlborough Gallery. Myers initiated a massive lawsuit against the painter and Marlborough which tied them up and dramatically reduced Rivers' presence in New York right at the moment that Johns and Rauschenberg were in the ascendant, and a couple of artists called Andy Warhol and Roy Lichtenstein were making their presence felt. Pop art was becoming a serious business, and Rivers, though not calling himself a Pop artist, had been ahead of the game since at least 1953, with *Delaware*'s inbuilt irony and ambiguous camp. He'd stayed bluntly wedded to figurative art, standing against Greenberg and the waves of Abstract Expressionism that crashed through American art and wiped out almost everything else. But at the moment he should have been hitting his peak, he was caught up in a legal battle, and by his own admission didn't get anything like the support from Marlborough that Myers and Tibor de Nagy had given him for so many years.

On 6 February 1960, a Welsh twenty-two-year-old called Clarice Price arrived in New York to take up a position as Rivers' au pair-cum-housekeeper. Rivers had custody of his teenage son Steven, who came to stay with his father in Greenwich Village on weekends from his Connecticut boarding school. Price had trained in Cheltenham, England as a teacher, and she and a friend had tried to get teaching posts in the States. After being told they'd need college degrees, they settled on trying to find au pair work instead. Price's American friend Ann Schwartly was headed back Stateside and said she'd find Price a job – which she duly did, with Rivers. Rivers, in *What Did I Do?*, writes that Schwartly was the connection too, though he remembers her as the painter Franz Kline's girlfriend, who first showed him a photo of Price in New York's Cedar Tavern.

By early 1961, Rivers and Price were in a relationship; in the autumn, they moved to Paris together. In mid-November, they went to London to get married. There they stayed with Price's friend, the artist Elisabeth Frink, then a visiting lecturer in the Sculpture School at the RCA (the art critic David Sylvester was another). After the Price–Rivers marriage at the Chelsea Town Hall, Frink threw the newlyweds a party, with the group ending up at Finch's on Fulham Road. Rivers remembered that among the assembled were Stephen Spender and David Sylvester; the Tate Gallery's director Sir John Rothenstein, who'd expanded the

Tate's modern and contemporary collecting, had written the seminal *Modern English Painters* in 1952, and opened the gallery up to temporary exhibitions such as the 1960 Picasso show that had been such a revelation for Hockney and his peers; and the artists Lynn Chadwick, Kenneth Armitage and Joe Tilson. Rivers' connection at this time to Sylvester is significant; in May of the following year, in his first solo show in London at Gimpel Fils Gallery, Rivers included a painting called *Mr Art*, an affectionate portrait of the critic.

It seems likely it was either Sylvester or Frink who arranged Rivers' talk at the RCA while he was in London to get married. And, as the secretary of the Painting School, it would have been Ann Quin's job to oversee the details. Clarice Rivers thinks the talk must have been before the wedding, because they returned to Paris very soon afterwards. Rivers confirmed this in his book too, writing: 'I was anxious about my exhibition [at Galerie Rive Droite, in April 1962] and wanted to return to Paris and my studio and Clarice's soups.'

The year 1961 was an odd one for Rivers. As Sophie Cras has shown, his move to Europe was for the sake of his career. In January of that year, Georges Marci, a dealer at Galerie Rive Droite, wrote to Rivers about having a series of European shows with sympathetic galleries, including his own and Gimpel Fils in London. That same month, Rivers and Price headed on a cross-country American road trip: their final destination Dwan Gallery in Los Angeles, where Rivers had a solo exhibition that ran throughout February. Conversations with the directors of Rive Droite and Gimpel Fils continued, and Rivers began to focus on the idea that he would create mini-retrospectives to give British and European audiences an overview of his work.

Back home in New York, an exhibition with Tibor de Nagy had been, commercially speaking, a flop. As Cras shows, Rivers' dealers on both sides of the Atlantic wanted him to make new work for London and Paris, and to push into new territory. Cras quotes a letter Myers sent Rivers in December 1961, in which he points out that Rivers had already made quite an impact in London, and that this gave him the potential to develop new audiences for his work. A big part of that impact, Myers wrote, was a result of 'your lecture' – clearly referring to the talk Rivers had given at the RCA in November.

In the decade to come, Rivers would get to know many of the young British artists then at the RCA: Derek Boshier, Hockney and, most of all, Frank Bowling. But in November 1961 Rivers was the big-shot American painter roughly fifteen years their senior. Some of them would have seen him in *Pull My Daisy* when it was screened at the National Film Theatre in June. Rivers visited the RCA painting studios, and was impressed by Hockney's work in particular. And he gave a lecture called, significantly, 'A Self-Portrait'. Rivers subsequently recorded a version of the talk for the BBC's Third Programme. It was broadcast in two parts: the first on Christmas Eve 1961 and the second on New Year's Eve (Bates's birthday).

There are two immediately striking features of Rivers' lecture. The first is how much it was a culmination not just of his own thoughts but also of the particular energies and enthusiasms that had, in essence, created him in New York during the 1950s. In particular, it bore the marks of a generational collegiality – a group of young artists, critics and poets who had forged their ideas and their relationships in the shadows of Abstract Expressionism, and who now, in their thirties, found themselves close to the institutional centre of things. They were becoming, in a sense, part of the American Establishment. Even so, they potentially provided the young British artists in the room with a blueprint for resistance, given how the most talented students among them were then trying to get beyond Abstract Expressionism and Francis Bacon's figurative painting. The specific influence of O'Hara on Rivers' thinking was also clear: short passages of the lecture match, almost word for word, an interview he conducted with Rivers that was published in *Horizon* in September 1959.

The second – and just as consequential – feature was implied by the lecture's title: 'A Self-Portrait'. This was a performance of self by the 'Wonder Boy' with his many sides. 'Since this is going to be about me,' Rivers opened, 'I will introduce myself. When I say myself, I mean what interests me, what irritates me, what bores me, what can never satisfy me, my immediate responses, my reflective ones, my history, and so forth. And I am going to take advantage of some undirected spleen to carry this through.'

That 'undirected spleen' was, in fact, pretty direct: an introductory lashing out at what he saw as the sentimental notion that an artist ought to love their subject matter – or even be interested in it – to make a great work from it. 'Obviously love of some sort moves us finally to end up in front of a canvas,' he said,

> but what you love becomes clear only as you proceed, only as you see – and the procedure is not natural and hardly ever feels right. Painting was never natural. It only becomes natural after it is invented and used and digested and discarded and finally filters down as a cliché to be used by those who remove themselves from the conflicts it takes to make a work of art today, here. You don't have to be enthusiastic about yellow to spread it generously over the surface. Do you love stones? There is a window, break it. I cannot even say that I love painting.

After voicing these thoughts, he returned to his autobiographical performance, which is worth quoting at length for the way it sets the scene for his much larger and more important advice to the assembled young artists. 'I am thirty-eight years old,' he said,

> giving me at this moment a particular view on my birth and another on my death. I am a native New Yorker; I literally grew up in the streets of what

was much less inhabited in those days – the Bronx. From the age of six until I was about ten years old I went to the zoo four or five times a week. I loved the big cats more than any other animal. I used to trail behind men until they dropped their cigarettes and then I'd pick them up and smoke them. My parents are from Poland, which was Russia before the first world war. They are no more or less interesting than the peasants who lived and worked in the same area. In conformity with the times, I was spanked, but not too much. The only thing in our house resembling art was a cheap tapestry with dark figures, a cross between a Fragonard and a Minsky stripper, popular in some dining rooms of the nineteen-twenties, and a five- and ten-cent store 8 by 10 reproduction of a very Spanish señorita holding a flower just above an exposed breast, and, to make matters worse, it followed us from one apartment to another and always across the moulding on the wall. But, mind you, when I took my mother to her first exhibition of paintings after her having had such a profound dining-room experience in art, she told me which were good paintings and which were very bad, with a strong voice that never showed for one moment that I could have thought her an innocent but none the less complete idiot.

So if I have inherited natural bad taste, that is in talking about my parent in that way, it is at least compounded with an obnoxious sense of who I am.

The cruel assessment of his parents and their bad taste, and his memories of weekends spent at the Bronx zoo rather than at the theatre or wandering the halls of museums, would have chimed with the experiences of the working-class students in the room. But there was a larger iconoclasm at play here: much of Rivers' lecture was in fact a rallying cry for contemporaneity – a call to the students to kill their parents off and ignore their influence. He used his own experience to illustrate the point, suggesting that *Washington Crossing the Delaware* was driven largely by a desire to irritate the hell out of New York's Abstract Expressionist Establishment:

> Pollock, a few years before, decided the brush inhibited him and began putting paint on with a stick. He laid canvas on the floor. Everybody told me he was great. I couldn't tell; I wasn't prepared. It was too gorgeous. I didn't like him. De Kooning's painting from a distance seemed to touch on objects and landscapes, but as you drew closer everything disappeared, and you saw a dipsy-doodle energy that kept pestering you long after looking. At this time I had not heard of Mark Rothko and disliked Gorky, because it all seemed like a romantic animated cartoon with the digestive tract as the still-life he painted from. My closest friends were three poets out of Harvard a few years, who were mad about a great deal of my work, and this was quite nourishing for me and inspired all sorts of activities.
>
> I was energetic and egomaniacal and, what is even more important, angry enough to want to do something contrary – a 'George Washington Crossing the Delaware' – something no one in the New York art world would doubt was disgusting, dead, and absurd; rearrange the elements; and throw it at them with great confusion.

This was not to imply that he'd dispensed with influence altogether. Many of Rivers' most important works from the fifties had been deliberate attempts to lock horns with Old Masters. As O'Hara later pointed out in an exhibition catalogue from 1965, Rivers' first major work, 1951's *The Burial*, was an attempt to best Gustave Courbet's *A Burial at Ornans*; his nude portrait of O'Hara from 1954 was him taking on Géricault's *Study of a Nude Man, c.* 1810–20, which the Metropolitan Museum of Art had purchased just a couple of years earlier; and then there was the influence of Jacques-Louis David. These battles, though, seemed more to do with Rivers' ego and quest for greatness than academic imitation. Far more important, he implied in his lecture, was for artists to find an art appropriate for their times. 'Van Gogh laboured to make a yellow cornfield,' he said:

> He gave us the stalks, the air, the sky. Seventy-five years later the accumulative labour of a few marvellous painters, and many less than marvellous, allows

me in the presence of just enough yellow and just so much off-white in relation to it to experience a similar sensation. I don't need the stalks. I was never interested in corn, not even to eat it. *His* sky can never be *the* sky. Seventy-five years ago you had to go to the well to get water. Today you turn the tap. Is it any the less sweet? Any the less water? Thank your grandparents and parents for what they did, but stay out of the covered wagon, you are blocking the highway.

Rivers argued that one of the most important elements of painting (again, in an implicit rebuke to the Abstract Expressionists and their high priest of 'form and flatness', Greenberg) was to let one's 'life' into the painting – which is to say, the external world of objects, people and ideas as they are experienced by the self: 'everything, but everything as it moves through the individual, depositing mountainous amounts of material, adding and destroying and organizing on new bases as it passes through, creating associations, memory, and passion, and all those uncontrollable elements embodied either in yourself or the observer of a painting'.

In that same 1965 essay, O'Hara confirmed this as the essential element in Rivers' own output. 'Rivers veers sharply,' he wrote, 'as if totally dependent on life impulses, until one observes an obsessively willful insistence on precisely what he is interested in. This goes for the father of our country [Washington] as well as for the later Camel and Tareyton [cigarette] packs. Who, he seems to be saying, says they're corny? This is the opposite of pop art. He is never naïve and never oversophisticated.'

Forget sentimentality. Kill your parents, and your sentimental darlings. Forget about needing to love your subject matter, and look up, and out, at the world around you for inspiration – not deep into your tormented soul, but at Life.

'I can't see anything in my work that will elevate anyone,' Rivers closed:

> I am not from the sunset school. My work has nothing to do with gorgeousness. It isn't virile in the sense of 'power'. The hard edge is too handy for spearmint gum. I don't know what to say. It might be funny. Perhaps it is only a visual gossip column that depends for its life on juicy bits of cigar-box covers, cigarette packages, grilles of large cars, trucks, playing cards, politics; dying and already dead Civil War veterans, and so forth. All these things do appear and disappear. I suppose it is enough to paint them. It will never make anyone who looks a better person. I'm sure that this is all building up to something, no matter how camouflaged, that will be really flattering to me. Well, when I was very young, and went to the zoo a lot, I once went with my father. He was feeding a deer through the wire fence and then began playing with the deer's antlers. Suddenly the deer backed away and a part of its antlers broke off, and there was my father holding them in his hand, and the deer charging off into the distance. Aside from expectations of glory, all I can hope for from my work is that it arrests your attention with no more or less insistence than the breaking of a deer's antlers; that something in my work obliges you to forget for a few moments the absurdity of your life.

With this lecture Rivers cut straight into the mainline of the most ambitious work at the RCA and gave it an American jolt. And the student most electrified by it was Bates.

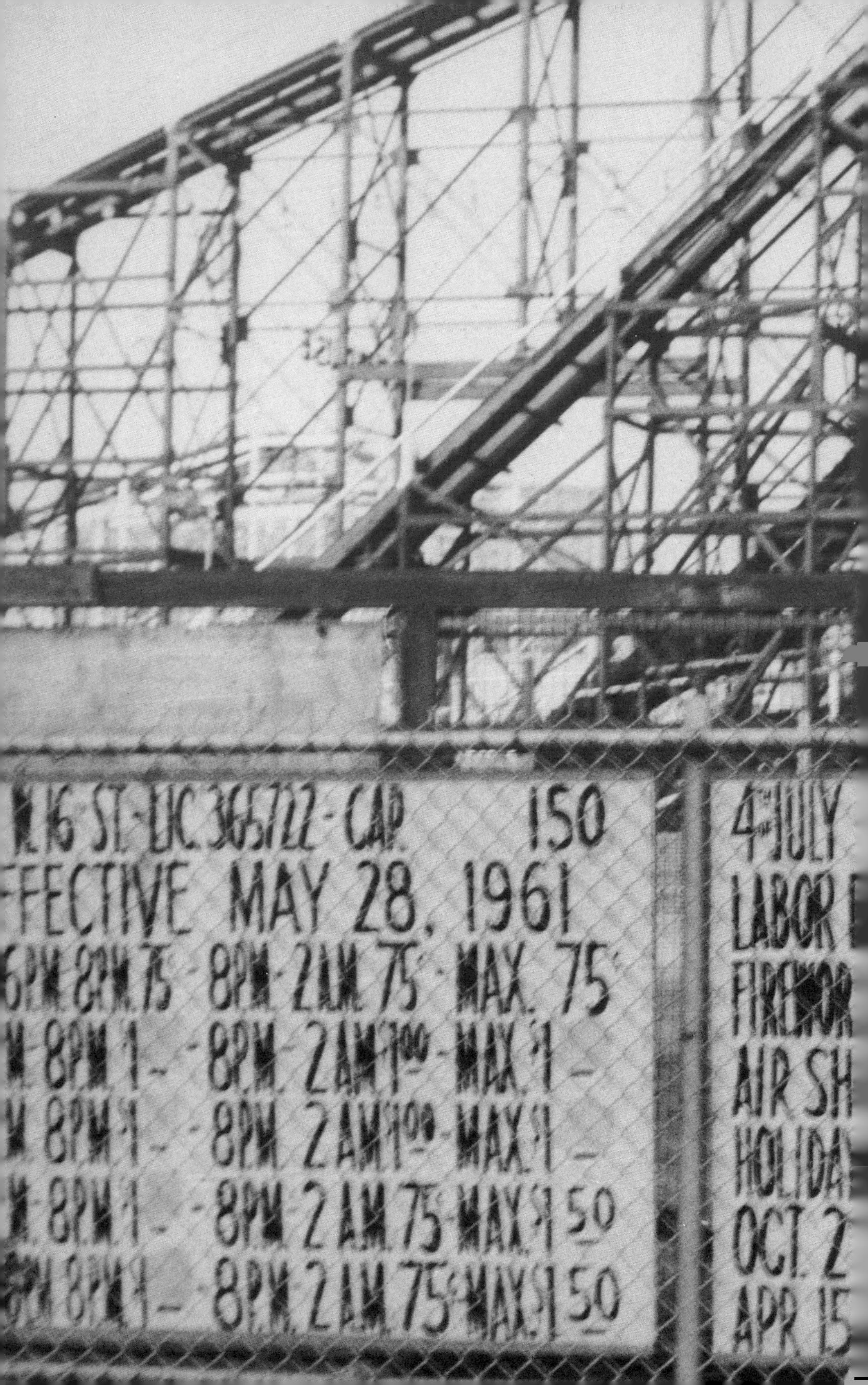
16 ST. LIC. 365722 - CAP. 150
FECTIVE MAY 28, 1961
4th JULY
LABOR
AIR SH
HOLIDA
OCT. 2
APR 15

PART III
MIRROR/MIRROR

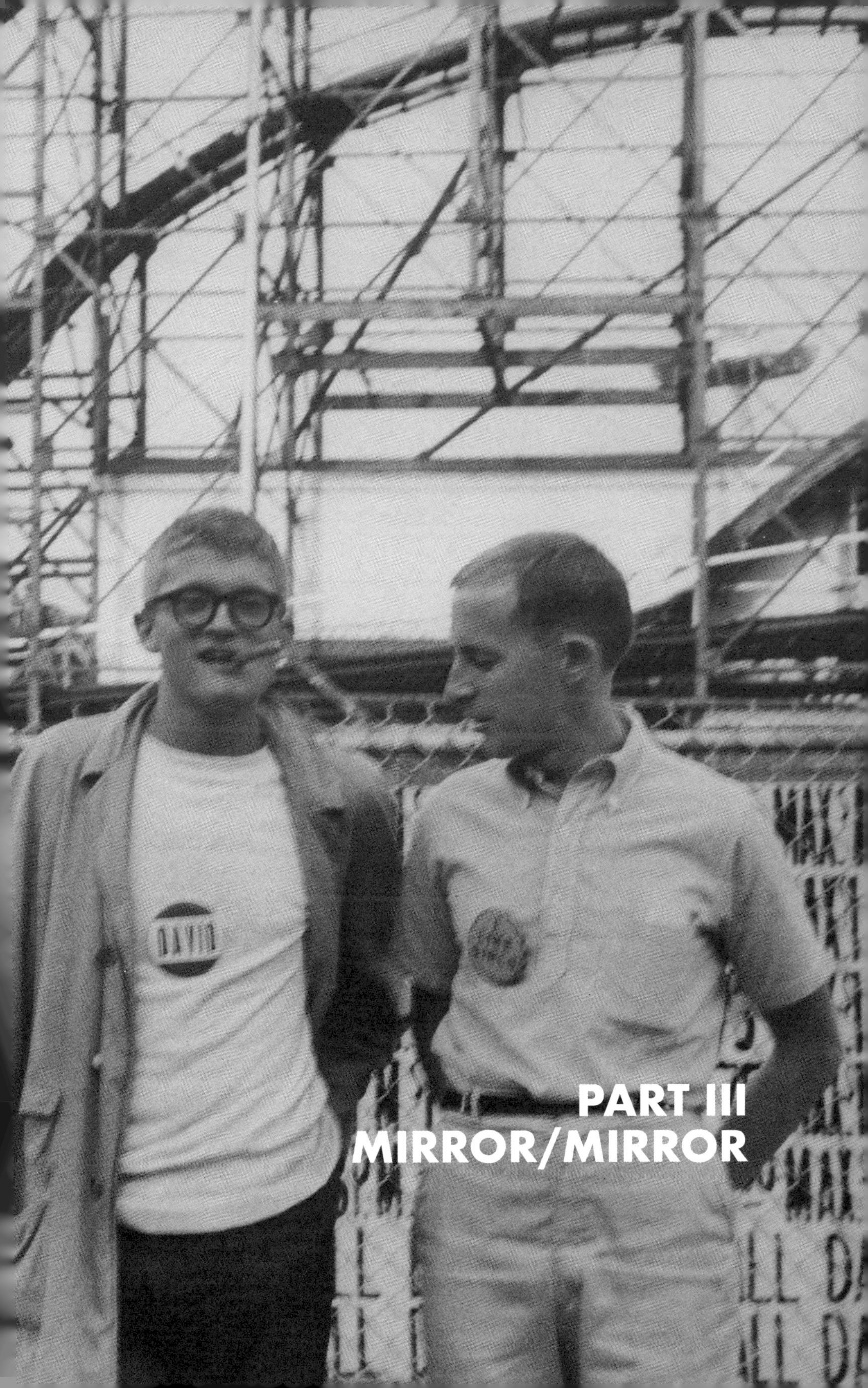

[I]f the fate of twentieth-century man is to live with death from adolescence to premature senescence, why then the only life-giving answer is to accept the terms of death, to live with death as immediate danger, to divorce oneself from society, to exist without roots, to set out on that uncharted journey into the rebellious imperatives of the self.

— NORMAN MAILER, 1957

FOR BATES, Rivers embodied so many of the things he either valued or aspired to after his first trip to New York: a deep and genuine connection with jazz music; a contrarian attitude to art-world orthodoxies; the sense that you didn't have to love your subject matter to make great art from it; a committed individualism; and a capacity for personal branding and self-mythologising. Rivers had landed at the RCA right when Bates needed inspiration most. The American would also, in a proxy way, solidify Bates's relationship with Ann Quin.

Apple doesn't remember exactly how or when Bates and Quin got together, but thinks it was likely at the start of his final year of study, in October or November 1961. He also thinks the romantic relationship was a side-consequence of Bates's 'art director' mentality: he needed a talented writer, badly, and Quin, along with Frank Bowling's wife Paddy Kitchen, was the best writer he knew.

Towards the end of their second year, the RCA students had been given General Studies dissertation topics. General Studies had been an unpopular aspect of the RCA programme since its introduction in 1958. But it was seen by the likes of Robin Darwin as an essential component of an RCA student's education: a way to introduce an element of intellectual rigour into their training. It was part of the larger revolution in art education that Darwin, Weight, Guyatt and others had been overseeing at the RCA since the 1940s, and a forerunner to the theory and philosophy classes that are such a feature of art schools today.

Hockney's antipathy to the RCA's General Studies requirements is well documented. He was already immersed in a heady intellectual and political environment alongside Kitaj, Berg and others, and the extra work was an unnecessary distraction from the studio: 'there were too many lectures', he wrote in 1976, 'and it was taking you away from painting.' He was, though, fond of the programme's head, Michael Kullman, who wasn't much older than the students.

Peter Webb describes Kullman as 'a very clever and rather self-opinionated man who struck some people as an eccentric genius, whilst others considered him mad'. There's plenty of evidence to suggest Kullman was closer to the students than most of the faculty. In Ron Fuller's photo of Hockney and Bates together at Michael Adams' Cornwall wedding, the shortish man wearing glasses running towards the camera in the background, adjusting his tie, is Kullman. His Mini van is also exactly the vehicle that would be immortalised by Hockney in *Flight into Italy – Swiss Landscape*, 1962, its licence plate '101TPC' as clear as day in both photograph and painting.

But Quin, Kullman's RCA colleague, evidently found his presence in London's artistic and literary scenes less charming. 'I wish you had been at that "Lit" party the other night', she wrote to Bates in early 1962:

> we might have been able to send it up together – as it was I was too tired I think to even 'twist' not that anyone was doing it properly apart from some tight-jeaned queer waving his arse in all the pretty boys' faces. Colin Wilson – rather out of the limelight now dancing a sort of ring a ring roses, while I listened to his ghost-writer saying things like: Life is so dull, yeah I've been abroad, Spain, Monte Carlo, Italy; O.K. so I'm another undiscovered genius but the only way I can make money is to ghost.' While Quin haunts the walls and stares at the blonde broads Kullmann [*sic*] brings in, deposits, leaves, meeting on the stairs – 'Hallo Anquin' Fuck – if I could have vomited that was the time and spot – I never have the conviction of my courage!

On paper at least, the General Studies course requirements were fairly draconian. In their first and second years, students were required to attend weekly lectures and tutorials, write essays and answer question sheets, and contribute to class conversations. In the final year, General Studies was required only in the first two terms, leaving the final term free for students to focus on their graduating exhibitions. But in those first two terms, they were required to submit both a spoken and written dissertation, the topics for which were handed out before students broke up for the summer at the end of their second year. The course was also compulsory: students couldn't get their RCA diploma without having satisfactorily completed it.

Bates was given Vincent van Gogh as his dissertation topic. Before he and Hockney headed off to New York, however, Bates negotiated with Kullman to do his dissertation on Dada instead. There's no documentation of Bates's rationale for this, but the direction his work was heading in provides strong clues: already, before his New York trip, he was moving towards a conceptually driven approach, using found objects, directing others, and integrating image and text. Dada, then, was an infinitely closer art-historical precedent to his own work than van Gogh's sunflowers and wonky bedrooms.

Bates's presentation in October 1961 was a disaster. On the day he was due to give it, he arrived to class late, and found it being run by a tutor he'd never met before: Peter de Francia, who would later replace Weight as the head of the RCA's Painting School. De Francia evidently didn't know about the change of topic, Bates performed badly, and they had an argument. Unsurprisingly, Bates was failed.

This created a problem not just for Bates but for Guyatt – his great defender – and Kullman too. Bates may have been gifted, but he'd already established a reputation among some staff and students as being aloof, difficult and arrogant. In a letter dated 30 October 1961, the RCA's assistant registrar Sybil de Boer wrote:

> He [Bates] has now seen Michael Kullmann [*sic*] and I think apologise (as much as Barrie ever could apologise) for his behaviour. . . .

> In fact, he has an outsize inferiority complex and this results, as it does in many people, in making him self-opinionated, rude, and his own worst enemy.

This wasn't a new assessment. As early as May 1960, Guyatt had written: '[a]lthough I regard Bates as my private pin-up boy, I appear to be the only member of the entire staff, including craftsmen, who does so. On all accounts he is the most abominable pain in the neck to everybody.' And in a remarkably unprofessional exchange of letters between the RCA's registrar J. R. P. Moon and Stewart Maclennan, the head of New Zealand's National Gallery (and the man overseeing Bates's government bursary), Maclennan suggested that a girlfriend might 'infuse a little frivolity into his make-up' – the 1960 equivalent of saying that maybe getting laid would help Bates lighten up. Guyatt couldn't even raise his enthusiasm in Bates's final report for 1961/62, scribbling five short sentences:

> Got everyone against him. Gave up TV. Took to fine art. Great compulsion to be a bomb. May well be one.

In early 1962, there was also a vicious little piece in the student rag, *Newsheet*, aspects of which seem a likely stab at Bates. 'ARE YOU A GENIUS?', its headline asked. 'It is never too early to decide.'

> (a) Do you repeat your name many times in the hope that it will sound as easy on the tongue as say Michaelangelo [*sic*], Goethe, Mozart?
> (b) Have you ever thought of changing your name?
> (c) If you take the art out of Mozart, what are you left with?
> 1. An organist with two left feet?
> 2. A childhood genius who 'whistled down the womb'?
> 3. Moz?
> (d) Have you one of the following physical/psychological defects, such as are

regarded as essential to being a genius?

1. Dwarf
2. Transvestism
3. New Zealand nationality
4. Protruding ears
5. Bed-wetting
6. Cupid-bow lips
7. Colour blindness

(e) What is your concept of the posterity for which you are working?

1. A babe in arms and a sucker for your charms?
2. A world full of your present tutors, hitting people over the head with your name?

It's difficult not to see Bates in some of this: the New Zealand reference; the colour-blindness (Apple, though not colour-blind, has seventy percent eyesight loss in his left eye); the reference to changing names – which suggests that Bates may have been contemplating it much earlier than November 1962.

Kullman hadn't completely abandoned Bates though. After the presentation disaster, the faculty decided that Bates should spend his entire second term focused on General Studies, under Kullman's direct supervision. To keep him interested, Kullman set it up so Bates could study with Professor Colin Cherry, an expert in human communication at Imperial College London, just a short walk from the RCA's home base in the Victoria & Albert Museum. This was an acknowledgement that Bates was becoming someone the RCA didn't have the internal resources to manage. And, in retrospect, Cherry was a potentially brilliant match for the young artist who was feeling his way towards what would eventually be called conceptual art.

Cherry's book *On Human Communication* was first published in 1957, a primer for the new and growing interdisciplinary field of communication studies, which Bates's interests in language and advertising sat squarely within. Cherry had delivered lectures at the RCA, and was an influential figure, particularly for some of the more intellectually inclined young artists and thinkers connected to the ICA and *ARK*. Marshall McLuhan also quoted Cherry's work at length in *The Gutenberg Galaxy*, 1962. Language was the key to Cherry's intellectual framework. 'The development of language reflects back on thought,' he wrote, 'for with language thoughts may become organized, new thoughts evolved. Self-awareness and the sense of social responsibility have arisen as a result of organized thoughts. Systems of ethics and law have been built up. Man has become self-conscious, responsible, a sociable creature.'

Sadly, the match-up seems never to have occurred: Apple has no recollection of meeting Cherry, and the work Bates eventually handed in shows no sign whatsoever of Cherry's influence. Despite the fact that Kullman was trying to do right by the young man, Bates, perhaps still injured by the encounter with de Francia and certainly charged up with a post-New York confidence, decided to go his own way – with the essential help of Ann Quin.

Apple remembers Quin fondly, particularly for how she helped him out of a bind, but he is also clear that theirs wasn't some great lifetime-defining love affair. He does, however, describe it as a strong intellectual connection, which evolved into a sexual relationship. He remembers that they would never go to her flat, but equally that she would never stay the night at his – possibly because this was when she would work on her own writing. In 1966, she wrote that she'd been kicked out of one flat because her 'typing late at night disturbed the land lady'. A letter she sent Bates around the time is headed with '1 a.m., Tues. morning' rather than the date.

Quin would come around to Bates's Cornwall Gardens flat once or twice a week. They'd have sex, but also talk – particularly about the project he'd asked her to write for him: his RCA dissertation. Apple points out that there's no way the pair would have been able to discuss this at the RCA, because Quin would likely have been sacked if they were found out. They also had to keep their relationship secret from the RCA faculty, following the fallout from the marriage of their friends Bowling and Kitchen. In that same letter in which she lampoons Kullman and Colin Wilson, Quin writes that:

> AWAY from Weight and Co., (who by the way caught us yesterday morn in corridor did you know and said to me in front of Sir Roger 'Now now we can't have students man-handling our secretary, at least not in College hours' . . . .) Shit I'm just waiting for you to have more than convictions, much more, in fact, a horse's (or a dog's if and as you prefer?) courage to come in and lay me down on that red plush couch of Carel's underneath Frank Aurbach's [*sic*] mighty of mightiest paintings. . . .

But Apple also says the couple went out in public together regularly, usually to one of three pubs nearby, all of which were popular with RCA students and London's wider literary and artistic scenes: The Queens Elm, The Hoop & Toy, and Finch's.

Quin's decision to risk her job to write Bates's dissertation suggests a few possible motivations. One is that she loved him enough that she wanted to see him do well. Another is that she just found the whole thing amusing. But another is that the 'intellectual connection' between the pair served a useful purpose for her, too – and that the writing she did for Bates either fed into, or drew from, the manuscript she was working on at the time, and which would eventually become her first published novel, *Berg*.

The letter Bates sent to his friend Leon Lesnie soon after his return from New York, which Apple is convinced Quin must have written, certainly has something of her tone about it: literary and sinewy and erotic, cut with little flashes of her vocabulary and preoccupations.

'There are so many camp people in N.Y.', Quin/Bates writes,

> I came back almost camp myself. Those boys, really sweet. . . . I got involved with a lot of gay guys on the beach at Long Island after some very gay parties. The boys here (there, that is) are very beautiful. I got involved with a lovely nymphomaniac negress, but she was studying opera. Also, a scizo [*sic*] from Columbia Uni. who let me f—k her in front of the whole of New York. She lay in front of an open window (on the Columbia campus) with the blinds up and the light on in the middle of the night and with a guy over the road cleaning his teeth and having an orgasm. She psychanalysed [*sic*] my every plunge and withdrawal. I am writing a song called 'I've left my balls in New York'. So what's new, what else is there to vomit out. Saw Rocco and his Bros. F—king good movie.

This teasing focus on Bates's sexual ambivalence is a clue that the letter was by Quin, because it also appears in pieces of writing she is known to have produced – most notably 'B. B's [Barrie Bates] Second Manifesto'. The manifesto is a brutal, darkly humorous collaboration, marked by the spikiness that characterises much of Quin's fiction. It is also dripping in the language of 'Hip', which had been such a feature of *The Connection*, and of the jazz scene in which Bates had been immersed in New York. The 'Manifesto' opens like this:

> Yeah maybe I ought to get organised, trouble is I don't know what I really want to do. O.K. so I could earn five thousand a year, but I'm not ending up like those other slick ad chaps. Christ they're so mass-consumed they can't even shit straight. And the exhibitions these other jerks have they're for the birds, so provincial. I want to do something no one has ever done as good, if only to drive a van better than anyone before...

Later, on Bates's behalf, Quin has a direct dig at his classmates:

> Like the other night I got sloshed, brought back some chap, we did a painting together, that's the real stuff, let it out first go, leave it at that, all these other crappy painters, they would be better if they used their pricks. Not that I dig this pop art, they haven't anything to say.

The painting Bates/Quin refers to here is possibly *Two Cobbers in Central Park*, which Bates made in collaboration with Reg Fisher, another Painting student in their year, with whom Bates was close. *Two Cobbers* appeared in 1962's 'Young Contemporaries' exhibition. Quin's writing clearly shows how outside the core group of young Pop painters – Boshier, Phillips, Boty, and previous RCA students like Peter Blake – Bates already felt in early 1962. She was also writing these words just two months before Ken Russell's film *Pop Goes the Easel*, the documentary that thrust Boshier, Boty, Phillips and Blake into the living rooms of Britain, was screened on the BBC. Bates, as their peer, and Quin, as the secretary in the Painting School, would certainly have known about its filming.

If Bates and, by proxy, Quin, really did find Pop art so dreary, what exactly was 'B. B's Second Manifesto' aligning them with? After the swipe at their contemporaries, the answer comes in the next line: 'Now Mailer could do anything and get away with it', Quin writes on Bates's behalf, 'I suppose you've got to be a genius, or something, to do that, otherwise it's sheer hard work.' This is the key that unlocks Bates's dalliance with the language and ideas of young America, and explains how he separated himself from the London drab of British Pop – because the novelist and essayist Norman Mailer was the self-appointed prophet of 'Hip'.

In 1959, Mailer's collection of essays and fragments, *Advertisements for Myself*, was published in the US: a self-consciously strange miscellany of previously published pieces with accompanying introductions and explanations, which Mailer described consistently throughout as 'advertisements'.

At the time, Mailer was struggling: by his own admission, he'd been smoking an awful lot of marijuana, and had seen his cultural stature slip after the muted critical reception of his second and third novels, *Barbary Shore*, 1951, and *The Deer Park*, 1955. He'd briefly written an incendiary column for the countercultural newspaper he'd co-founded, the *Village Voice* (which counted Nat Hentoff among its columnists), and had written a daft essay for a gay magazine called 'The Homosexual Villain', which Mailer himself described as 'beyond a doubt the worst article I have ever written, conventional, empty, pious, the quintessence of the Square' (one of the many quirks of *Advertisements for Myself* is that it includes his disasters alongside his better work). The fifties had not been kind to the young star who'd published arguably America's greatest World War II novel, *The Naked and the Dead*, in 1948.

Advertisements for Myself put him back on the literary map. But then, in November 1960, Mailer undid himself again. Having decided that he was going to stand for New York City mayor, Mailer threw a party at his apartment, and, in the early hours of the morning, stabbed his wife Adele Morales, almost killing her. He was, once again, America's most notorious writer: the genius, in Bates's manifesto, who could do anything and get away with it. (Morales didn't press charges, though Mailer was committed for psychiatric evaluation.)

Andre Deutsch, the British publishing company that had made its name and reputation in 1949 when it released Mailer's *The Naked and the Dead*, published *Advertisements for Myself* in the UK in 1961. The book's most controversial essay, but also its most important, was one originally published in *Dissent* in 1957: 'The White Negro: Superficial Reflections on the Hipster'.

One of the arguments of 'White Negro', at least when it came to the 'negro' part, was essentially that the adoption of black culture by young white America – specifically jazz music and the language of Hip

– was part of a potential revolution in American cultural life. Mailer wrote the essay during the aftershocks of *Brown v Board of Education* and the debates about desegregation gripping the country. He argued that, because African-Americans had already lived for generations with fear and violence, to gain equality via the civil rights movement would mean that they would become the superior cultural group. And the terror this represented for America's whites, he stated, was '[l]ike all conservative political fear . . . the fear of unforeseeable consequences, for the Negro's equality would tear a profound shift into the psychology, the sexuality, and the moral imagination of every white alive.'

Mailer then doubled down on his strange prediction of a new American racial-sexual chaos. 'With this possible emergence of the Negro,' he continued,

> Hip may erupt as a psychically armed rebellion whose sexual impetus may rebound against the antisexual foundation of every organized power in America, and bring into the air such animosities, antipathies, and new conflicts of interest that the mean empty hypocrisies of mass conformity will no longer work. A time of violence, new hysteria, confusion and rebellion will then be likely to replace the time of conformity.

Though Mailer declares himself a sexual libertarian who has no personal objections to whites and blacks sleeping with each other, he sees this underlying sexual threat as a far more defining fear than desegregation: '[W]hen it comes,' he wrote, 'miscegenation will be a terror, comparable perhaps to the derangement of the American Communists when the icons to Stalin came tumbling down.'

James Baldwin's famous condemnation of Mailer's essay, 'The Black Boy Looks at the White Boy', published in *Esquire* in 1961, came not in the immediate aftermath of the publication of 'White Negro' but after the infamous events of that evening in 1960 in Mailer's apartment. With that night, Mailer had laid himself out on the cultural canvas, becoming a figure both of ridicule and sadness. But he was also a writer with whom Baldwin shared a complicated mutual respect, and one-time friendship, before Mailer criticised Baldwin's work in *Advertisements for Myself*.

'But *why*', Baldwin asked of 'White Negro',

> should it be necessary to borrow the Depression language of deprived Negroes, which eventually evolved into jive and bop talk, in order to justify such a grim system of delusions? Why malign the sorely menaced sexuality of Negroes in order to justify the white man's own sexual panic? Especially as, in Norman's case, and as indicated by his work, he has a very real sense of sexual responsibility, and even, odd as it may sound to some, of sexual morality, and a genuine commitment to life.

Mailer, in other words, knew better. The central problem with his essay was the wild generalisations he made about the collective character of the 'Negro': 'it is no accident,' he opined, 'that the source of Hip is the Negro for he has been living on the margin between totalitarianism and democracy for two centuries'. There's his assertion that: 'Any Negro who wishes to live must live with danger from his first day.' And later still: 'Hated from outside and therefore hating himself, the Negro was forced into the position of exploring all those moral wildernesses of civilized life which the Square automatically condemns as delinquent or evil or immature or morbid or self-destructive or corrupt.'

When viewed like this, it is, of course, an insanely silly and racist piece of writing: psychosexual racial bombast dressed up as political nihilism. But it is also Mailer's important attempt to define the singular figure of the 'American existentialist', who, in his framework, was the hipster.

In Mailer's view, the hipster was distinct from European existentialists precisely because of the influence of black culture; the language of Hip and the abstract vocabularies of contemporary jazz gave expression to a singularly American experience of personal crisis and death. For blacks, these were survival mechanisms in a culture that discriminated against them and, at worst, wanted them dead. But World War II had inserted a fragility into white America's comfortable, dominant existence too: the horrors of the Holocaust, the brutalities of Stalin which had shattered the utopianism of American communists, and America's use of the atomic bomb to wipe out two Japanese cities all illustrated the real risk of societal annihilation. The hipster, then, is,

> the man who knows that if our collective condition is to live with instant death by atomic war, relatively quick death by the State as *l'univers concentrationnaire*, or with a slow death by conformity with every collective and rebellious instinct stifled (at what damage to the mind and the heart and the liver and the nerves no research foundation for cancer will discover in a hurry), if the fate of twentieth-century man is to live with death from adolescence to premature senescence, why then the only life-giving answer is to accept the terms of death, to live with death as immediate danger, to divorce oneself from society, to exist without roots, to set out on that uncharted journey into the rebellious imperatives of the self.

This last handful of words is key: the exploration of the individual self rather than the collective self was essential to the hipster's status as a kind of creative and existential libertarian. The war had shown how collective identity could lead to conformity, and that conformity could lead to fascism, totalitarianism, and oppressive moral and racial structures in society. To participate in a collective identity, then, was to run the risk of participating in state-sanctioned murder – as the Nazis, the Soviets and Americans had all proved.

The two pathways to this individualist freedom, Mailer suggested, are art and sex. Art, first of all, is the essential element in being able to 'swing': the vital condition of the hipster. And to swing, Mailer argued, 'is to be able to learn, and by learning, take a step towards making it, towards creating. What is to be created is not nearly so important as the hipster's belief that when he really makes it, he will be able to turn his hand to anything, even to self-discipline.'

The sex paradigm is the more important in Mailer's hipster universe. Orgasm, and the pursuit of it in ever-improving or 'apocalyptic' forms, was in his thesis an energetic life-force rather than the release of one: a little death that aspires to nuclear proportions, with long-term consequences. Sex was a physical expression of love with the potential to accelerate culture. 'It is not granted to the hipster to grow old gracefully,' he wrote, 'he has been captured too early by the oldest dream of power, the gold fountain of Ponce de Leôn, the fountain of youth where the gold is in the orgasm.' This is also where Mailer starts to get himself in trouble, conflating the outsider status and oppression of the 'Negro' with perceived sexual prowess. And what is jazz, Mailer asks, if not the (black-dominated) expression of this wild, primal, apocalyptic orgasm-chase?

It's a dumb conceptual leap to make. More important is *why* Mailer placed orgasm at the heart of the American existentialist condition. And this has much less to do with miscegenation than with the huge influence on him of Wilhelm Reich.

Well before Mailer published 'White Negro', the Kinsey Reports had placed the discussion of sex front and centre in post-war America. Kinsey's work is often cited as the start of a 'sexual revolution' that culminated in the collision between the freedoms granted by the contraceptive pill and the late-sixties counterculture. But this focus on Kinsey tends to overlook the work of Wilhelm Reich, who had coined the term 'sexual revolution' in the 1930s – and who would himself fall victim, eventually, to the moralising cruelties of 1950s America.

Reich was an Austrian Jew who had been one of Sigmund Freud's star students but eventually split with his mentor. Freud's psychoanalytic framework argued that the unconscious is the location for our infantile and antisocial feelings. This, Reich didn't dispute. But he argued that the unconscious 'also contains many impulses which represent natural biological demands, such as the sexual desire of adolescents or of people tied down in an unhappy marriage' – in other words, our perfectly normal sexual urges. Provided they didn't harm anyone and were expressed in consenting physical relationships with people of our own or similar age, these were nobody else's business and the key to good mental health.

Reich expressed this thesis in his groundbreaking book *The Sexual Revolution*, first published in German in 1936 and then in English in 1945. It was a kind of pre-Kinsey rallying cry for the rights of everyone to have a positive sexual life on their own terms. As its title implies, Reich was deeply influenced by Karl Marx, and called for a restructuring of society based on 'sex-economic' factors. We live, he argued, in sex-negating cultures, where genital gratification, as 'the decisive sex-economic factor in the prevention of neuroses and establishment of social achievement – is at variance, in every respect, with present-day laws and with every patriarchal religion'.

His was not a call for promiscuity but for satisfaction. If one had found their perfect sexual match in a single partner, as many people do, then it was perfectly acceptable in Reich's framework to live out a monogamous life. But, he argued, '[c]ompulsive morality as exemplified in marital duty and familial authority is the morality of cowardly and impotent individuals who are incapable of experiencing through natural love capacity what they try to obtain in vain with the aid of the police and marriage laws.'

In 1939, Reich emigrated from Norway, where he'd been teaching for several years, to take up a position at the New School in New York. It was there that things started to get a little kooky. Reich had already raised eyebrows in Norway for some of his biochemical experiments, but it was in the States that he fully developed his theory of 'orgonomy':

the study of 'orgone energy', which Reich argued was a literal thing – a tangible force in the atmosphere that, when concentrated, could do everything from cure cancer to dramatically improve orgasm.

The next step in proving his theory was to build 'orgone energy accumulators': essentially, metal-lined cupboards that individuals sat in to concentrate orgone energy. Reich's biographer Christopher Turner points out that the orgone box became popular in the 1940s and 1950s, and was used in particular by writers, including Allen Ginsberg, J. D. Salinger and Saul Bellow. William Burroughs apparently claimed to have once had a spontaneous orgasm inside one. Mailer had several accumulators. 'To bohemians,' Turner writes, 'the orgone box was celebrated as a liberation machine, the wardrobe that would lead to utopia, while to conservatives it was Pandora's box, out of which escaped the Freudian plague – the corrupting influence of anarchism and promiscuous sex.'

Reich later also invented a 'cloudbuster': a machine that aimed to manipulate orgone energy in the atmosphere, to make it rain in the desert. All of this was, from a scientific perspective, complete bunkum. As early as 1941, he'd met with Albert Einstein to discuss orgone energy, and Einstein even carried out his own tests on an accumulator, eventually declaring that it had no scientific merit at all.

A man trying to recreate society by putting healthy sex at its core, and building machines that could free us from our sexual repression, improve our orgasms and solve the problems of climate change, seems both harmless and very cool by contemporary standards. But the America of the McCarthy fifties was different. Reich was a brilliant psychoanalyst, but his machines – and, clearly, his own slip into a kind of madness – were his undoing. The Food and Drug Administration eventually shut down the accumulator business on account of its 'fraudulent' scientific claims. When some accumulator parts were later shipped across state borders, Reich was arrested – and convicted – in 1956. Meanwhile, Kinsey had published *Sexual Behavior in the Human Female* in 1953.

As Turner argues, '[i]f Kinsey's libertarianism was attracting attention, bringing Reich to trial promised to stem that tide.' Sexual liberation was, in McCarthy's America, a communist conspiracy, and Reich became one of its fall guys. He was also the victim of an event that he'd doubtless never expected to see in America after escaping the Nazi push across Europe: in June and August 1956, his books were burned by the authorities – including copies of *The Sexual Revolution* and, ironically, his other great work, *The Mass Psychology of Fascism*.

Reich died just over a year later, on 3 November 1957, in Lewisberg Federal Penitentiary. He was sixty years old. His prosecution, imprisonment and death made brutally real his own words two decades earlier in *The Sexual Revolution*: 'If one investigates ecclesiastical, fascist and other reactionary ideologies for their unconscious content, one finds that they are essentially defense reactions. They are formed for fear of the unconscious inferno which everyone carries within himself.'

Mailer, at the time of 'White Negro', was in thrall to Reich's ideas, and placed them at the heart of his new agenda for creativity and liberty in America. Mailer's hipster was the product, at least in his mind, of the twentieth century's greatest forces and traumas: Freud, Marx, sexual liberation, technology, totalitarianism, nuclear war, jazz, urbanity, and art as the expression of the inner self. Little wonder that Mailer wanted so badly to be a hipster himself, and even wanted to write the great hipster novel – which, like his own Hip status, never quite arrived. Baldwin, in 'The Black Boy Looks at the White Boy', can't resist pointing out that the black jazz musicians he and Mailer had hung out with in Paris in the fifties thought of Mailer not as one of them but as a kind of lovable square: exactly what he desperately wanted not to be. Nat Hentoff was critical of Mailer's hipster vision too, writing in *The Jazz Life* that it was out of touch with present realities. 'The amoral hipster,' Hentoff wrote,

> in short, is now a rare figure in jazz. As the music has become an object in itself, a discipline and responsibility is required of the jazzman which the 'authentic' hipster cannot regard as worth that much time and trouble if the only values are right now. The act of Sonny Rollins – withdrawing from the jazz life entirely for more than a year to re-examine the content and technique of his playing – is not the act of a hipster. The months of listening and sketching through which Miles Davis prepared a flamenco album signifies an involvement with the future that is not 'hip' in Mailer's sense.

In 'B. B's Second Manifesto', Quin and Bates collaborated to turn Bates into a singular embodiment of Mailer's hipster: a young loner fixated on American style and jazz, who wants to remake himself and shake off his past, who'd been to New York and become obsessed with the inner workings of American advertising – not just for its creative potential, but also for the way it was reshaping mass culture, in the here and now, through sublimation, manipulation, and the exploitation of the repressed desires Reich believed we had to release if we were to build a healthier world.

Quin and Bates's faithfulness to, and playfulness with, Mailer's vision come through especially clearly in the manifesto's condensation of bisexuality, art and the psychic force of miscegenation. 'This club in New York we all went to,' they have Bates say,

> they stood around just staring, some in drag, quiet music and all that crap in the background, sure I've thought about it; maybe I ought to sleep with some guy. Told myself lately I don't need sex any more, gone so hip I don't think I do now. Wish I hadn't had so many women, like a machine in the end. This chick I lived with, just a convenience, screwed her every night, again in the morning, get up at eleven and know she had cooked some breakfast, Jesus it gets so boring. She was a nymphomaniac, that was her trouble. I want it to mean something, not just sex. All these chicks dote on one, that's why I've given them up. Now take these crazy negros in their white sneakers,

> paisley ties, two vents in their jackets and all that crap, not really wild, just conservatively wild you know, watch how they treat their chicks. One in the subway went up to this broad and said Get in there I'm going to fuck you, she did too, right there and then in the tube, isn't that great, I mean it's real, that's how a movie should be made.

The subway incident seems too preposterous and convenient to be believable, except as an attempt to vividly illustrate Mailer's more dubious points about the societal overthrow that miscegenation promised. The manifesto, then, wasn't just an expression of Bates's frustration with his life in London and the ascendance of the Pop artists he was surrounded by and thought mediocre. It was also a masterclass from him and Quin in how to turn a complicated theoretical idea into a living art work.

By drawing on Mailer's figure of the hipster, the pair created a framework for Bates to understand his outsider status in relation to his peers, and also to British culture and the wider art world. The young New Zealander was clearly more drawn to the changes going on in America than to anything he was seeing around him at the RCA. This recognition would be the thing that finally separated him from his British Pop colleagues. He and Quin had also recently encountered someone who already embodied so many of Mailer's ideas: that saxophone-playing, hyper-individualist, sexually free painter, Larry Rivers. Seen through this lens, it becomes clearer just why Bates had been so affected by Rivers' talk.

The lecture became the basis for Bates's and Quin's most substantial collaboration: his RCA dissertation, otherwise known as 'Pop Corn (Being a Conversation between Vincent Van Gogh & Larry Rivers at "The Five Spot" Jazz Club, New York)'.

'I wanted the following piece to really swing, so I took a painter like Larry Rivers, whose ideas I dig in more ways than one,' Quin and Bates wrote as the very first line of the foreword. The dissertation takes the form of an imagined dialogue between Rivers and van Gogh, the link having been provided by Rivers himself. 'Van Gogh laboured to make a yellow cornfield,' he'd told the RCA students:

> He gave us the stalks, the air, the sky. Seventy-five years later the accumulative labour of a few marvellous painters, and many less than marvellous, allows me in the presence of just enough yellow and just so much off-white in relation to it to experience a similar sensation.

This wasn't just a comment on van Gogh's use of yellow: it was a call for contemporaneity – something Bates had been striving for in his own work, and something that was becoming even more urgent for him as he saw the growing success of his painting peers at the RCA who were engaged in what he saw as a pretty conservative set of pursuits. This is arguably what began to separate him from Hockney, too: as much as Hockney's work was a breath of fresh air, it was deeply concerned with looking to the likes of Bacon and Hogarth – those 'grandparents blocking the highway'. Bates, the New Zealander, wasn't burdened with the same historical legacies.

Apple says that Bates came up with the title and concept for 'Pop Corn' as a play on Rivers' status as a proto-Pop artist and van Gogh's cornfields. But it's just as likely it was a dig at 'corny' classmates like Peter Phillips, who was being championed as one of the young trailblazers in British Pop. Apple is also clear that it was Quin who stitched together the seamless conversation between the artists, one living, one dead, by using quotes from van Gogh's letters to his brother Theo and quotes from Rivers' lecture, and a conversation she had with Rivers himself at Finch's Pub (Quin references the conversation in the dissertation's bibliography).

Reading 'Pop Corn', it's hard not to infer the influence on Quin of Samuel Beckett (later, they'd share a publisher in John Calder), who had himself been heavily influenced in his early years by Dada (and its successor Surrealism), the ostensible subject of Bates's aborted dissertation. This is seen in the overlapping, slightly disjointed conversation she constructs between van Gogh and Rivers, a kind of hipster *Godot*:

> V.G. You talk about plants – that may be, but you are corn, and your place is in the cornfield, and in order to grow one must be rooted in the earth. Take root in the soil you will germinate there – don't wither on the sidewalk brother
>
> L.R. Sure if one remains at a railroad station too long he must die, for nothing comes along to give you substance. No one cares about your personal problems, and the dead can't talk
>
> V.G. Brother I wouldn't say that. Lately I've been thinking of doing a drawing of my father the way he looked at a funeral
>
> L.R. My old man played the violin, but let's clear that up. My parents are from Poland, which was Russia before the first World War. They're no more nor less interesting than the peasants who lived and worked in the same area. I can't think of anything they did which, if I had had the chance, I would do – no matter, if I did, I'd then be them
>
> V.G. Which reminds me Father had a windfall, Uncle Stricker sent him 100 guilders, which I thought was very kind of Uncle S. you know, but then as far as money goes I haven't profited from being here

The dialogue continues like this for over thirty pages. In it, van Gogh comes across as an earnest trier grappling with his lack of success, his theories of painting and colour, and his relationship with Paul Gauguin. Rivers acts as his deadpan foil, giving the dead Dutchman the occasional acerbic Hip reality check.

The presence of van Gogh, though, served more than just a dramatic purpose: it was also a chance for Quin and Bates to make fun of the RCA and the disaster that had led to Bates's General Studies probation in the first place – the fact he hadn't wanted van Gogh as his dissertation topic. 'Well here's the thesis of all thesis,' Quin wrote in the letter she sent Bates with the finished document,

> will it cool Kullmann's [*sic*] tongue and/or scroo scroo Darwin's b . . . s? You will see it swings a little more than it did in places, I put a bit more in and took a lot of the duller bits out – take a look at that BIBLIOGRAPHY man it's really wild don't you fink fink? By the way did you manage to squeeze Pete Collins enough for the snaps of L. R. in wedlock bowler hatted? that'll really send 'em up – and hey what about acknowledgements to QUINOLOGY also Secretary, plus typist and not forgetting Patience . . . .

Pete Collins was a photographer and friend of Elisabeth Frink, who'd taken photos of Rivers' and Clarice Price's wedding. Rivers includes one of these in his autobiography *What Did I Do?* and he is, as Quin suggests, wearing a bowler hat for the occasion.

It's easy to write off 'Pop Corn' as juvenilia for both Bates and Quin. But it's a serious, experimental work, which clearly served a purpose for both of them. Bates couldn't possibly have thought that handing in something so far from what he'd been assigned – whether van Gogh or a studentship with Colin Cherry – would earn him the pass he needed. And Quin would have lost her job if the collaboration had been discovered. Nor was she a writer who was messing around: she'd already completed two novel manuscripts (both rejected by publishers) and was on her way to finishing a third.

'Pop Corn' is, in retrospect, a nuanced document of the period Quin and Bates were living through together. There was van Gogh, obviously, who'd been brought back to life by Rivers in his talk. Henry Miller, in *Tropic of Cancer*, had written that van Gogh's letters had a perfection beyond either Dostoevsky or Turgenev, and that they represented 'the triumph of the individual over art'. The publication in the US of Miller's *Tropic of Cancer* in 1961 by Barney Rosset of Grove Press had been a linchpin of the obscenity debates. The Grove edition – 'The book they are trying to ban!' – was advertised in those same *New Yorkers* Bates had flicked through in John Craddock's apartment. But copies from its original French publisher, Obelisk Press, had been circulating in London for years, particularly among art students. 'How's Henry Miller', Quin asked Bates in the letter she sent him with 'Pop Corn', 'but I don't suppose "genius" No. 2 (guess No. 1?) has had much time for peering at the printed word . . .'

'Pop Corn' also makes clear that the pair were actively working through Mailer's influence. At one point in the foreword they suggest of van Gogh that 'here was a man more "hip" than the many potential hipsters of today – what Mailer would call "very much with the scene" . . .' The foreword also closes with a quote from Mailer: 'The final purpose of art is to intensify, even, if necessary, to exacerbate the moral consciousness of people.' This comes directly from the 1961 Andre Deutsch edition of *Advertisements for Myself*, from an interview with Mailer conducted in the wake of 'White Negro'.

Beckett, sex, hipsterism and existentialism – all were present in this strange, semi-Dadaist collaboration. But there is one more big presence in its foreword: the psychiatrist R. D. Laing, whose *The Divided Self* had been published in 1960, and who would become a strong influence on Quin's writing.

Like 'White Negro', *The Divided Self* was an existentialist text, which defined mental illness not as something solely located in our subconscious, but as a state of being shaped and defined through our existence in relation to others. Madness, Laing argued, might in fact be a form of 'ontological insecurity': an inability to experience one's own subjectivity as complete, coherent and whole in the world. Laing wrote that if the ontologically insecure individual,

> cannot take the realness, aliveness, autonomy, and identity of himself and others for granted, then he has to become absorbed in contriving ways of trying to be real, of keeping himself or others alive, of preserving his identity, in efforts, as he will often put it, to prevent himself losing his self. What are to most people everyday happenings, which are hardly noticed because they have no special significance, may become deeply significant in so far as they either contribute to the sustenance of the individual's being or threaten him with non-being.

In an echo of this, Quin/Bates wrote of van Gogh that:

> Even with the psychiatric treatment that is now taken as a matter of course, could anyone have brain-washed the destructive element, which in its own way is creatively wild, of such a painter, and would he still have preferred to drive himself 'mad' rather than face the strain of a supposably [*sic*] sane world – I think he might well have done.

There may have been a measure of self-identification for both of them here: Quin, creatively wild with a self-destructive streak, who had already received psychiatric treatment after her breakdown in Cornwall before she started working at the RCA ('I went to see a psychiatrist, more from curiosity, and spent a few hours entertaining the horrified lady'); and Bates, increasingly recognising his own outsider status as he became more isolated both from his New Zealand home and his London classmates – with his own capacity to self-destruct too.

> My job at the art college lasted three years, and before leaving I finished the third novel, of which I did three or four versions. This was accepted. Soon after I went down with glandular TB and spent several happy months revising the book while convalescing; dreaming in fact of months, years

> maybe, of being in a sanatorium somewhere in the mountains, and writing masterpieces. Instead I had to face the world again, and the problems of being published. The proofs finally arrived, I couldn't open them, and spent the whole day vomiting from anxiety and depression. Eventually the galleys lay all over my room. The dream had been realized, but reading what I had written seemed someone else's dream. A kind of involuntary commitment. And like Camus I became aware that: 'There is in me an anarchy, a frightful disorder. Creating costs me a thousand deaths, for it involves an order and my whole being rebels against order. But without it I should die scattered.'

That 'third novel', which Quin says she finished at the RCA in her brief 1966 autobiography in *London Magazine*, was *Berg* – the first book she published, in 1964. Quin resigned from her secretarial position at the end of 1962. She would go on to publish three more novels after *Berg*, but it's still widely regarded as her best book.

The novel's titular hero is Alistair 'Aly' Berg, immortalised in the book's opening line: 'A man called Berg, who changed his name to Greb, came to a seaside town intending to kill his father. . . . ' It seems likely he was named after the painter Adrian Berg (his first name has the same initial too), who was studying in the RCA's Painting School for two of the three years Quin worked there. Berg had done a degree in English literature before his arrival at the RCA, so books may have been a connection between the pair. But Quin may have been just as attracted by the easy reversal of his surname, to Greb, because *Berg* is ultimately a book about reflections: about doubles, mirrors and their images; about temporary identities and their effects on our sanity.

Aly Berg, out to avenge the emotional hurt caused to his too-forgiving mother by his estranged father Nathaniel, identifies his father in a seaside town and takes a room in the same boarding house. Nathaniel is there with Judith, his current lover. Berg's room adjoins theirs, and through the thin partition he can hear the full mess of their lives: the fights and the reconciliations, the fucking, the night-time grinding of his father's teeth, the squawks of a pet budgie. It's an obviously Oedipal set-up: a three-way situation in which the father doesn't recognise the son and the son eventually takes the father's place in bed, becoming just as obsessed with Judith as he is with murdering Dad.

Quin expert Jennifer Hodgson has made the point that there was a widespread revival of the Oedipus theme in sixties culture: 'recovered and reinvented to describe the limits upon the individual that are imposed by social reality and internalised, etched upon the self by ideology. It was employed to describe the ways in which the anarchic productivity of unconscious desire is sublimated and regulated.' Shades again, then, of the way Quin had described van Gogh's madness in 'Pop Corn', and strong echoes of the idea of the individualist outsider in Mailer's 'White Negro'. But perhaps even stronger is the connection here to Laing's 'divided self', and the way, Laing suggests, madness is constructed socially. Hodgson also points out that the Oedipus complex became the cornerstone of Freudian psychoanalysis – which both Wilhelm Reich and Laing worked so hard to expand and reinvent. Throughout Quin's writing, Hodgson states, 'Quin turns to the Oedipus story as a mythic master code with which to articulate the human existential plight and her profound ontological distrust of the normative.'

Aly Berg, of course, is different from the Oedipus of myth: he knowingly wants to kill his father, knowingly wants to fuck his father's lover, and eventually does. As if to emphasise the maternal confusion, Aly is obsessed with Judith's breasts. At one point, as they make love, Judith tells him how much better – how much bigger – he is than his father, before she calls him by his father's name as she climaxes. 'The gap in the wall seemed wider from the angle of his head,' Quin writes, at the moment of Judith's mistake. 'He closed his eyes.' (Oedipus, of course, blinds himself after his mother-lover commits suicide.)

Judith's name is no accident either: it is the name of that great widow and beheader of Holofernes (her surname, 'Goldstein', is Jewish too, hammering home the point). There are other references in the book to the great emasculators of myth. Berg – significantly, given what Hockney and Bates were up to with their personal images at the time – is a travelling hair-tonic salesman. In his suitcase are bottles, wigs, and pamphlets that read, in caps: 'BUY BERG'S BEST HAIR TONIC DEFEAT DELILAH'S DAMAGE: IN TWO MONTHS YOU WILL BE A NEW MAN'.

Oedipus was also a convenient building block for Quin's fixation with three-way relationships. *Berg* is basically an incestuous love triangle; her second novel *Three* is about an older couple's sensual fixation with a younger woman who has disappeared; her book *Passages* is about a woman and her lover trying to find the woman's brother. And, of course, *Berg* is about reflections: Oedipus is his father's younger double; so too Berg is to his father Nathaniel (emphasised when Judith calls out the wrong name during sex). Jennifer Komorowski has written that: 'When Berg changes his name to Greb, with the intention of disguising his true identity in order to get closer to his father, he is also (unwittingly?) changing his own reality; rather than creating a new identity separate from his father, Aly Berg becomes his father's mirrored double.'

Berg encounters his reflection ('Greb'), either crystal-clear or partially fogged and warped, everywhere: 'Berg grinned into the mirror, at the landscape accustoming itself to the interior planning'; 'He cooked the beans and the bacon, until the steam curled over the window and mirror'; 'he stared at his reflection in the plate, a faint glimmer of someone barely recognisable'; 'they sat either side of a glass-topped table, above them a cherub-garlanded mirror, into which Berg gazed at the blind man thumping the piano'; 'He drew a circle in the mirror and wrote NON OMNIS MORIAR'; and, when Berg encounters his father having a bath, 'The mirror steamed over.'

As Berg's grip on reality slips, we see his world not so much through his eyes but as a series of framed images – not just reflections, but also scenes spied through keyholes, through windows, through partially opened doors and cracks in the partition walls: '[i]dea and image juxtapositioned,'

Quin writes early in the novel, 'spinning between myth and rationality'. At one point, Berg hatches a plan to hide from Judith and his father by stealing some of her clothes and putting on one of the auburn wigs he has in his 'hair tonic' case: shades of Alfred Hitchcock's 1960 classic *Psycho*, in which its lead character Norman Bates dresses up as his (dead) mother to carry out murders at the family motel.

Just as with Norman Bates, Berg's drag is less about masquerade than a literal reinvention as, or stand-in for, his absent mother – the ingenuous woman jilted by his deadbeat dad Nathaniel. But there's another stand-in too, which in many ways defines the novel. Early on, Berg encounters his father – his ultimate reflection – in the street. The older man reveals that he's trying to escape from Judith, and gives Berg a room key so he can collect his personal effects for him, including Berty, the budgie, '[a]nd there's also a ventriloquist's dummy, actually he's most important, in the wardrobe, at the back, I think on the left side. You see I'm going on tour with a friend, a sort of vaudeville act, hope to make a bit of lolly, doing the resorts as soon as the season begins.'

It's the ventriloquist's dummy – yet another reflection of his father, and of him – that really does for Berg's grip on reality. When he finally believes he's killed Nathaniel, he bundles the corpse in an eiderdown: 'At last action has supplanted idea and imagery,' Quin writes. It's not until later, after he tries to dispose of the body, rolled up in a rug, that Berg discovers that all he's managed to kill is his father's wooden doppelgänger. Nathaniel is still alive, and instead it's the dummy – a kind of brother he never had – that becomes his tormenter.

'The purpose of the ventriloquist's dummy,' Komorowski writes, 'is to allow the spoken voice of the other to speak. That is to say, the dummy possesses neither a literal voice nor an internal voice of its own: it is an object.' This might seem obvious, but it also points to the influence on Quin (and, by association, Bates) of Laing's *The Divided Self* and his idea of ontological insecurity. Giles Gordon, in his 2001 introduction to *Berg*, suggests that Quin had to have known about Laing's book.

Hodgson, too, is clear on the influence: '[w]hile she frequently peoples [her novels] with Laingian fellow travellers . . . she does so in order to indict their vain and hubristic attempts to summon the Dionysus within. Their ecstatic release never arrives. To be insane is always to suffer; toying dilettantishly with these dark and formidable forces can be deadly and by "going over the edge" her characters sacrifice themselves to more authentic truths that are at length revealed to be trivial and insubstantial myths.'

In *The Divided Self*, Laing writes that for the ontologically insecure person,

> one is open to the possibility of experiencing oneself as an *object* of his experience and thereby of feeling one's own subjectivity drained away. One is threatened with the possibility of becoming no more than a thing in the world of the other, without any life for oneself, without any being for oneself. In terms of such anxiety, the very act of experiencing the other as a person is felt as virtually suicidal.

This is precisely the situation Aly Berg finds himself in, as his autonomous identity comes unstuck in the face of not just the father who didn't raise him but his father's dummy – the empty shell, the object his father seems to have held in greater affection than the son he abandoned. Eventually, he can only see himself as a reflection: as 'Greb', as the dummy, as his father's lover's lover. So as not to see himself when Judith mistakes him for his dad as they fuck, he closes his eyes.

It's easy to see the connections in *Berg* to Quin's own life, born as she was in Brighton, the assumed 'seaside town' of the novel, and the fact that she was estranged from her father for most of her childhood. There is also the fact that her mother had left her first child, her son John, when he was a boy, not to encounter him again until he was fully grown. Nathaniel's aspirations to be part of a vaudeville act hint at Quin's own desires to be an actor. Then there are the Oedipal themes: 'At eighteen,' she wrote, 'I went up to London to spend Saturdays with my father (he had left my mother when I was ten) and pretended he was my lover.' When Berg thinks he has his father's body rolled in a rug, he stashes it at the train station's left-luggage office. In 1934 there were two separate murders in which the victims' bodies were found inside trunks at the Brighton station left-luggage office. That was the year Quin's mother Anne first arrived in the town. The novel, in truly ambivalent form given these details, is spikily dedicated: 'For Mother'.

But to read Quin's work strictly autobiographically undermines the deep theoretical and conceptual thinking underpinning it. *Berg*'s greatness lies not in its riffing on the classical story of Oedipus but in its cultural and psychological contemporaneity. This is a novel shaped by a deep awareness of existentialist thought, both in literature and new psychoanalysis; by an understanding of the new dynamics of sex in literature, exemplified by the obscenity trials that had taken place in London and the States, particularly around Lawrence and Miller; and by an intense, deep understanding of the complex relations between the framed image and language. The reflections in *Berg* turn the novel's confused hero into a man at sea in a world of objects: wigs, budgies, dummies, lovers, breasts, mouths, fathers, glasses, mirrors, pubs, beans and bacon. There's a strange distancing effect, where Berg seems never to fully touch anything but, rather, always to observe the act of touching. Everything turns into a kind of fetish: a way either to sublimate or release his desires.

The connections with what Bates was starting to do in his own work, and the way he was thinking about his own place in the world, are strong. When he and Quin collaborated on 'Pop Corn', it seems each was using the other to inch towards something personally revelatory.

Bates handed in the dissertation, probably at the end of January or the very start of February. In his student file is a confused if conciliatory note from Michael Kullman to the RCA administration from 6 February: '. . . though he may not have done quite the work specified,' Kullman wrote in a pretty remarkable understatement, 'I don't feel like holding him to blame for it because he has been going through a crisis. He seems to have decided against the world of advertising, and now wants to be, as he puts it, an "Ideas Man".' The following day, Guyatt chipped in with support too: 'For my part,' he wrote, 'I would strongly recommend that we keep him on and just accept the fact that he is a quirk . . . He is a very talented man and is painfully trying to find his true direction as an artist.'

Though theirs might not have been an earth-shattering love affair, there is enough to suggest that Quin played a role in accelerating Bates's discovery of that true direction – which would lead, before 1962 was out, to the disappearance of Bates forever. What she'd created through his manifesto, his correspondence and his dissertation was a language and a framework of existentialism and Hip that he'd been feeling his way towards but been unable to articulate on his own. After his time in New York, his encounter with Rivers and his time with Quin, Bates was starting to assemble the equipment he needed for a radical change.

Bates didn't know about the correspondence between the RCA faculty about 'Pop Corn'. At the same time, his friend Hockney was also in trouble over General Studies: his own lack of enthusiasm for it had resulted in his half-arsed dissertation on Fauvism, which was deemed not up to scratch. But neither man was particularly perturbed by the crisis building for them at RCA – because, at the start of 1962, they had an exhibition to get ready for.

If 'Young Contemporaries' in 1961 had put Hockney on the radar of British art-world figures like John Kasmin, the 1962 iteration of the exhibition cemented his reputation as London's most promising painter. It is also the exhibition that, in the hands of historians like Marco Livingstone and several contemporaneous art critics, established a new school of British Pop.

Hockney's bravura moment in the 1962 show was delivered in the form of his 'Demonstrations of Versatility' – four canvases, completed between 1961 and early 1962. There was: *A Grand Procession of Dignitaries in the Semi-Egyptian Style* – that big painting he'd started after returning from New York; *Tea Painting in an Illusionistic Style* – that seated figure trapped inside Hockney's tea caddy; and an early version of *Flight into Italy – Swiss Landscape* called *Painting in a Scenic Style* (the later one includes Michael Kullman's Mini van dashing through a mountain range, the words 'thats [*sic*] Switzerland that was' shooting out of its exhaust). The painting documents a trip taken in the winter break at the end of 1961, and there are three figures in the car: Hockney, crammed in the back; Kullman driving; and Ferrill Amacker, Hockney's sometime lover and flatmate in Brooklyn, who'd come to Europe to travel. The group of paintings was completed by *Figure in a Flat Style*, made up of a small canvas for the head, a much bigger one for the torso, and two angled wooden batons for legs (this was the Hockney work for sale in the 2016 Christie's catalogue that Apple and I had pored over in his living room).

There's an oft-quoted line from an interview with Hockney in 1965, about the motivation behind these works: 'I deliberately set out to prove I could do four entirely different sorts of picture like Picasso,' he'd said. 'They all had a sub-title and each was in a different style, Egyptian, illusionistic, flat – but looking at them later I realized the attitude is basically the same and you come to see yourself there a bit.' Just as interesting is the identity of Hockney's interviewer: Larry Rivers, who was writing about the young British artist for the Summer 1965 edition of *Art and Literature*, a publication edited by Rivers' friend John Ashbery.

One of Hockney's key prints from this period was also included in the exhibition: *My Bonnie Lies over the Ocean*, 1961–62. As Martin Hammer writes, this is the earliest known work associated with Hockney's first New York trip: it is dated 'July 1961', and was made at the Pratt Institute, where William Lieberman had arranged for Hockney to have access to the printing facilities (Apple still owns a print of it, inscribed to Bates).

Hammer juxtaposes this work with a print from the portfolio 'Stones', which was a collaboration between Rivers and Frank O'Hara, published in 1960. The affinities are compelling, including, as Hammer writes: 'the integrated lines of hand-written text, sometimes floated at eccentric angles; the passages of dense scribbling located towards the bottom centre of each image; a general effect of improvisation and of pockets of artistic incident, from legibly figurative to abstract, dispersed as if randomly within the compositions.'

It's notable that Hockney made this *before* Rivers showed up at the RCA and visited him in his studio, and illustrates that the older painter was already being treated as an influence. There are other aspects to the work that show Hockney's new American enthusiasms: a vertical American flag held aloft by a tiny figure with the initials 'Dh' (Jasper Johns's 'Flag' paintings were another key touchstone for these young British artists), and the head of George Washington on another figure (again, a potential reference to Rivers' *Washington Crossing the Delaware*, if the 'Stones' connection is correct). The theme of a wistful transatlantic love – Hockney's bonnie over the ocean – plays out in the figure on the opposite side of the etching with a Union Jack: a reference to Peter Crutch, Hockney's crush, back in London. But as Hammer also points out, this is Hockney once again using a pop music reference: the guitarist Duane Eddy had a 1960 transatlantic hit with his instrumental version of the traditional tune, called 'Bonnie Come Back'.

Bates had several works in 1962's 'Young Contemporaries'. He had also come up with a canvas that wasn't included, which combined poster, invitation and work label as a proposition for the show's visual identity (he'd been responsible for the 1961 identity too, with his strange eyeball-target form). 'Young Contemporaries 1962' is spelled out in bold black type at the top, just above all the details of the exhibition – address, dates, opening times and so on. Below this are several strips in which information about each work could be entered: the artist's name; title of the work; the price; and the school the artist attended. Christina Barton writes that 'the work has since become a defining marker in [Apple's] conceptual trajectory'.

It may have missed the mark with his fellow students, but some of Bates's works in the exhibition garnered him the attention of London's critics, most notably *Two Cobbers in Central Park, New York on Wednesday 19 July 1961 at 2pm*, 1961 (its title, obviously, referencing the same timeframe in New York as Hockney's *My Bonnie*). This was, in fact, a collaborative painting Bates made with his close friend Reg Fisher. The work is made up of two joined canvases, a policeman's arm spilling from one to the other, while two disembodied heads float freely. (Given Hockney's use of heads in 'A Rake's Progress', this is further evidence of the cross-fertilisation between the men at this time.) Both heads wear hats: one a boater with a red-and-blue band; the other an American-style trilby. This figure also wears tā moko on his nose and chin – traditional Māori tattoo, which Bates and Fisher borrowed from Horatio Gordon Robley's late-nineteenth-century book on the subject. (Apple tells me Bates had pinched a copy of the book from the New Zealand High Commission in London.)

Near to where the painting was displayed, Bates also presented *Love for Sale*, a sculpture that picked up, like the boater's ribbon, the iconic colours of both the Union Jack and the American flag: a white plinth with three perfect blue stripes painted on it, supporting a single glossy red heart, stuck with a butcher's price tag: 'London's Best 2'8 per LB.' The heart was in fact the wooden buck used to shape the tea caddy from Bates's 'we all love tea' campaign, painted red. Bates made the work at his Cornwall Gardens flat. Quin must have seen this and the collaborative painting in progress there at the same time she was working on 'Pop Corn'. '[S]o how's the stripes, red white and blue', she wrote in the letter she sent to Bates with the finished dissertation, '(say how about an all-over red – no scarlet bedspread for Valentine's Day?) butcher's enterprize, and that crazy boater building?'

All of the RCA up-and-comers were included in 'Young Contemporaries' that year. Reviews in the British press were mostly positive, and the smarter critics clearly recognised that a significant shift, particularly in contemporary painting, was underway. The *Times*'s critic described it as a 'brilliant' exhibition that 'fairly bubbles with bright ideas and visual excitement'. The exhibition was, apparently, full of intelligence 'and it is interesting to see in what directions it is currently aimed –':

> Larry Rivers, Henry Mundy, Vasarely, Pasmore, 'hard-edge' Americans, and two markedly influential 'art-school movements', the girder-and-iron-plate painted sculpture at St. Martin's, and the raspberry-blowing 'new surrealist school' (for want of a better name) at the Royal College of Art.
>
> This last dominates the first room, particularly in the person of its present star turn, David Hockney, and in the tougher, harder-hitting talent of Peter Phillips. But its weird mixture of impudence, whimsicality and beautifully tender painting is also well exemplified by Derek Boshier, Michael Upton, Barrie Bates and, in a somewhat different vein, by Malcolm MacLeod.

Ray Watkinson, writing for *The Arts Review*, sensed that something was up too, describing the show as:

> . . . fundamentally a flood of imagery, half-resolved because continuously experienced; not collected in neat tranquillity, but raw, tasteless, and living. Pin-ups and pin-tables, space fiction and city construction, the pabulum of admass and the monitory shapes of motorways, are all pouring furiously through the shifting sieve of consciousness into the patterns of a fully

> urban art. Behind this visual babel, these youngsters are pressing towards comprehension and communication. Is the language sometimes frightening? It's a world full of frightful, as well as wonderful, possibilities.

John Berger, writing for the weekend *Observer*, even tried to offer up a working thesis for the new Pop art on display, which hugged close to some of Marshall McLuhan's ideas: 'Pop art is an art of social comment,' he wrote,

> both satirical and poetic. It rejects the whole tradition of fine art as useless sugar coating a bitter pill. It is anti-authoritarian, anti-military, anti-snob. It affirms the individual *unnoticed* imagination which can transform the commercial pulp fed to it. A film is dismissed as trash by the pundits, but the couples who watch it in the dark put it to uses never considered by the experts.

Terence Mullaly, writing for the *Telegraph and Morning Post*, was less convinced, and Bates was his symbolic villain: 'A red heart marked "London's Best 2s 8d per lb" hardly seems a just reward for all the money spent on our art schools,' he wrote. 'Nor should the appallingly shoddy craftsmanship that provides the common factor in this exhibition be accepted.'

Accepted or not, the buzz around the RCA generation was confirmed when on 25 March, just a month after 'Young Contemporaries' closed, Ken Russell's film *Pop Goes the Easel* screened on the BBC. Though neither Bates nor Hockney was among the featured artists (Hockney has an incredibly brief cameo on a dancefloor), the film's screening was a crucial moment in the trajectory of that year, helping the young artists at the RCA define exactly what they were – and what they weren't.

The film's four heroes are Boshier and Phillips, Pauline Boty and Peter Blake. At the film's start, they frolic at an amusement park, driving bumper cars and playing arcade games. Then we see Blake in bed, caught in a creepy fever dream about French film star Brigitte Bardot, set to the bizarre soundtrack of the tribute to her by the band Achilles and His Heels, released in 1961: not just a pop reference but a clear allusion to Boty's resemblance to Bardot. Out of bed, we see Blake's flat is pasted in pin-ups. 'This is like living in Girls' Town' comes the unfortunate opening line of Blake's voiceover.

Phillips' eventual arrival is just as weirdly pitched: he is chauffeured to his flat in a top-down American convertible by a black driver. Blake's Elvis-era pop songs are gone; instead, Phillips is consistently accompanied by jazz. As he enters the flat, we see Bates's poster for the 1961 'Young Contemporaries' show pasted to the wall next to the mirror Phillips checks himself out in. The place is packed with Phillips' paintings. In the first room, he flings a horror magazine at a Hip woman sitting on a bed in the corner; in the next, a good-looking blonde plays a pinball machine while Phillips flicks through girlie mags (pinball machines and dirty pics were regular subject matter in his paintings).

Apple, in 2013, said of Phillips that he was 'not an intellectual but he was stylish, like a James Dean from Birmingham'. Phillips' paintings from 1961 and 1962 are arguably the most archetypically Pop works produced by any of the RCA artists associated with the movement at that time, in the sense that they most obviously – and least critically – reference American popular culture and its effects. Paintings like *Motorpsycho/Tiger*, 1961–62 (which Phillips is seen working on at the end of *Pop Goes the Easel*) seem to venerate the implicit 'cool' of American biker culture. And 1962's *Star Card Table* is a monochromatic image of Bardot seen through the aperture of a star, sliced into a green surface – meant to evoke a baize table-top. Many of Phillips' other paintings from the period reference playing cards.

Next is Boshier's McLuhan-esque breakfast experience, followed by his declaration of his love for the dead American pop star Buddy Holly. And finally, there's Boty, with whom Russell's camera spends much of the next twenty minutes fixated. Boty, like Blake, enters in the midst of a dream: trapped in a curving hallway where she lays out pictures, only to have instructions barked at her by grumpy German nurses before she's chased by a wheelchair-bound woman wearing dark glasses who eventually catches up to her in the lift and rises from the chair just as Boty shakes herself awake. When she does wake up, she finds Boshier, Phillips and Blake waiting to be let into her flat. Boty explains how much her vivid dreams feed her collages: clearly the most surreal and least obviously Pop works of the group. Blake and Boty talk about her new works; Boshier reads the back cover of a science-fiction pulp mag to a grinning Phillips. Soon after, Boty, dressed in suit and top hat, lip-syncs Shirley Temple's 'Good Ship Lollipop' to camera.

The foursome flick through comic books together; go to professional wrestling together; twist together at a student party (where Hockney briefly head-bangs his way through the crowd). The final few seconds are of all four painting, alone in their respective studios, accompanied by classical harpsichord. It's an inadvertent affirmation of the conventionality of their work. Despite new subject matter, in the end, they are figurative painters in a British figurative tradition, wedded to the same workaday studio practices of previous generations. In 2013, Marco Livingstone all but confirmed Russell's implicit thesis when he wrote that many of the stars of early-sixties British Pop were 'devoted to finding a personal voice through an insistence on the hand'.

Russell's film was seen as both a breakthrough and controversial; innovative for its subject matter, shocking to many regular Britons sitting at home watching the BBC. But its scripted nature meant that all four artists became tools towards the expression of a flawed notion: that British Pop, as the film presented it, was something new and radical. With the exception of Boshier's brief McLuhan-inspired musings, the film failed to grapple with the fundamentally existential questions of what it meant for these artists to make Pop work in an age of mass communication. Instead, their work was presented as something to be read simplistically and iconographically – as a series of signs that pointed to things elsewhere: celebrities, brands, musicians, space rockets. It inadvertently confirmed the worst fears that British Pop was something entirely superficial. Berger's definition of Pop in the *Observer* had been far more acute, and closer to the mark.

Little wonder, then, that Hockney and Bates didn't feature: their sophisticated explorations of the self in the age of mass communication would have blown the film up like an atomic bomb. In fact, Russell had tried to get Hockney for the film's original line-up, but the artist declined, confirming to Lisa Tickner in 2011 that '[h]e didn't see himself as part of a group or as having a significant connection to Pop, and so "backed down and left it to the purists".'

Despite the fact Michael Kullman and Richard Guyatt both felt Bates shouldn't be failed for 'Pop Corn', he was one of five students that year who, in early April, were informed that they couldn't graduate. Hockney was another. Apple remembers the meeting with the RCA's registrar J. R. P. Moon clearly. Bates and Moon hadn't had much time for each other even before the General Studies fallout, as evidenced by numerous letters in Bates's file between Moon, other faculty members, and Stewart Maclennan back in New Zealand. This culminated in the very last letter in Bates's file, from Moon to New Zealand's High Commission in London. 'Barrie Bates has made a very considerable and highly individual contribution to the life of the College,' Moon wrote dryly, 'although perhaps his contribution has not always been as outstanding as Barrie Bates has thought.'

The five students were summoned into Moon's office and informed of their fate. The three others, according to Apple, said nothing. Bates and Hockney, meanwhile, laughed it off, saying that they'd like to make their own versions of a diploma and stamp it with 'FAILED'. (Hockney did make a version of the certificate, the five downcast students at the base of the work, echoed in the five anonymous Bedlam inmates in the final plate of 'A Rake's Progress'.)

Their cockiness, to be fair to them, was by this stage pretty well grounded. Hockney was still basking in the aftermath of 'Young Contemporaries' and the fact almost every critic in London who mattered had mentioned him by name. Rivers and other artists had passed through the RCA studios and identified him as a standout too.

Bates was also doing well, clearly framed by the critics as part of the RCA's rising generation, as well as receiving attention, alongside Frank Bowling, for his contributions to 'Young Commonwealth Artists', in April. Perhaps his most important work from that exhibition was the one plastered around London: his poster for the show – a plain white Union Jack, with red pencil scribbled into the top half of its English cross and a couple of the bars of the saltire. Its strapline was as pithy as anything a Madison Avenue copywriter could have come up with: 'A Union, Jack!', its perfectly placed comma turning it into a sharp piece of street slang, as well as a summation of the context – artists from around the Commonwealth, exhibiting in the heart of London. It won Bates – or Apple, as he was by then – a prestigious D&AD award for best poster the following year.

Unbothered by what was unfolding at the college, Bates decided to spend the April break in Europe: specifically, Yugoslavia. His mother Marija was a Croatian New Zealander, and Bates decided to make contact with his relatives there. But he also stopped off in Paris to do two things: to see Larry Rivers' solo exhibition at Galerie Rive Droite (10 April – 7 May 1962) and to drop in on the artist himself.

This exhibition, along with his solo show at London's Gimpel Fils in May, were watershed moments for Rivers, signalling a substantial shift in subject matter and its treatment. In paintings like *Washington Crossing the Delaware* and other works like his nude double-portrait of his mother-in-law, he'd established himself as one of the great figurative painters of the time. But in his RCA talk he'd indicated that he was in the middle of a change. That change would become crystal clear in the Paris and London shows.

As Sophie Cras argues, the heart of that transformation was his move away from working from models towards found images. In particular, he began to work with Camel and Tareyton cigarette packets and French banknotes. There's hardly any time between Rivers doing this in Paris and Warhol making his own dollar-bill and 'Campbell's Soup Can' paintings in New York (Warhol's first show of the soup can paintings took place in Los Angeles, in July 1962). Rivers' treatment of his found subject matter was far more painterly than Warhol's, though, and far more about the subject of painting itself. His works often included, for instance, the kinds of grid-lines that painters use for perspectival guidance or translation from preparatory sketches.

As Cras writes, 'The banality of these images, together with the profanation evident in the appropriation of official banknotes (bearing the portrait of the national hero Napoleon) or the reduction of painting to a pathetic diagram . . . produced a spirit of impertinence and dark humour that became the trademark of Rivers's new style.' There is evidence, though, that this 'impertinence and dark humour' didn't land well with the young London artists who saw the Gimpel Fils exhibition.

In May, Rivers gave a lecture at the ICA that was sufficiently contentious to warrant a long mention in the *Guardian*. On 21 June 1962, in an article called 'The Anatomy of Pop', George Butcher wrote that:

> One of the interesting things about the 'pop' label is that it comes nearest to suiting that variety of the movement which is most at home in London. That there is a peculiarly local expression was very evident from the discussion

> between Rivers and the 'pop' painters in the audience at the ICA in May. Neither side really understood much of what the other was trying to say. It was almost as though some Academician from Moscow were on the platform instead of an ex-jazz musician from Brooklyn [*sic*: Rivers grew up in the Bronx]. Rivers really did sound like the opening lines from his catalogue [written by John Ashbery], where it is said that he 'paints whatever comes within his reach. This is what Lautréamont was thinking of when he wrote of the sublime logic of making love to the first person who comes along.' Busting up the whole mood, the young 'pop' artists kept pursuing the thread of 'responsibility,' and trying to pin Rivers down to some form of social commitment. They failed.

Butcher doesn't name the young artists haranguing Rivers. He does, however, go on to unpack his view of the specificities of British Pop and the young artists who best embodied it. The two he singles out are R. B. Kitaj and Hockney. Butcher drew attention to Hockney's *A Grand Procession of Dignitaries in the Semi-Egyptian Style*, and also focused on Kitaj's *Red Banquet* from 1960: a 'history painting' that includes the Russian anarchist figures Mikhail Bakunin and Alexander Herzen, and one of several paintings Kitaj made with explicitly socialist content.

Is this, then, why the young Pop artists were interrogating Rivers? Against the likes of Kitaj, painting about socialism, or Hockney, painting openly about homosexuality, Rivers' banknotes and cigarette packs might well have looked tame, perhaps even reactionary. But some of the younger artists may also have arrived at the ICA talk forearmed; several would have attended Rivers' lecture at the RCA or heard the broadcast version on the BBC. Allen Jones, who was there, remembers Rivers saying at one point that if you didn't know what to put in the bottom left-hand corner of a painting, maybe it was finished already. According to Jones, Hockney was there too, and when Rivers discussed a painting in which the main figure was incomplete, Hockney heckled from the crowd. 'Yes, but hands are hard to draw!'

Jones, of course, had long been expelled from the RCA, so hadn't heard Rivers speak the previous November. He had nonetheless encountered Rivers' work well before the ICA talk. He had first seen Rivers' painting *The Next to Last Confederate Soldier*, 1959, on the cover of the March–April 1960 edition of *Evergreen Review*. (This was a journal published by Barney Rosset of Grove Press, the same man who had published *Lady Chatterley's Lover* in 1959 and faced down the US courts.) He says he was deeply impressed by Rivers' ability to corral the painterly language of Abstract Expressionism and direct it towards figurative painting. He realised that what had become stale, in the hands of educators like Carel Weight, Ruskin Spear and others, was the *language* around figuration's potential. But Rivers' work was a reminder that the *actual* potential of figurative painting hadn't yet run out. And this, he says, was an important realisation for many of the young Pop artists who were struggling under the weight of American abstraction.

Apple recalls that when Bates saw the Paris show, it wasn't the lack of political content or 'responsibility' that irked him as much as the painting itself. The young artist didn't see what was gained in remaking the found images, and in such a painterly way. For him, that process of translation just got in the way of the conceptual significance of the subject matter. Bates had needed, desperately, the ideas Rivers had offered up at the RCA in November. But the man's paintings – not so much. He did, nonetheless, drop in unannounced on Rivers and his wife Clarice while in Paris. He didn't stick around for long, and Apple doesn't remember anything particularly significant about the exchange, though does recall seeing more banknote paintings in Rivers' studio – likely for the forthcoming Gimpel Fils show in London. Nor did Rivers seem particularly excited to have the London art student on his doorstep. Evidently, Bates's brief obsession with Rivers had – while leaving a lasting impact on him – run its course.

The subsequent Yugoslavia visit is an unusual incident in Bates's story. Between the late nineteenth and early twentieth centuries, hundreds of Croatian men, mainly from Dalmatia, left their homeland for New Zealand. The motivation for many was to avoid conscription into the army, as the Austro-Hungarians basically used Dalmatia as a rump against the Ottoman Empire. For many Dalmatians, the Austro-Hungarians were an occupying force, and so they left for 'Amerika' – which just as often meant Australia and New Zealand. Since that time, Dalmatia had become part of Tito's Yugoslavia, a Soviet satellite state.

Many of the men who came to New Zealand settled in the northern regions of the North Island to work in the gumfields, where they would dig up large chunks of gum from ancient kauri forests. The gum was a prized furniture resin in Europe and the US before synthetic resins became widely used. Later, many of those Dalmatian families would go on to found New Zealand's wine industry. Some became great market gardeners too.

Evidently, Bates still held his family history in some affection. Quin, writing as Bates, hinted at this. 'I want to do something no one else has ever done as good,' she has him say in his manifesto,

> if only to drive a van better than anyone before, thought of motor racing once, well maybe I'll end up growing cabbages. Take my grandfather, he potters about the farm, all these years doing shit all, apart from watering a few plants, that's why he's lived so long. Man of ideas though, bought two trawlers for herring fishing, made anchovy paste, sold for miles around, yeah he's really wild.

Bates's entire trip to Yugoslavia took place between 16 and 22 April 1962. In that time, he visited relatives in four cities: Rijeka, then Zagreb, Sarajevo, and finally Split. At each stop, Apple recalls, he felt as though the relatives were keen to move him on to his next one, quickly. To this day, Apple isn't sure whether they just didn't want him there, or whether they were worried about informants, given that Bates was a 'Brit' from London. Either way, the trip did little to make him feel connected to his roots, and helped confirm that he was ready to break with his New Zealand past.

In May 1962, Bates received a letter from Moon confirming he'd failed his diploma. Sykes writes that Hockney received similar correspondence. To pass, both men would have to re-present their work for assessment after an extra term at the college. Neither had the remotest interest in doing so. Believing this was the final word on the matter, Bates booked a second trip to New York for July. He planned to stay with Craddock again, and to build on the connections he'd made the summer before. But he was also interested in making links in New York's art world, rather than mainly focusing on Madison Avenue as he had in 1961.

A big factor in his ability to make these connections was his friendship with the slightly older artist Richard Smith, who, as the first artist to receive a Harkness Fellowship to the States in 1959, had made serious connections of his own in New York. There were two major aspects to this: his friendships with artists including Ellsworth Kelly, Barnett Newman, Agnes Martin, Tom Wesselmann, Jim Dine, James Rosenquist and Robert Indiana; and his working relationship with the art dealer Richard Bellamy (who had played the bishop in *Pull My Daisy*, acting alongside Rivers). Smith had met Bellamy through Henry Geldzahler, the curator at the Metropolitan Museum of Art, and had his first show at Bellamy's Green Gallery while he was still in New York in 1961. 'It was a very exciting time,' Smith recalled in 1992. 'It was exciting and it was hip in a way that was so easy. Hearing jazz at the Five Spot, and you know, eating at Ratner's [a Jewish deli, and a Lower East Side institution], and just being around.'

New York, and specifically his time as part of the thriving art scene in the Manhattan neighbourhood of Coenties Slip, gave Smith a taste for large, loft-style spaces that doubled as apartments and studios. When he returned to London in 1961, he set about finding something similar there. He found one, in Shoreditch, not far from Moorfields

Eye Hospital. Smith took over the top two floors of a building at 13 Bath Street which were connected by a 'loading bay' that allowed him to transfer paintings and materials between the two levels. Soon after he moved in, he held an exhibition in his studio, which was sponsored by Alan Power, son of the collector Ted Power. Smith's loft also became the backdrop for one of *Pop Goes the Easel*'s most memorable scenes: the party where we see Derek Boshier and Pauline Boty twist, and Hockney crash his way through the crowd. Some of Smith's big canvases are just visible, leaning against the walls.

Since the mid-fifties, Smith had been a regular contributor to *ARK*. This kept him closely connected to the RCA, and in the Summer 1962 issue he published an article on the work of Boshier, Phillips and Hockney. As much as it was an analysis of them as individuals, it was also Smith – slightly older, more established, the Harkness already under his belt – validating their interest in contemporary culture as subject matter. 'In using this material,' Smith wrote, 'the painters are not either saying "We love it" or "We hate it". They accept it for what it is; a part of the visual world with more associations, more complexities and more impact than St. Ives, Shoreham, or the antique room at the Slade. The material functions in different ways in their work, though they all inhabit a similar world.' There are strong echoes here of Rivers telling the young artists that they should consider their contemporary world as valid subject matter, and that they needn't love their subjects to create great works of art from them.

Despite the fact that Smith is best known for his large abstract paintings, he and Bates shared interests, most notably in American films and advertising (many of Smith's seemingly abstract works from the time take their cues from found images or concepts, with titles like *Revlon*, *Chase Manhattan* and *Product*). Apple recalls that Smith was obsessed with movie trailers as a format, and in 1961 made a short film with the photographer Robert Freeman called *Trailer*, which was shown at the ICA that November. According to Martin Gayford, a row broke out in the audience straight after the screening: many were supportive of the film, while others thought its subject matter – advertising – was outrageous. Apple doesn't recall if he was at that particular screening, but remembers Smith's and Freeman's *Trailer* films well. Both men – as well as Smith's loft – would end up playing vital roles in Bates's story at the end of 1962.

In early June, Hockney's graduation fate took a turn. The RCA's principal, Robin Darwin, had decided he wanted Hockney to receive the college's prestigious gold medal for the most outstanding student, from any of the schools. To his dismay, he discovered that Hockney was ineligible, not just for the award, but to graduate at all, because of his General Studies failure. Rather than letting the matter lie in the hands of the faculty who had assessed Hockney's half-hearted dissertation, Darwin cooked the results. He convened a faculty panel, which included Weight and Kullman, and changed the grades: Hockney and one other of the five failing students could graduate after all.

Bates wasn't the other; a letter in his RCA student file from Moon, dated 6 June, confirms that he would have to re-submit the following year. But when the corrected results were posted on a college noticeboard, Hockney immediately protested to Moon, insisting that all five of the previously failed students should be passed. Whether Hockney had recognised just how much sway he now had over the RCA faculty, or whether he saw this as a basic matter of fairness, is difficult to know. But the result was that on 22 June Bates received a letter from Moon saying that he had, in fact, passed General Studies, and could therefore receive his diploma.

The RCA's convocation that year took place on 13 July. Again, this is one of the most famous moments in early Hockney lore, as the college's golden boy took to the stage with his golden hair, wearing a gold lamé jacket.

He also won the college's life-drawing prize. Several schools awarded silver medals to their top students. In Painting, the silver went to Frank Bowling – the man who'd been kicked out in their first year for marrying Ann Quin's best friend, Paddy Kitchen. Reg Fisher, Bates's painting collaborator in the 1962 'Young Contemporaries' show, won a medal for mural painting. Bates was nowhere on the prize list (interestingly, Guyatt chose not to award a Graphic Design medal at all that year), nor was he even at the ceremony. By that stage, he was already back in New York.

Despite all the ructions and plot twists in their RCA journey, both Hockney and Bates pushed on relentlessly with their respective art practices through 1962, laying foundations for the work that would, over the next decade, come to define them. 'Young Contemporaries' in February had been confirmation that the paths they were on were the right ones. After that show, both of them picked up pace dramatically.

Bates's work had started to move towards a tougher, more conceptual approach – though one still deeply rooted in what he'd picked up from Herb Lubalin, Ernie Smith and others on Madison Avenue. One of his breakthrough works in this regard was *Relation of Aesthetic Choice to Life Activity (Function of the Subject)*, 1961–62, which had its origins in the RCA's publication, *ARK*. Bates saw the plates for the image leaning up in the Graphic Design School's printing room, and asked the RCA's lithography technician Roy Crossett if he would print it four times on canvas, using offset lithography, for him.

The image was eventually used in an *ARK* article from its Autumn 1962 issue called 'Twist Drunk' by Keith Branscombe. The picture is of an officer who worked aboard the MV *Daffodil* (the subject of Branscombe's article), a boat that sailed out from Gravesend and was popular with university students as a party venue beyond the reaches of restrictive British licensing hours.

This aspect of Bates's image choice feels more student in-joke than truly relevant detail. Far more important is the work's central conceit: that there is ostensibly no difference whatsoever between the four reproductions, but that the first in the grid of four is marked by a neon tick. The neon tick comes through the canvas, via two neat holes: an early use by Bates of a commercial technology hugely popular in American signage and advertising, and that would become a major art material in New York in the mid-1960s (and used by Billy Apple, who was briefly one of the pioneers of neon art in the United States). The function it was performing had its origins in New York, too, in Bates's Madison Avenue experiences. Marking up proof sheets with ticks and crosses was exactly the process commercial photographers like Bert Stern and art directors like Helmut Krone used to identify the images that would eventually find their way into the advertisements that graced the pages of magazines like the *New Yorker*. The way the work was printed would become crucial to Bates, and later to Apple: Apple would continue to use Crossett as a technician to make some of his most important works well into the 1970s.

Bronze casting became an essential process for Bates in 1962, too: another technique that relied wholly on others making the work for him – both the Angeloni brothers at the RCA's foundry, and the technicians at the Art Bronze Foundry. In anticipation of the transformation he'd undergo at the end of the year, much of this work involved creating moulds from fruit – some of which, Apple says, were eventually bought by Ted Power. One of Bates's kookiest objects from this period is a grinning orange with a full set of white false teeth, a work that likely had its origins in George Lois's Wolfschmidt vodka ads that had so affected Bates when he first saw them.

Mimicking the orange's grin is a slice of watermelon, half eaten and cast in bronze. There were bananas too, always half-peeled, their skins splayed in three. In one set-up Bates had photographed, a banana and the smiling orange face each other, the banana's tip bending towards the pearly whites (its title: *Smile, Slim, We're Having our Photo Taken*). In another, a banana, with its skin drawn back, stands on a plinth with a sign that reads 'Revlon's Low Down Pink', its tip nibbled and stained with the same shade of lipstick – leaving no doubt as to the work's real subject. (Apple remembers that it was eventually purchased by the collector Chuck Diker, then an executive at Revlon.)

This idea of using common objects to stand in for an individual, absent body – Bates's – began to develop into an essential element of his work. Again, in a strangely anticipatory gesture, Bates made a bronze cast of his own very prominent Adam's apple. (As Apple, he'd later be fond of saying that the eponymous fruit Adam and Eve ate in the Garden of Eden was 'the world's first product' – which would presumably make the serpent the world's first advertising director.)

In 1962 he also made a series of works that are still regarded as essential to the evolution of Billy Apple: a group of bronze castings collectively known as *2 minutes 33 seconds*. Each group is made up of three apples mounted on a white base, at various stages of consumption: whole; a single large bite taken; a well-chewed core. The work's title refers to the time it took him to eat the fruit while amused technicians waited for him at the Art Bronze Foundry. Two early sets were painted – one red, another green – while a later third set was gold-plated – archetypal apple colours, both natural and mythical, that would come to be the trademarked colours of the later Billy Apple brand. *2 minutes 33 seconds* would also play a key role in his debut in London as Billy Apple, at Victor Musgrave's Gallery One, in 1963.

The strangeness of these works lies in the ways they so clearly carry marks of a real body: a real mouth that has taken big, crunchy bites from the fruit, which itself has such heavy religious and mythical connotations of bodies, sex and original sin. (Bates had also bitten the tip from the wax mould of the Revlon banana, and munched away at the watermelon slice.) There are shades here too of his Bilston Gallery series of photographs, back in 1960, in which he and another male subject were photographed with their mouths wrapped around opposite sides of the same apple. He also made a work during this time called *William Tell Junior* – a cast apple pierced by a single arrow, its puncture wound reaching back to *B.E.A. Flight over East Berlin*, that painted Union Jack shot up at a shooting range.

There was one final, strange nod to Bates's New Zealand roots around this time. One of the most intriguing works he made in 1962 is the sculpture *Long Life Beer*. In it, a single, shot-up beer can (like the can in his *Tin Star* poster) stands on top of an ostensible fence post. Apple remembers that Bates, Hockney and Reg Fisher went to stay with Fisher's family in the Midlands town of Dudley, near Wolverhampton. Bates found the piece of wood there, and his travelling companions helped him lug it back to London. In the art work Bates eventually made with it, the post is standing on a strip of artificial grass, and it's pierced by five thin metal rods, evoking wire. It's a portrait of the world Bates left behind, the wire fences of New Zealand's countryside that delineate the nation's farms. In a single surviving photo, the work is installed outside, in a lane next to the entrance to the RCA, at the back of the V&A Museum: like the artist himself, a small piece of the Commonwealth returned to the centre of the Empire, ready to change it from the inside.

Off the back of his work in 'Young Contemporaries', Hockney was invited to show in the summer of 1962 at the ICA, in an exhibition called 'Four Young Artists'. He was also included in 'Image in Progress' at London's Grabowski Gallery in August with other young stars like Phillips, Boshier and Jones. 'Their sources are plain,' Nevile Wallis wrote in his review of the show, 'Francis Bacon and the Americans Larry Rivers and Jasper Johns are as influential as the environment of pin-ups, advertising slogans, and pinball alleys to which the wayward school alludes. The pity is that a flippant irony still takes the place of penetrating satire.' Hockney also entered into the formal agreement with dealer John Kasmin that they hadn't been allowed to officially sign while Hockney was a student. As confirmation of Hockney's ascendancy in London's art world, Kasmin was able to sell many of Hockney's key student works in that first year of their contractual relationship.

Like Bates's, Hockney's work developed substantially and rapidly through the rest of 1962. Two of his best-known works were made as a kind of nose-thumbing, yet again, at the course requirements imposed on him by the RCA. The first was *Life Painting for a Diploma*, its title referring to the fact that all Painting students needed to submit a final work made from a life model. Hockney had been refusing to use the RCA's life models for a while, and instead painted his own nude, based on the cover of an American male physique magazine (like the ones Mark Berger had introduced him to). He then attached a beautifully precise anatomical drawing of a skeleton to the canvas.

Hockney also made a partner work for this: *Life Painting for Myself*, a more Bacon-esque exploration of nudity, in which two figures – one standing, the other seated with knees raised – emerge barely formed out of grey paint and areas of untouched canvas. Both works involved pairs: the skeleton and the bodybuilder, the two (presumed) lovers. This was an extension of the pairings and reflections he'd explored the year before in works like *We Two Boys Together Clinging* and *Mirror, Mirror on the Wall*. But there was something new about them too; a hint that Hockney was moving towards the more naturalistic portrayals of gay love and relationships that would, eventually, become crucial to so many of his greatest paintings made between the mid-1960s and mid-1970s.

This approach was confirmed on Hockney's own travels that summer. Rather than returning to New York, he headed to Italy with the American artist Jeff Goodman. In Florence, Hockney and Goodman met up with Berger and, once again, Ferrill Amacker. The pair then travelled on to Munich, and to Berlin, where they visited the Pergamon Museum. They lost each other for a while, and when Hockney stumbled upon

Goodman standing in the museum's Egyptian section with a sculpted figure, he had an epiphany of sorts. The comical 'couple' became the subject matter for Hockney's painting *The First Marriage (A Marriage of Styles I)*, 1962, in which a suited man stands alongside a seated Pharaonic figure, a single palm tree behind them. *Man in a Museum (or You're in the Wrong Movie)*, 1962, continues the theme, a man standing with his back turned to a more totemic figure.

These works would quickly, over the course of 1963 and 1964, evolve into his double portraits of gay men in domestic scenes. But there is one more intriguing work from 1962, and it was included in 'Image in Progress' that August: *In Memoriam of Ceccino Bracci*. It is another of Hockney's shaped works, this one a coffin, constructed from two parts. Lying in the coffin is a body swathed in white fabric, its hands folded across its chest. Resting on its torso is a wreath, and inside it, in block letters, is the dead man's name – 'Ceccino'. The work is a reference to the teenager Ceccino Bracci, who had worked for Michelangelo and was known to be extraordinarily beautiful.

Michelangelo subsequently designed the boy's tomb, and wrote epitaphs for him. Hockney inscribed one of them on the painting:

> If buried here those beautiful eyes are closed
> forever. This is now my requiem:
> They were alive and no one noticed them.
> Now everybody weeps them dead and lost.

The inference is clear: Michelangelo, the great gay hero of the High Renaissance, was in love with the boy. The forbidden relationship between man and teen resembles the graffiti Hockney had scrawled on *The Third Love Painting*: 'my brother is only 17'. More than this, though, the work exemplifies the qualities that would come to define so much of Hockney's best work in the coming years: genuine love, and not just physical encounters, between men; his continued obsession with literature; and his lifelong grappling with the most important figures of European art history.

When Bates touched down again in New York in July 1962, he did so armed with a crucial introduction from Richard Smith. It was to the artist Robert Indiana.

Indiana was seven years older than Bates, and had begun to establish himself as a significant figure in the New York art scene. Bates met Indiana at the warehouse he shared with fashion designer John Kloss in Coenties Slip. He was deeply impressed by Indiana, but impressed most of all by his work, particularly his seminal 'EAT/DIE' series of paintings, which date from 1962. Apple remembers that the very first pair in the series was in the studio when he visited. The existential diptychs were stark statements, with each word painted in block letters on a canvas, inside a circle. For an artist as committed to conceptual reduction as Bates was, they were a revelation – they did, in his opinion, everything an art work needed to do.

There is another aspect to Indiana's influence on Bates: he was, like Rivers, an artist with a fabricated name. In Indiana's case, he'd taken as his surname the state he originated from. As Apple has always said, this was a little like calling yourself 'William of Orange' – a name as geographic identifier. It was, nonetheless, another forerunner to Bates's own eventual transformation.

Indiana then made Bates an introduction to Jasper Johns. Again, Bates visited the older artist in his studio, and Apple remembers that Johns had one of his iconic *Map* paintings propped on cans against a wall. Apple recalls a funny exchange in which Johns asked Bates about what he'd been working on. Bates pulled out an idea for a work: seven 7 Up logos, taped together, in a row. Apple says Johns asked him why he needed seven of them. Bates replied that it was because it was 7 Up, as though the answer was self-evident. Johns, according to Apple, didn't see the need for the multiple. The difference says something about the generational shift that was starting to occur in the early days of American Pop art, from the uniqueness of Johns's paintings of targets and flags and maps, to the embrace of the multiple, of corporate logos and commercial printing techniques by Warhol and Apple, among others.

Johns asked Bates if there was anyone else in New York he'd like to meet. Bates replied instantly: Leo Castelli. Castelli, who represented Johns, had opened his commercial gallery in 1957, and was clearly the most interesting art dealer in New York. Johns went over to the wall-mounted phone and put in the call. Castelli said Bates should ring him the following Monday, which he duly did. The dealer and the young London artist met up, but the significance of that meeting with Castelli wouldn't be fully felt until Bates returned to New York, in 1964, as a completely different person. In the meantime, Apple says, Johns drove Bates back uptown in a white Jaguar.

Meeting Indiana and Johns left an undoubted and profound imprint on Bates. But there was one more artist he met on that same trip: someone who, like him, had a background in commercial art and an interest in found images, had worked for Herb Lubalin, and was starting to use multiples and printing processes to make his work. His name was Andy Warhol.

Bates visited Warhol at 1342 Lexington Avenue, the house Warhol shared at the time with his mother Julia. Apple remembers entering the living room and seeing some of Warhol's early paintings. He remembers Warhol's *Telephone*, 1961, and a Campbell's soup can with a can opener sticking out the top – which is very likely to have been *Big Campbell's Soup Can with Can Opener (Vegetable)*, 1962. That very month, July 1962, was when Warhol was having his first solo exhibition, of thirty-two soup can paintings, at Ferus Gallery in Los Angeles – widely regarded as the first show of Pop art on the West Coast. There were clear affinities between the two men and their work. With Warhol, Bates also met the art critic Gene Swenson, who would go on to write some of the crucial early texts on Warhol's practice, and the curator at the Metropolitan Museum of Art, Henry Geldzahler (who, later, would also become close with Hockney). Both of them were, give or take a few months, Bates's exact contemporaries.

In the space of just a month, then, Bates had met three of the most important artists in New York's contemporary art scene, all of them older than him: Johns by five years, Warhol and Indiana by seven. There had been his Paris visit in April to Larry Rivers, too. And he'd seen key works by all of them, not in museums or galleries but during studio visits (if Warhol's living room can count as a studio). He'd also been introduced to three crucial art-world figures in Castelli, Geldzahler and Swenson. The entire experience was confirmation enough for the New Zealander that he was on the right track, and that his work belonged alongside theirs. In fact, it wouldn't be long before his fruit sculptures were shown in New York, at Allan Stone Gallery, in a group show called 'Nuts & Bolts'.

But although it seems star-studded in hindsight, the importance of Bates's second trip to New York can be fully understood only when his first is taken into account. All of these men – Johns, Indiana, Rivers, Warhol – were using the images of their day: trying to paint their times rather than their lives, and spearheading a change in American art in the process. But Bates was slightly different, still deeply committed to an ideas-based approach that he'd picked up on Madison Avenue, in his conversations and collaborations with Ann Quin, and in his deep interests in jazz and the language of Hip. Like those artists he met in New York, he was a man of his time. But he also wanted to be ahead of it. The moment had arrived for a more radical change. So on 22 November 1962, Barrie Bates disappeared forever.

As the London winter set in, Bates, back after that second New York trip, was staying with Richard Smith at the Bath Street loft. On a November afternoon, he began to tell Smith he'd been thinking about rebranding himself. He had been talking to Victor Musgrave about having an exhibition at Musgrave's Gallery One. The tiny gallery in fact already had New Zealand connections. Kasmin, the dealer then riding the Hockney wave, had lived in New Zealand for a while in his late teens, and on returning to London worked for Musgrave briefly. The New Zealand writer Kevin Ireland, a friend of Kasmin's, worked there too, to be replaced eventually by the New Zealand artist Michael Illingworth. But rather than wanting to make anything to do with his homeland, Bates saw a rebrand as potential subject matter for the show.

As Apple remembers it, Bates and Smith thought up his change together. Smith had a notepad, and they began to brainstorm new names. Both of them, of course, knew Robert Indiana. But Bates wanted to do something more extreme. He'd been interested, for example, in Malcolm X as a figure (which seems consistent with his wider interests in African-American culture: in jazz, Hip, James Baldwin, and Norman Mailer's 'White Negro' controversy), seeing the X as a remarkable piece of self-branding, in both senses: as a 'brand name' but also an indelible burn on his personhood, which had its own violent undertones given X's motivation to abandon his slave surname. At the more absurd end of things, Bates also liked the name of Peter Pears, a well-known British opera singer and the partner of composer Benjamin Britten. Bates was also keen that his new name should sound instantly like a product – like Babe Ruth, or Hershey's.

The pair came up with a list. Apples had been present in Bates's practice for a while, and particularly in recent months with his bronze sculptures. He also had that prominent Adam's apple he'd cast from bronze. And he liked the idea of the apple in the Garden of Eden being the world's first product; the very beginning, in a sense, of advertising as temptation. As a child, he'd had a teacher who'd called him 'Billy the

Pirate' – a reference to the pirate Billy Bones in Robert Louis Stevenson's *Treasure Island*. Bates was supposed to have worn an eye-patch to correct a lazy eye. He'd refused to wear it, which meant his optic nerve didn't develop properly.

'Billy Apple', then, became the choice. Bates decided to mark the transformation using the same product he, Hockney, Berger and Amacker had fooled around with in New York in the summer of 1961: Lady Clairol. He went blonde again, and bleached his eyebrows this time too. Smith photographed Bates's transformation, culminating in one of the most well-known images of Billy Apple: the twenty-six-year-old, looking into a mirror, seeing his new self for the very first time. He was, essentially, a new man – a subject without a past. As Apple said to me in 2012, on Apple's fiftieth 'birthday': 'The brand was also a way to get away from the New Zealand connection. Suddenly, you're from nowhere, you're brand new. I became British – I was created there in 1962. I could say: "Billy Apple was born in London," and a lie detector wouldn't twitch.'

In 1974, London's Serpentine Gallery staged a mid-career retrospective, called 'From Barrie Bates to Billy Apple'. In the accompanying catalogue, Apple reproduced Smith's image of that first moment of self-revelation. 'In London in 1962', Apple wrote,

> I began an extended work which was part of an effort to break down the separation between 'art activity' and 'life activity'. I decided to use my own identity as the vehicle with which to explore the concept of the artist as 'art object'. This began by my changing my name (identification) and my physical appearance. Recreating myself became the art work. I relinquished my given name Barrie George Bates and chose the name Billy Apple to replace it. Then I assumed a new appearance which was Barrie Bates's conception of Billy Apple's image . . .
>
> At this point the art process-work-object and the artist became interchangeable. This change of identity which was done initially as an

> 'art act' became a life situation and as such is a continuing process. During the time between the conception of the idea and its execution, the invented identity evolved into the actual identity.

Like Robert Indiana and Larry Rivers and even Malcolm X, the change, in other words, was for good. Apple cut himself off completely from his past to such an extent that Bates's mother Marija, in Auckland, had to contact London's Metropolitan Police to track him down to make sure he was still alive. Which he was, and wasn't.

The creation of Billy Apple was one of the most radical art works of the early 1960s. Its importance partly lay in its permanence: this was no act of masquerade, nor was Bates assuming an artistic alter-ego. He was replaced, and never appeared again. In his place stood one of the most complicated art objects of the era – a living human being who was simultaneously subject, verb (because he was also the actor-creator) and object. In that sense, Billy Apple was a perfectly formed, and perfectly embodied, 'art-political statement'.

The emergence of Billy Apple was unquestionably informed by Bates's experiences on Madison Avenue: his deep awareness of the power of branding on the way we perceive and desire products, and the notion that the best visual expression of an idea is often the most stripped down. Apple became all three – the brand, the product and the idea – starkly realised, with no embellishment, just a shock of blonde hair and the eyebrows to match. That the transition was marked by the same product that had changed Hockney – Lady Clairol – is significant but not so much for the parallel between the two. More important is that it was, at the time, one of the archetypal products of mass consumerism, and a carrier of mass communication's ability to commodify our unconscious anxieties about self and our sexual desires. There was an aspect of morbidity here, too: America's most iconic blonde had died just three months earlier: ever since, Marilyn Monroe has occupied the popular and mythic consciousness both as an image and an object. Warhol, unbeknown to Bates/Apple, had begun to make his 'Marilyn' silkscreens. Another factor that made Bates's transformation different from Hockney's was that Apple's blonding was only ever used to mark the transition. In December, Smith's friend Robert Freeman photographed Apple as a blonde from the front and back. But that was the last time he bleached his hair.

One of the most complicated aspects of Billy Apple as art work is the fact that, in his creation, he was so ambivalent: unlike the Pop paintings made by many of his peers, it was impossible to know whether Apple's creation, when it came to the politics of mass communication, was an act of celebration or critique. By the time Apple emerged, McLuhan had published *The Gutenberg Galaxy: The Making of Typographic Man*. Whether Apple knew that text by then or not, he crystallised many of McLuhan's ideas about the consequences of typography and reproduction, and the profound shift the world was undergoing as televisual technologies created the 'global village'. 'Today we live on the frontier between five centuries of mechanism and the new electronics, between the homogeneous and the simultaneous,' McLuhan wrote. Indeed, new technologies – television, neon, lasers, Xerox and others – would come to define much of Apple's work in the 1960s and 1970s. (The two men would eventually meet when Apple had an exhibition in Toronto in 1970.)

It has always been difficult to draw Apple on the full psychological complexities of Bates's disappearance. But it seems clear that there was something in it to do with escaping his New Zealand past – the idea that he was born in London, that a 'lie detector wouldn't twitch'. There's no question Bates had aspired to transcend his Commonwealth roots ever since he arrived at the RCA in 1959. Quin's writings for him, from late 1961 and early 1962, also show an artist grappling with his past: nostalgic reflections about his grandfather and New Zealand's black-sand beaches, counterbalanced by the idea that he was a young man on the verge of change. The confusing lack of hospitality he encountered from his Yugoslav relatives may also have contributed to his sense that it was time to move on. The sheer fact he took the trip in the first place, under his own steam rather than at the request of his mother Marija, suggests he may have been unconsciously searching either for familial connection or finality.

By the time Apple emerged, Bates and Quin were well and truly through – Apple thinks they had drifted apart before he went to New York on his second trip in July 1962. But it seems reasonable to suggest they left a lasting impact on each other. Quin wrote in *London Magazine* that she finished *Berg* – her novel about a hair-tonic salesman who changes his name to kill his father and thus erase the cause of much of his past trauma – before she left her job at the RCA. She gave her notice on 26 November 1962 – just four days after Apple had been created.

The most intriguing through-line between *Berg* and Billy Apple is the influence on both 'art works' of R. D. Laing, and specifically his idea of ontological insecurity. It's already been noted that Quin's novel is full of reflections and reversals, objects, images and doubles, ultimately embodied by Nathaniel Berg's dummy. It feels no accident that the most iconic image of Apple's emergence is of the young man looking at his new self in the mirror. Hockney had used mirrors and doubles extensively at the time, too. This is where Laing's existentialism becomes significant: because it changed, dramatically, the dynamic between the interior and exterior self, introducing a new understanding that identity, subjectivity and madness were formed in relation to a culture, rather than strictly within a subject's unconscious. This intersected neatly with McLuhan's ideas about the ways in which the products of mass consumerism and mass communication were reshaping the sense of self, both at a collective and individual level.

From the moment Bates became Apple, he was as much an artist 'done to' as one in control of his own destiny. He regularly used his own body to examine the forces of technology that were reshaping wider society.

In one of the long case studies Laing used to illustrate his theories in *The Divided Self*, he described his treatment of Peter, 'a man of twenty-five and . . . the picture of health'. Peter's and Bates/Apple's stories are very different, but in Laing's diagnosis, there are intriguing parallels between Peter and the psychological ambiguities of Apple-as-art-work. Peter, Laing wrote, had developed a method of 'uncoupling' as a way to cope with the world, a way to 'sever the ties that related different aspects of his being together'. Central to this was Peter's relationship with his own body. As Laing wrote:

> The body clearly occupies an ambiguous transitional position between 'me' and the world. It is, on the one hand, the core and centre of my world, and on the other, it is an object in the world of the others. Peter tried to uncouple himself from anything of him that could be perceived by anyone else. In addition to his effort to repudiate the whole constellation of attitudes, ambitions, actions, etc., which had grown up in compliance with the world, and which he now tried to uncouple from his inner self, he set about trying to reduce his whole being to non-being; he set about as systematically as he could to become nothing. . . . He belonged nowhere. He was going from anywhere to anywhere: he had no past, no future. He had no possessions, no friends. Being nothing, knowing nobody, being known by none, he was creating the conditions which made it more easy for him to believe that he *was* nobody.

Apple may not have been quite so anxious or nihilistic as Peter, but he did, at that moment of creation, become 'nobody': a man without a past or future. And he would, like Peter, soon become a wanderer, leaving London for good in 1964.

It's impossible to overlook the all-Americanness of 'Billy Apple' as a brand; as American, Apple said in 2012, as apple pie. It was also the perfect name for Mailer's figure of the 'American existentialist' – the hipster, inspired by black culture and by the radical object-ness of jazz. Much like Laing's patient Peter, a central condition for Mailer's figure was the necessity that he live entirely in the present – that he become a man without a past, to 'exist without roots, to set out on that uncharted journey into the rebellious imperatives of the self'. At the heart of this condition was something Bates had been mastering and Apple subsequently perfected – Hip. 'The unstated essence of Hip,' Mailer wrote,

> its psychopathic brilliance, quivers with the knowledge that new kinds of victories increase one's power for new kinds of perception; and defeats, the wrong kind of defeats, attack the body and imprison one's energy until one is jailed in the prison air of other people's habits, other people's defeats, boredom, quiet desperation, and muted icy self-destroying rage. One is Hip or one is Square (the alternative which each new generation coming into American life is beginning to feel), one is a rebel or one conforms, one is a frontiersman in the Wild West of American night life, or else a Square cell, trapped in the totalitarian tissues of American society, doomed willy-nilly to conform if one is to succeed.

The creation of Apple, then – with his sharp new look, his total existence in the present, his love of jazz, his American-ness – was as much about becoming Mailer's hipster, the true American existentialist, as it was about escaping his past. It also gave literal form to the figure Ann Quin had intuited, and first described, in the manifesto she'd written for Apple's predecessor, the late Barrie Bates.

Apple had only one major art outing around this time in London: the solo exhibition at Gallery One, in April 1963, which he'd discussed with Smith in November 1962, and which he called 'Apple Sees Red'. The invitation that was sent out showed the back of Apple's blonde head – one of the photos taken by Robert Freeman – facing a red ground. The exhibition also included what Apple called his 'Live Stills' (as opposed to 'still lifes'), which added up to a cumulative self-portrait.

It was a mix of works made by Bates and Apple. The red set of *2 Minutes 33 Seconds*, those groups of bronze apples, was included. *Love For Sale* – Bates's red heart on a plinth, pinned by a butcher's price tag – was there too. So was *Relation of Aesthetic Choice to Life Activity (Function of the Subject)*, its neon tick glowing from the back of the room. The artificial grass that had provided the 'New Zealand' ground for *Long Life Beer* was repurposed and lifted up onto a table, where it became the cushioning for a cluster of apples, one of them bronze, presumably fallen from an absent tree of life – but also, Apple says, a reference to the way the freshest produce in markets was referred to as the 'top brass'. And *Smile, Slim* – his grinning orange and his banana – was on display in the window.

But the most important works in the exhibition were definitively Apple's: a series of twelve self-portraits, each identical, which ran along one wall. Each stretched white canvas had two Robert Freeman images on it: one of Apple's face against a green ground; the other the shot from the invitation, of the back of his head against a red ground. It was impossible to know where the 'real' Apple was. He was, by this stage, not so much an individual as a product, endlessly repeatable, capable of multiplying forever (this, six decades before his cells began to do the same in an American human-tissue collection).

Apple's expression in the images is utterly ambiguous. There is the hint of a smile, his lips parted just slightly. But there is something quizzical in his expression as well, his blonded eyebrows furrowed just enough to suggest that this is a young man wondering how he's ended up here. There are shades of the mugshot, too; or, with the back and front portraits together, the scientific or eugenic specimen. Apple's shoulders are bare in the shots, simultaneously making it impossible to date the images based on fashion while also suggesting something cadaverous: a young corpse on a vertical slab hung from the wall.

Critics struggled to know what to make of it, or of Apple, this man who'd come from nowhere, only to offer up a troubling and kaleidoscopic portrait of an absent subject, brought into being by multiple, and multiplying, objects. Edward Lucie-Smith, writing in *The Listener*, described it as 'the oddest [exhibition] London has seen for some time.' There was one other piece of critical feedback too. During the exhibition's run, someone shot a bullet through the gallery's front window: Apple, a modern-day William Tell, used for target practice.

In the same month, April 1963, Hockney was photographed by Lord Snowdon for the 2 June issue of the *Sunday Times Magazine* dedicated to 'British Painting Now'. In one of Snowdon's photos, Hockney is shown walking down a London street, his hair freshly bleached, wearing his trademark specs and white sneakers. Dangling from his finger is a gold bag, and he's wearing the gold lamé jacket he'd worn on the RCA stage the year before to receive his gold medal.

Two golden men, fresh with new identities that London spring: two new ideas of what an artist could, and should be, at the end of a love story, striding down opposite paths.

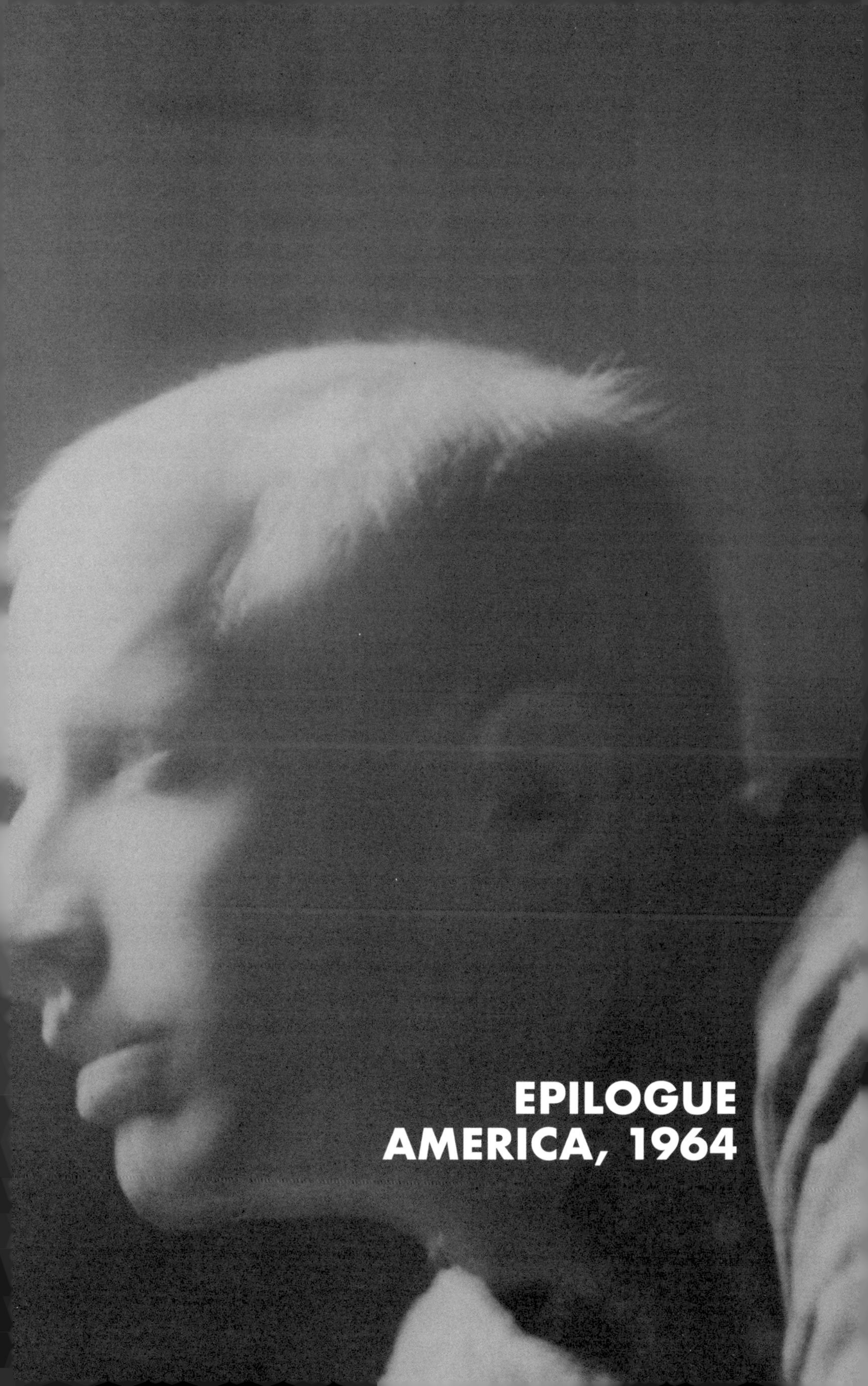

EPILOGUE
AMERICA, 1964

I could do with a dozen pep pills, a hundred dozen Barrie pecks and pulls at the moment – instead I will wind myself off, into my narrow virginal bed and hope to dream nice dreams of us lying in long long grass or lying in deep soft white sand, naked, under a huge – no not that – well why not THE SUN? and crushing corn between our inseparable lips?

— ANN QUIN TO BARRIE BATES, EARLY 1962

THE FINAL EXCHANGE of letters in Ann Quin's thin RCA staff file is between her and the college's principal, Robin Darwin. It was almost exactly two years after she'd finished working there. The first letter, dated 1 November 1964, is from Quin to Darwin, asking him if he'd write a letter of support for her application for a Harkness Fellowship. In it, she mentions that *Berg* has recently been published by Calder; that it has also been sold to Gallimard in Paris and Mondidori in Milan; and that Scribner's in the US is interested too. She also mentioned that she'd already finished another novel.

The timeframe was tight; she apparently needed to submit her application by 12 November. In arguing her case, Quin wrote that 'I do feel some active acquaintance with writers such as John Hawkes (with whom I have now some contact); Robert Duncan, Robert Creeley, and such people as James Schevil [*sic*] at the Writers' Workshop, San Francisco and Thom Gunn.' She also provided a copy of her proposal with the letter. Her 'literal plans', she wrote, were to visit New York briefly; travel in the Southwest ('Taos where Lawrence stayed – i.e. a place so actively used by an English writer I much admire'); and spend time in San Francisco.

It was clear she'd started to tap into America's more experimental writing circles. What she didn't mention to Darwin was that she had already been in an intimate relationship with the poet Robert Creeley, who was based in Placitas, New Mexico, with his wife Bobbie Louise Hawkins, and that this was likely as much a motivation to visit the Southwest as the Lawrence connection. John Calder had bought the rights to Creeley's novel *The Island*, and published it in 1964 – the year he published Quin's *Berg*. Quin met Creeley in London, and the pair had an affair. Creeley then became one of her referees for the Harkness. According to his biographer Ekbert Faas, he also began negotiating on her behalf to get her the D. H. Lawrence Fellowship at the University of New Mexico.

Darwin turned Quin's request down in a polite note dated 3 November, stating that he was supporting other candidates from the college instead. Quin then turned to another prominent writer with whom she'd recently had a complicated affair: a man more than forty years her senior, the British novelist Henry Williamson. The pair had met on 13 February 1964 at The Queens Elm, where Williamson had been stood up by another woman. He nonetheless met 'an Irish girl there [Quin had some Irish heritage], 27 years, who had written a book accepted by Calder, BERG, by Ann Quin'. He took her for dinner at the Renaissance Club, and by the end of the evening declared to an acquaintance that he was in love with her.

He attended the publisher's party for *Berg* on 20 June, where he noted the Bowlings – Frank and Paddy – among the other guests. But Williamson's diaries make for sad reading about their torrid affair: enormous arguments; the disapproval of his family; his own inability to cope with Quin's unpredictability ('while with A.Q. one is always as it were alerted for any moment *crisis de nerfs* in her, major or minor . . . but the SHOUT . . . devastated me. It is this shout in her that is manic, & devastates me'); and pathos-laden accounts of clumsy sexual encounters, culminating in Williamson accusing Quin of giving him a venereal disease. This caused her a great deal of understandable distress, given it later emerged he didn't have one at all.

Their relationship is clearly the inspiration for Quin's story 'A Double Room', the details of which mirror Williamson's diary entries. In it, a young woman has an affair with a much older man. 'On her single bed they had gone so far. Fully clothed.' The pair head off on the train from London for a weekend in a seaside town; on the train, she has a paperback copy of an autobiographical novel (Williamson's major literary achievement was his fifteen-volume autobiographical novel *A Chronicle of Ancient Sunlight*). When they arrive, they find a hotel. As they move through the town, the young woman feels the eyes of its inhabitants on them, snickering at their age difference. He struggles with impotence; she's driven mad by his snoring. The next couple of days unfold with a brutal awkwardness, until they finally part ways back in London.

Like the characters in her story, Quin and Williamson drifted apart. But on 11 November he received a letter from her asking him to recommend her for the Harkness. He initially refused, using the excuse that he hadn't known her for the required minimum of two years. But by 30 November he'd changed his mind. This was after the submission date Quin had mentioned to Darwin, which suggests that she resorted to asking Williamson only after Darwin had rejected her request.

The letters of recommendation from the two established writers with whom she'd had relationships in 1964 worked. Quin received the Harkness Fellowship for most promising Commonwealth writer under thirty, *and* the D. H. Lawrence Fellowship. She travelled to the US in 1965. She hated New York, and arrived in Placitas, according to Faas, around 20 May, and stayed with the Creeleys for about a week. While there, Creeley read around seventy pages of *Three*, and was impressed: a book about a couple who become obsessed with the memory of a much younger woman who had briefly lived with them. When *Three* was published in 1966, it was dedicated 'For Bobbie and Bob'.

Another consequence of Quin's relationship with Williamson was that through him she met Brocard Sewell, a Carmelite friar based in Kent, friend to British writers and publisher of the literary journal the *Aylesford Review*. After first visiting his priory in April 1964, Quin maintained a correspondence with Sewell until her death in 1973. Their letters map the period during which all four of her novels were published, and during which she traversed America and Europe, living on almost nothing: meagre royalties, occasional advances from her publishers, and the odd arts grant or award.

In 1982, in his book *Like Black Swans: Some People and Themes*, Sewell offered his recollections of Quin, quoting extensively from her letters. 'I seek stillness,' she wrote to him, a few days after her first visit,

> as that is the vital reservoir needed for creating, and only by living on my own am I able to achieve that – it is possible that I have not learned to really give, and basically fear a permanent relationship having in my childhood never known family life as such. . . . I am glad (though apprehensive!) that you have a copy of Berg – the best part of which, at the moment anyway, for me seems the cover! The rest is dead. The book was a necessary struggle to free myself from inhibiting constrictions . . .

By this stage Quin was already well advanced on her second novel, *Three*. Quin wrote to Sewell in mid-1964 about it. 'I don't know about the book I'm on at the moment', he quotes her as writing,

> as being in another vein, expressing more truly myself. I think it will take many years before I strip off the layers of 'spectres' in my own nightmarish way. In the present work I am still dealing with three people, this time a girl who lives with a couple. The relationships between three has always fascinated me, being I suppose partly because I have never known the family unit, and partly the influence of the Roman Catholic convent I spent my childhood in (the trinity etc.). In reality I have often found myself at my best, a kind of security when with two other people, most of my friends are couples, and I suppose automatically I play the role of the child. Does all this sound too Freudian for words?!

For Apple and Hockney too, it was clear by 1964 that America was where their future successes lay. Apple had had his Gallery One show, and his films had been screened at the ICA. He'd also won a D&AD design award in 1963 for his 'A Union, Jack!' poster for the 1962 'Young Commonwealth Artists' exhibition. Despite these early successes, he was unable to get a solid foothold in either London's art world or its advertising industry. In May 1964, he took a short trip to New York, during which he visited Leo Castelli again. According to Apple, Robert Rauschenberg – one of the gallery's artists – was there too. Apple had brought with him one of his *Self-Portraits* from the Gallery One show (the ones printed with the Robert Freeman photographs), unrolled it and placed one of his bronze apples on top. Castelli was impressed. Apple returned to London enthusiastic about his prospects for an art career in New York, and decided to make a permanent move in August. When he got there, Castelli's assistant Ivan Karp arranged for him to have the studio of sculptors Eva Hesse and Tom Doyle, who were out of town for a while.

Though Castelli decided not to add Apple to the gallery's stable, the art dealer arranged for him to go around to Bianchini Gallery, where Ben Birillo was organising the exhibition 'American Supermarket'. It opened in October 1964, and has since become a seminal moment in the story of American Pop. Apple's bronze fruit were included alongside Warhol's soup cans and Brillo boxes, a plastic turkey by Tom Wesselmann, Jasper Johns's beer cans, chrome eggs by Robert Watts, and works by Roy Lichtenstein. The exhibition was made to look like a functioning supermarket, complete with turnstiles, designed by Richard Artschwager. On 20 November 1964, *Life* magazine – the same publication that had declared Larry Rivers a 'wonder boy' six years earlier – ran an article about the exhibition by Calvin Tomkins, with photographs by Henri Dauman. Two of the prominent images were of Warhol with his Brillo boxes, and Apple with his watermelon slice.

It was an auspicious start to Apple's New York career. Just a couple of weeks earlier, Hockney had also had his New York debut – a solo exhibition at Alan Gallery, which sold out. Hockney had finished 'A Rake's Progress' in May 1963, and the proceeds from selling the publication rights to Editions Alecto had funded his move to the US – to California rather than New York. There, he began to make the paintings which would come to define his work – and that are still arguably his best: nude men sunbathing by swimming pools, through to *A Bigger Splash*, 1967; *Portrait of an Artist (Pool with Two Figures)*, 1972; and his remarkable double-portraits like *Henry Geldzahler and Christopher Scott*, 1969.

Apple doesn't remember if he went to Hockney's exhibition at Alan Gallery. He does, though, remember Hockney visiting him in Hesse and Doyle's studio around that time. From that point on, Apple was in New York for a quarter-century, exhibiting regularly, setting up one of the city's first artist-run spaces in 1969, and working intermittently with some of the top people in New York advertising, including Bill Bernbach, Bert Stern and Helmut Krone. Hockney settled into California life too, using it as one of his long-term bases. Quin, meanwhile, bounced between the States, the UK and Europe until her death. She drowned at Brighton in 1973.

It's significant that, in 1964, all of them clearly saw a brighter future for their work in the States than in London (Frank Bowling wasn't far behind them, moving to New York in 1966). All three were still comfortably shy of thirty; all three had major achievements under their belts on both sides of the Atlantic. It was the identities they'd forged in London around 1962 – and their intense explorations of *how* identity is forged – that had launched them. Within three years at the RCA – and in that year between the summers of 1961 and 1962 in particular – they'd discovered not only themselves, but new strategies and ideas for how to represent the self, in the age of mass communication.

This interrogation of selfhood was what, in the end, elevated them beyond their contemporaries, many of whom were more fixated on the literal signs of mass consumerism – products, pin-ups, pinball machines, cereal boxes – than the human, subjective consequences of these cultural shifts. Rather than a break with the existentialism of the previous generation, Quin, Apple and Hockney represented a new phase for it: one in which – as Laing, McLuhan and Mailer had all argued – the individual had to push back against their pasts, against conformity and against the madness of the masses. Larry Rivers had invited them to do something similar too ('Thank your grandparents and parents for what they did, but stay out of the covered wagon, you are blocking the highway').

For much of the sixties, all three were at the coal-face of their respective disciplines: Quin in experimental writing on both sides of the Atlantic; Hockney in figurative painting; Apple in New York Pop, then conceptual art, all the while keeping a toe in the advertising world. By the late sixties, much of what they'd achieved in their personal explorations of individualism and self – the sexually, creatively, political-liberated artist – was starting to crumble at a wider societal level: Laing, McLuhan and Mailer all disappearing down different countercultural wormholes; the civil rights movement, with race riots and assassinations, heading towards the racial 'chaos' Mailer has anticipated in 1957; anti-Establishment self-absorption in free love and LSD twisting the sexual revolution and psychotherapy into new and monstrous forms; the failures of the 1968 student revolts; and the creeping rise of a new, conservative individualism – neoliberalism – which would become the dominant force in economics and politics, both in the US and the UK. The art world wouldn't be immune to its effects, either.

In 1962, though, the liberated individual – freed from their history, freed from collective morality and a restrictive society, freed to be who they wanted to be – felt like a figure worth fighting for. Something had changed in the corridors and studios of the RCA. And it was three brilliant young people, all outsiders when they'd arrived in 1959, who would recognise the full potential of that transformation – looking in the mirror and asking serious questions of their reflections, and coming up with radical, culture-changing answers in reply.

SOURCES AND FURTHER READING

BIOGRAPHICAL SOURCES

For David Hockney:

Marco Livingstone, *David Hockney* (London: Thames & Hudson, 1996).
Paul Melia (ed.), *David Hockney* (Manchester: Manchester University Press, 1995).
Nikos Stangos (ed.), *David Hockney by David Hockney* (London: Thames & Hudson, 1976).
Chris Stephens and Andrew Wilson (eds), *David Hockney* (London: Tate Publishing, 2017).
Christopher Simon Sykes, *Hockney: The Biography, Volume 1, 1937–1975* (London: Century, 2011).
Peter Webb, *Portrait of David Hockney* (London: Chatto & Windus, 1988).
The David Hockney Foundation website: https://thedavidhockneyfoundation.org/
Email correspondence between the author and David Hockney, November 2019.

For Barrie Bates/Billy Apple:

Christina Barton, *Billy Apple®: A Life in Parts* (Auckland: Auckland Art Gallery Toi o Tāmaki, 2015).

——*Billy Apple®: British and American Works 1960–1969* (London: Mayor Gallery, 2010).

——*The Expatriates: Frances Hodgkins and Barrie Bates* (Wellington: Adam Art Gallery, 2004).

Anthony Byrt, 'Brand, New', *frieze*, no. 151, November–December 2012, pp. 134–41.

——'The Immortal Artist', *Metro*, issue 392, April 2015, pp. 74–82.

Wystan Curnow, 'Blond Ambition: Barrie Bates to Billy Apple 1959–1963', in *Sold on Apple: The Complete Wystan Curnow Writings* (Auckland: Auckland Art Gallery Toi o Tāmaki, 2015), pp. 158–67.

Leanne Pooley (director), *Being Billy Apple*, 2007.

Barrie Bates's student file, Royal College of Art (RCA) Archives, London.

Details of Apple's early life as Bates discussed and verified in numerous conversations with Billy Apple between 2016 and 2019.

For Ann Quin:

Robert Buckeye, *Re: Quin* (Champaign: Dalkey Archive Press, 2013).

Nell Dunn, *Talking To Women* (London: Silver Press, 2018; first published by MacGibbon & Kee, 1965).

Ekbert Faas with Maria Trombacco, *Robert Creeley: A Biography* (Montreal: McGill-Queens University Press, 2001).

Jennifer Hodgson, '"She finds a metaphor for her condition without defining it": Ann Quin and the British "Experimental" Novel of the Sixties', PhD thesis, University of Durham, 2013.

Paddy Kitchen, 'Catherine Wheel', *London Magazine*, vol. 19, no. 3, June 1979, pp. 50–57.

Ann Quin, 'Leaving School', *London Magazine*, vol. 6, no. 4, July 1966, pp. 63–68.

Brocard Sewell, *Like Black Swans: Some People and Themes* (Padstow: Tabb House, 1982).
Ann Quin's staff file, Royal College of Art (RCA) Archives, London.
Email correspondence between the author and Jeremy Ward, Ann Quin's nephew and the representative of her estate, October 2019.
Excerpts from Henry Williamson's diaries, transcribed and provided to the author by Anne Williamson of The Henry Williamson Society.

For Frank Bowling:

Elena Crippa (ed.), *Frank Bowling* (London: Tate Publishing, 2019).
Okwui Enwezor (ed.), *Frank Bowling: Mappa Mundi* (Munich: Haus der Kunst, 2017).
Martin Gayford, *Modernists & Mavericks: Bacon, Freud, Hockney & The London Painters* (London: Thames & Hudson, 2018).
Email correspondence between the author and Rose Jones of the Frank Bowling Archive, 2017–19.
A visit by the author to the Frank Bowling Archive, London, February 2018.
Derek Boshier recorded in interviews with Hester Westley, 'National Life Stories: Artists' Lives', British Library Sounds, 2007–09.

For Larry Rivers:

Brad Gooch, *City Poet: The Life and Times of Frank O'Hara* (New York: Alfred A. Knopf, 1993).
Larry Rivers, 'A Self-Portrait', broadcast in two parts by the BBC's *Third Programme* on 24 and 31 December 1961. The transcript of the broadcasts was published in *The Listener*, also in two parts, on 11 and 18 January 1962.
Larry Rivers with Arnold Wildstein, *What Did I Do?: The Unauthorized Autobiography* (New York: Harper Collins, 1992).
Phone interview by the author with Clarice Rivers, 17 April 2018.
Email correspondence between the author and David Joel of the Larry Rivers Foundation, 2017–19.

NOTES

Prologue: Auckland, New Zealand, October 2016 – London, England, May 2017

pp. 5–6: Details of his 1961 wedding from email correspondence between the author and Michael Adams, February 2017; and a meeting with Jake Fuller, February 2018, whose father Ron Fuller photographed Bates and Hockney together at Adams' wedding.

p. 6: 'fascinating and droll character', email correspondence between the author and David Hockney, November 2019.

p. 7: 'And all those pretty boys . . .', from 'Untitled (Neh Man It's Like This)', a fragment Quin wrote as Bates in late 1961 or early 1962. Included in Ann Quin, *The Unmapped Country: Stories and Fragments*, edited and introduced by Jennifer Hodgson (Sheffield: And Other Stories, 2018).

p. 8: 'We had a relationship . . .', Byrt, 'The Immortal Artist', *Metro*, p. 77.

p. 9: 'identity [was not] some inner essence . . .', Barton, *The Expatriates*, p. 12; 'riposte to modernist depth', ibid., p. 22. This publication accompanied an exhibition of the same title at Wellington's Adam Art Gallery in 2004. Barton included 'Pop Corn' in the exhibition, and her essay briefly discusses Bates's relationship with Quin. *The Expatriates* therefore played an essential role in opening up the historical space this book explores at length.

pp. 11–17: Alice Butler suggests Adrian Berg may have been Ann Quin's titular source in *Ann Quin's Night-Time Ink: A Postscript*, which Butler produced for the Royal College of Art Graduation Show 2013. http://www.alicebutler.org.uk/wp-content/uploads/2016/03/Butler_AnnQuin_Book.pdf

Part I: The Connection

p. 19: '1 a.m. Tues. morning . . .', Ann Quin, undated letter to Barrie Bates, early 1962, Billy Apple® Archive.

p. 23: 'Ten or eleven years ago . . .', Robin Darwin, *Royal College of Art Annual Report 1959* (London: Lion & Unicorn Press, 1960), p. 20.

p. 23: 'In severing the links with landscape . . . ', Marco Livingstone, *Richard Smith: The Green Gallery Years 1960–1963* (New York: Richard L. Feigen & Co., 1992), p. 15.

p. 24: 'I was a great fan of Carel Weight's paintings . . .', Derek Boshier quoted in Marco Livingstone and Amanda Lo Iacono, *When Britain Went Pop: British Pop Art: The Early Years* (London: Christie's, 2013), p. 291.

p. 24: 'Burri remade Blow in his image', Michael McNay, 'Sandra Blow Obituary', *Guardian*, 23 August 2006.

p. 24: 'Christ could I really get sloshed right now . . .', Ann Quin, undated letter to Bates, early 1962.

p. 25: '[t]he staff said that the students that year . . .', in Stangos (ed.), *David Hockney by David Hockney*, p. 42.

p. 25: 'They stuck a pin in the list . . .', Allen Jones quoted in Livingstone and Lo Iacono, *When Britain Went Pop*, p. 302.

p. 25: 'Jones says it was a dreadful moment . . .' and 'legs cut off', phone interview by the author with Allen Jones, 11 November 2019.

p. 27: 'The Hockney literature has been . . . dominated . . .', Chris Stephens, 'Play Within a Play', in Stephens and Wilson, *David Hockney*, p. 20.

p. 28: 'imitated the painter by walking about . . .', Webb, *Portrait of David Hockney*, p. 13.

pp. 32–38: All quotes attributed to Quin and Kitchen are taken from Quin, 'Leaving School' and Kitchen, 'Catherine Wheel'.

p. 35: 'terrific snob' and 'spinning in her grave', email correspondence with Jeremy Ward.

pp. 44–45: *The Report of the Committee on Homosexual Offences and Prostitution* (The Wolfenden Report), 1957. Kenneth Robinson quotes from Hansard, HC Deb 29 June 1960, vol. 625, cc1453–514.

p. 47: 'Made a lamentable start . . .', Bates's student report in his student file, RCA Archives.

pp. 48–49: Thomas Crow, *The Long March of Pop: Art, Music, and Design, 1930–1995* (New Haven: Yale, 2014); Alex Seago, *Burning the Box of Beautiful Things: The Development of a Postmodern Sensibility* (Oxford: Oxford University Press, 1995).

p. 49: 'If the rise of image consciousness . . .', Seago, ibid., p. 25.

p. 54: 'Barrie Bates shows some eye-catching themes for posters . . .', 1960 newspaper clipping in the Billy Apple® Archive.

p. 55: 'a desert scene . . .', Bates quoted in *Print: America's Graphic Design Magazine*, March/April 1961, no. 15, p. 11.

p. 56: 'A group, seen here for the first time . . .', Lawrence Alloway in *Young Contemporaries 1961 Exhibition Catalogue* (London: RBA Galleries, 1961).

p. 57: 'I remember looking at this show . . .', Jones quoted in Livingstone and Lo Iacono, *When Britain Went Pop*, p. 302.

p. 58: 'Abstract Expressionism had triumphed . . .', Brad Gooch, *City Poet: The Life and Times of Frank O'Hara* (New York: Alfred A. Knopf, 1993), p. 314.

p. 58: 'Indeed one often hears Existentialist echoes . . .', Alfred H. Barr in *The New American Painting: As Shown in Eight European Countries 1958–59* (New York: Museum of Modern Art, 1959), p. 16.

pp. 58–59: Frances Stonor Saunders, 'Modern Art Was CIA "Weapon"', *Independent*, 22 October 1995.

p. 59: '[T]his new painting does have qualities . . .', Frank O'Hara, *Jackson Pollock* (New York: George Braziller Inc., 1959), p. 22.

p. 60: James Finch, '*Adam*: An Early Exhibition and Ownership History', *Tate 'In Focus'* series, https://www.tate.org.uk/research/publications/in-focus/adam/early-exhibition-and-ownership

p. 60: 'In the 1960s the subject had been completely played down . . .', Stangos, *David Hockney by David Hockney*, p. 61.

p. 61: I have pieced together the specific paintings Hockney and others would have encountered at the Marlborough exhibition in 1960 by looking at the exhibition histories of paintings on the official website of the Estate of Francis Bacon: https://www.francis-bacon.com/

p. 62: James Beechey and Chris Stephens (eds), *Picasso and Modern British Art* (London: Tate Publishing, 2012).

p. 62: Joe Tilson references the Picasso and Matisse exhibition in Livingstone and Lo Iacono, *When Britain Went Pop*, p. 327.

p. 63: 'Ron Kitaj and I were at loggerheads . . .', Apple quoted in ibid., p. 277.

p. 63: '[t]he moment Ron Kitaj and David Hockney . . .' and 'I think they were jealous of anyone . . .', Adrian Berg in Paul Huxley (ed.), *Exhibition Road: Painters at the Royal College of Art* (London: Phaidon, Christie's and the Royal College of Art, 1988), p. 88.

p. 64: '[t]he source of all art . . .', Hockney quoted in Webb, *Portrait of David Hockney*, p. 24–25.

p. 66: Boshier confirmed Hockney's use of '4.2' was not a reference to his initials in email correspondence with the author, March 2018.

pp. 69–70: Charles Rembar, *The End of Obscenity: The Trials of Lady Chatterley, Tropic of Cancer & Fanny Hill* (New York: Random House, 1968). 'A thing is obscene . . .', ibid., p. 123; 'if books are to be judged . . . ', ibid., p. 97; 'An outstanding best-seller among books . . .', ibid., p. 42.

p. 71: 'The plot, Mr. Griffith-Jones said . . .', Mollie Panter-Downes, 'The Lady at the Old Bailey', *New Yorker*, 11 November 1960, https://www.newyorker.com/magazine/1960/11/19/the-lady-at-the-old-bailey

p. 72: 'the issue was morality . . .', Rembar, *The End of Obscenity*, p. 159.

p. 73: 'If Graphic Design is even to be raised . . .', 'H. D.', 'The Stereotype in the Economy of Abundance', *Newsheet*, Summer 1960, no. 16, RCA Archives.

p. 74: 'From enmeshed thoughts . . .' and 'In this case I closely directed . . .', interview with Bates in *Advertiser's Weekly:*

	The Journal of Advertising & Marketing, 2 June 1961, p. 16.
pp. 75–76:	'as close to Pop art as I ever came . . .' and 'To make a painting . . .', Stangos, *David Hockney by David Hockney*, p. 64.
p. 77:	'[a] whole gang of us went . . .', Brian Haynes quoted in Seago, *Burning the Box of Beautiful Things*, p. 194.
p. 78:	'Monk, Delonius . . .', Barrie Bates, undated letter to Leon Lesnie, mid-1961, Billy Apple® Archive.
p. 78:	'The jazz group, whose presence alone . . .', Donald Malcolm's original review is quoted in a 'Culture Desk' article, dated 10 Janurary 2009, archived on the *New Yorker*'s website: https://www.newyorker.com/culture/goings-on/the-connection-on-stage-screen-and-disk
p. 79:	'I'm not taking junk', Bates, undated letter to Lesnie, mid-1961.
pp. 79–80:	'The play is not a defence of dope . . .', Kenneth Tynan, introduction to Jack Gelber, *The Connection: A Play* (London, Faber & Faber, 1960), pp. 8–9.
pp. 85–86:	'After *The Connection* had been running for many months . . .', Larry Rivers with Arnold Wildstein, *What Did I Do?: The Unauthorized Autobiography* (New York: Harper Collins, 1992), pp. 353–54.

Part II: Flying Tiger

p. 91:	'Ideas. They brought around a plate and we spewed them out . . .', Bates, undated letter to Leon Lesnie (likely written by Ann Quin), late 1961, Billy Apple® Archive.
p. 93:	Details of Bates's arrival in New York and subsequent stay with Craddock from email correspondence between the author and John Craddock, March 2018.
p. 94:	'revelled in a Bohemia that went on night and day', email correspondence between the author and David Hockney, November 2019.
p. 94:	a'[f]ew old posters and things', Bates, undated letter to Lesnie, late 1961.

p. 95: Adrian Shaughnessy, *Herb Lubalin: Typographer* (London: Unit Editions, 2016).

p. 95: 'The American People react to ideas . . .', Lubalin quoted in ibid., p .8.

pp. 96–97: All four issues of *Eros* have been digitised at http://eros.110west40th.com/

pp. 96–97: 'First there were the "jumpers" . . .', Faye Emerson, 'We All Love Jack', *Eros*, Summer 1962, vol. 1, no. 2, p. 5.

p. 97: '"the touchers." . . .', ibid., p. 5.

p. 98: 'Time-table first day . . .', Bates, undated letter to Lesnie, late 1961.

p. 99: For discussion of *Madison Avenue. Lie$, Lie$, Lie$*, 1961, see Barton, *Billy Apple®: British and American Works 1960–1969*, p. 15.

pp. 99–100: '[I]t has long been plain . . .', Marshall McLuhan, *The Mechanical Bride: Folklore of Industrial Man* (London: Routledge & Kegan Paul, 1967), p. 34.

p. 100: 'I'm very interested in the whole set-up . . .', Derek Boshier quoted in Ken Russell (director), *Pop Goes the Easel*, 1962.

p. 100: 'In a 2013 interview . . .', Boshier makes this clear in Marco Livingstone and Amanda Lo Iacono, *When Britain Went Pop: British Pop Art: The Early Years* (London: Christie's, 2013), p. 290.

p. 100: 'extraordinary body of work . . .', Chris Stephens, 'Image in Revolt', in Paul Gorman (ed.), *Derek Boshier: Rethink/Re-entry* (London: Thames & Hudson, 2015), p. 34. Stephens also analyses the connections between Boshier's paintings from the time and the writings of McLuhan and Vance Packard.

p. 101: 'the fragmentation of identity', ibid., p. 45.

p. 102: 'As the literal or "the letter" . . .', Marshall McLuhan, *The Gutenberg Galaxy: The Making of Typographic Man* (Toronto: University of Toronto Press, 1962), pp. 111–12.

p. 105: 'a changing intellectual climate . . .', Nat Hentoff, *The Jazz Life* (New York, The Dial Press, 1961), p. 44; 'an object in itself, a non-functional music . . .', ibid., p. 38.

p. 106: 'In more and more clubs . . .', ibid., p. 41.

p. 106: 'like a world governing body of jazz', ibid., p. 47.

p. 106: 'a really great jazz film', John Craddock, 'Towards an Abstract Cinema? Not Yet', *Vision: A Journal of Film Comment*, vol. 1 no. 2, Summer 1962, p. 21.

p. 106: 'Saw every one who's any one in music . . .', Bates, undated letter to Lesnie, late 1961.

p. 106: 'Much has been written about . . . ' Hentoff, *The Jazz Life*, p. 21.

p. 107: 'That guy encourages miscegenation', ibid., p. 52.

p. 108: 'beginning what should be its most . . .', ibid., p. 39.

p. 109: 'warning to himself as well as to others . . .', Livingstone, *David Hockney*, p. 39.

p. 110: The reference to Theodore Dreiser is made in *The Tate Gallery Report 1970–1972*, although 'Dreiser' is misspelt 'Dreisler'. https://www.tate.org.uk/art/artworks/hockney-1-the-arrival-p07029

p. 110: Details about Hockney's thrill at New York's skyscrapers are from email correspondence between the author and David Hockney, November 2019.

pp. 113–14: 'The ordinary person . . .', McLuhan, *The Mechanical Bride*, p. 21.

p. 115: 'One evening, Mark and he . . .', Webb, *Portrait of David Hockney*, p. 41. For Sykes's version of the hair-bleaching incident, see Sykes, *Hockney: The Biography, Volume 1*, p. 97.

p. 115: 'Called round at 2 a.m. . . .', Quin, *The Unmapped Country*, pp. 69–70.

p. 115: 'Accidentally bleached my hair . . .', Bates, undated letter to Lesnie, late 1961.

p. 117: 'Like many of their fellows elsewhere . . .', Joshua C. Taylor, *Futurism* (New York: Museum of Modern Art, 1961), p. 11.

p. 118: 'I arrived back looking like Kennedy . . .', Bates, undated letter to Lesnie, late 1961.

p. 118: 'people were already grabbing places . . .', Stangos, *David Hockney by David Hockney*, p. 67.

p. 118: 'wry comment on human nature . . .', Livingstone, *David Hockney*, p. 40.

Interlude: A Self-Portrait

p. 123: 'There are four elements . . .', Larry Rivers, 'A Self-Portrait', a version of his November 1961 RCA lecture, broadcast in two parts by the BBC's *Third Programme* on 24 and 31 December 1961; the transcript of the broadcasts published in *The Listener*, also in two parts, on 11 and 18 January 1962. All quotes in this section attributed to this lecture come from this source.

p. 126: 'He showed them to me . . .', Larry Rivers with Arnold Wildstein, *What Did I Do?: The Unauthorized Autobiography* (New York: Harper Collins, 1992), p. 325.

p. 127: 'The paintings, made up of countless fragmentary images . . .', 'Wonder Boy and His Many Sides', *Life*, 20 October 1958.

p. 128: See Kate Taylor, 'Artist's Daughter Wants Videos Back', *New York Times*, 7 July 2010, https://www.nytimes.com/2010/07/08/arts/design/08rivers.html; and Michael Shnayerson, 'Crimes of the Art?', *Vanity Fair*, 3 November 2010, https://www.vanityfair.com/culture/2010/12/larry-rivers-201012

p. 129: 'The weather was pleasant and the afternoons vanished . . .', Rivers and Wildstein, *What Did I Do?*, p. 34.

p. 129: 'a formidable force . . .', Jenni Quilter, *New York School Painters & Poets: Neon in Daylight* (New York: Rizzoli International Publications, Inc., 2014), p. 14.

p. 130: '[n]ot only did she forge close relationships . . .', Eric Brown, 'Worlds in Her Eyes', in Jenni Quilter, *Jane Freilicher: Painter Among Poets* (New York: Tibor de Nagy Gallery, 2013), p. 5.

p. 130: '[inspired] unparalleled devotion . . .', Quilter, *Jane Freilicher*, p. 9.

p. 130: 'A pretty twenty-six-year-old painter . . .', Brad Gooch, *City Poet: The Life and Times of Frank O'Hara* (New York: Alfred A. Knopf, 1993), p. 177.

p. 131: 'when Frank was running herd on him' and '[a] lot of [O'Hara's] very unhappy, wretched, miserable poems . . .', ibid., p. 231.

p. 131: 'I liked his Ivy League dirty white sneakers . . .', Rivers and

Wildstein, *What Did I Do?*, p. 228.

p. 132: '[a]n affectionate grope at the door . . .', ibid., p.231; 'Sex with Frank . . . was not very thrilling', ibid., p. 235.

p. 132: 'very sweet but very stupid . . .', O'Hara letter quoted in ibid., pp. 232–33.

p. 133: 'How did I actually picture the crossing? . . .', ibid., p. 310.

p. 133: See Dong-Yeon Koh, *Larry Rivers and Frank O'Hara: Reframing Male Sexualities* (New York: The City University of New York PhD dissertation), 2006, https://academicworks.cuny.edu/cgi/viewcontent.cgi?referer=&httpsredir=1&article=2681&context=gc_etds

pp. 134–35: Quilter discusses Myers' importance in the poetry, art and theatre scenes in 1950s New York extensively in *New York School Painters & Poets*. Rivers and Wildstein also discuss him extensively in *What Did I Do?*

p. 135: For discussion of Merrill's gift to Rivers, see Langdon Hammer, *James Merrill: Life and Art* (New York: Alfred A. Knopf, 2015), p. 176.

p. 135: 'Rivers basked in the attention . . .', Gooch, *City Poet*, pp. 199–200.

p. 137: 'I was anxious about my exhibition . . .', Rivers and Wildstein, *What Did I Do?*, p. 381.

p. 137: For a discussion of Rivers' time in Paris, see Sophie Cras, 'An American in Paris', Tate 'In Focus' series, https://www.tate.org.uk/research/publications/in-focus/parts-of-the-face-french-vocabulary-lesson-larry-rivers/anamerican-in-paris

pp. 138–39: O'Hara's *Horizon* interview with Rivers is also included in Frank O'Hara, *Art Chronicles 1954–1966* (New York: George Braziller, 1975), pp. 106–20.

p. 139: For O'Hara's discussion of Rivers' engagement with art-historical precedents, see Frank O'Hara, 'Larry Rivers: A Memoir', reproduced in Quilter, *New York School Painters & Poets*, pp. 76–80.

p. 142: 'Rivers veers sharply . . .', ibid., p. 79.

Part III: Mirror/Mirror

p. 147: '[I]f the fate of twentieth-century man . . .', Norman Mailer, 'The White Negro: Superficial Reflections on the Hipster', in *Advertisements for Myself* (London: Andre Deutsch, 1961), p. 283.

p. 150: 'there were too many lectures . . .', Stangos, *David Hockney by David Hockney*, p. 42.

p. 150: 'a very clever and rather self-opinionated man . . .', Webb, *Portrait of David Hockney*, p. 21.

p. 150: 'I wish you had been at that "Lit" party . . .', Ann Quin, undated letter to Barrie Bates, early 1962, Billy Apple® Archive.

p. 151: Details of Bates's presentation disaster are taken from his student file in the RCA Archives.

pp. 151–52: 'He [Bates] has now seen Michael Kullmann . . .', letter by Sybil de Boer, RCA Assistant Registrar, 30 October 1961, in ibid.

p. 152: '[a]lthough I regard Bates as my private pin-up boy . . .', letter by Richard Guyatt, 16 May 1960, in ibid.

p. 152: 'infuse a little frivolity into his make-up', letter from Stewart Maclennan to J. R. P. Moon, 2 June 1960, in ibid.

p. 152: 'Got everyone against him . . .', Bates's student report in his student file, in ibid.

p. 152: 'ARE YOU A GENIUS? . . .', *Newsheet*, Spring 1962, p. 4, RCA Archives.

p. 154: 'The development of language reflects back . . .', Colin Cherry, *On Human Communication: A Review, A Survey, and A Criticism, Second Edition* (Cambridge: MIT Press, 1966), p. 4.

p. 154: 'typing late at night disturbed the land lady', Ann Quin, 'Leaving School', p. 68.

p. 155: 'AWAY from Weight and Co . . .', Quin, undated letter to Bates, early 1962.

p. 156: 'There are so many camp people in N.Y. . . .', Bates, undated letter to Leon Lesnie, late 1961, Billy Apple® Archive.

pp. 156–57: 'Yeah maybe I ought to get organised . . .'; 'Like the other night I got sloshed . . .'; and 'Now Mailer could do anything . . .', Ann Quin and Barrie Bates, 'B. B's Second Manifesto', signed by Ann Quin and dated 8 January 1962, Billy Apple® Archive.

p. 158: 'beyond a doubt . . .', Mailer, *Advertisements for Myself*, p. 199.

p. 159: '[l]ike all conservative political fear . . .' and 'With this possible emergence . . .', ibid., p. 300.

p. 159: '[W]hen it comes . . . miscegenation will be a terror . . .', ibid., p. 301.

p. 160: 'But *why* . . . ', James Baldwin, 'The Black Boy Looks at the White Boy: Norman Mailer', *Esquire*, May 1961, p. 105.

p. 160: 'it is no accident . . . that the source of Hip . . .', Mailer, *Advertisements for Myself*, p. 284; 'Any Negro who wishes . . .', ibid., p. 285; 'Hated from outside . . .', ibid., p. 292.

p. 161: 'the man who knows . . .', ibid., p. 283.

p. 161: 'is to be able to learn . . .', ibid., p. 295.

p. 162: 'It is not granted . . .', ibid, p. 297.

p. 163: 'also contains many impulses which represent . . .', Wilhelm Reich, *The Sexual Revolution: Towards a Self-Governing Character Structure* (London: Vision Press, 1969), p. 17.

p. 163: 'the decisive sex-economic factor . . .', ibid., p. 19.

p. 163: '[c]ompulsive morality as exemplified in marital duty . . .', ibid., p. 29.

p. 164: 'To bohemians . . . the orgone box was celebrated . . .', Christopher Turner, 'Wilhelm Reich: The Man Who Invented Free Love', *Guardian*, 8 July 2011, https://www.theguardian.com/books/2011/jul/08/wilhelm-reich-free-love-orgasmatron

p. 165: '[i]f Kinsey's libertarianism was attracting attention . . .', ibid.

p. 165: 'If one investigates ecclesiastical, fascist and other reactionary ideologies . . .', Reich, *The Sexual Revolution*, p. 20.

p. 165: 'The amoral hipster . . .', Nat Hentoff, *The Jazz Life* (New York, The Dial Press, 1961), p. 141.

pp. 166–67: 'This club in New York we all went to . . .', Quin and Bates, 'B. B's Second Manifesto', Billy Apple® Archive.

p. 167: 'I wanted the following piece to really swing . . .', Barrie Bates (ghost-written by Ann Quin), 'Pop Corn (Being a Conversation between Vincent Van Gogh & Larry Rivers at the "Five Spot" Jazz Club, New York)', London, Royal College of Art dissertation, 1962, p. 1, Billy Apple® Archive.

p. 168: 'Van Gogh laboured to make a yellow cornfield . . .', Larry Rivers, 'A Self-Portrait', a version of his November 1961 RCA lecture, broadcast in two parts by the BBC's *Third Programme* on 24 and 31 December 1961; the transcript of the broadcasts published in *The Listener*, also in two parts, on 11 and 18 January 1962.

p. 169: 'V.G. You talk about plants . . .', Bates and Quin, 'Pop Corn', pp. 4–5.

p. 170: 'Well here's the thesis of all thesis . . .', Quin, undated letter to Barrie Bates, early 1962.

p. 171: 'the triumph of the individual over art', Henry Miller, *Tropic of Cancer* (London: Harper Perennial, 2005), p. 19.

p. 171: 'How's Henry Miller . . .', Quin, undated letter to Barrie Bates, early 1962.

p. 171: 'here was a man more "hip" . . .', Bates and Quin, 'Pop Corn', p. 1.

p. 171: 'The final purpose of art is to intensify . . .', ibid., p. 2. The quote comes from 'Hip, Hell and the Navigator: An Interview with Norman Mailer by Richard G. Stern', which Mailer included in *Advertisements for Myself*, p. 326.

p. 172: 'cannot take the realness . . .', R. D. Laing, *The Divided Self* (London: Penguin Classics, 2010), pp. 42–43.

p. 172: 'Even with the psychiatric treatment . . .', Bates and Quin, 'Pop Corn', p. 2.

p. 172: 'I went to see a psychiatrist . . .', Ann Quin, 'Leaving School', p. 68.

pp. 172–73: 'My job at the art college lasted three years . . .', ibid., p. 68.

p. 173: 'A man called Berg . . .', Ann Quin, *Berg* (Champaign, Illinois: Dalkey Archive, 2001), n. p.

p. 174: 'recovered and reinvented to describe . . .', Hodgson,'Ann Quin and the British "Experimental" Novel of the Sixties', p. 115.

p. 174: 'Quin turns to the Oedipus story . . .', ibid., p. 119.

p. 174: 'The gap in the wall seemed wider . . .', Quin, *Berg*, p. 146.

p. 175: 'BUY BERG'S BEST HAIR TONIC . . .', ibid., p. 3.

p. 175: 'When Berg changes his name to Greb . . .', Jennifer

Komorowski, 'The Voice as an Object of Desire in the Work of Ann Quin', MA thesis, University of Western Ontario, 2017, p. 22.

p. 175: All of the following come from Quin, *Berg*: 'Berg grinned into the mirror . . .', p. 36; 'He cooked the beans and the bacon . . .', p. 38; 'he stared at his reflection . . .', p. 39; 'they sat either side of a glass-topped table . . .', p. 43; 'He drew a circle in the mirror . . .', p. 59; 'The mirror steamed over', p. 51.

p. 175–76: '[i]dea and image juxtapositioned . . .', ibid., p. 8.

p. 176: '[a]nd there's also a ventriloquist's dummy . . .', ibid., p. 38.

p. 176: 'At last action has supplanted idea and imagery . . .', ibid., pp. 75–76.

p. 176: 'The purpose of the ventriloquist's dummy . . .', Komorowski, 'The Voice as an Object of Desire', p. 23.

p. 177: 'While she frequently peoples . . .', Hodgson, 'Ann Quin and the British "Experimental" Novel of the Sixties', p. 103.

p. 177: 'one is open to the possibility . . .', Laing, *The Divided Self*, p. 47.

p. 178: 'At eighteen I went up to London . . .', Quin, 'Leaving School', p. 64.

p. 179: ' . . . though he may not have done . . .', letter by Michael Kullman, 6 February 1962, in Bates's student file, RCA Archives; 'For my part . . .', letter by Richard Guyatt, 7 February 1962, ibid.

p. 180: 'I deliberately set out to prove . . .', quoted in Webb, *Portrait of David Hockney*, p. 46.

p. 181: 'the integrated lines of hand-written text . . .', Martin Hammer, 'David Hockney's Early Etchings: Going Transatlantic and Being British', in *Tate Papers*, no. 27, Spring 2017, https://www.tate.org.uk/research/publications/tate-papers/27/david-hockney-etchings

p. 182: 'the work has since become a defining marker . . .', Barton, *Billy Apple®: British and American Works 1960–1969*, p. 11. For discussion of Bates's collaboration with Reg Fisher and Apple's involvement in 'Young Contemporaries 1962', see ibid., pp. 11–15.

p. 183: '[S]o how's the stripes, red white and blue . . .', Quin, undated letter to Barrie Bates, early 1962.

p. 183: 'fairly bubbles with bright ideas . . .', 'Art Students' Brilliant Exhibition', *The Times*, 13 February 1962. Clipping in the Billy Apple® Archive.

p. 183: '. . . fundamentally a flood of imagery . . .', Ray Watkinson, 'Young Contemporaries', *The Arts Review*, vol.14, no. 3, 24 February–10 March 1962 , p. 1. Clipping in the Billy Apple® Archive.

p. 184: 'Pop art is an art of social comment . . .', John Berger, 'The Harsh Predicament', *Observer Weekend Review*, 11 February 1962. Clipping in the Billy Apple® Archive.

p. 184: 'A red heart marked "London's Best 2s 8d per lb" . . .', Terence Mullaly, 'Young Contemporaries' Art is Trivial and Shoddy', *Daily Telegraph and Morning Post*, 20 February 1962. Clipping in the Billy Apple® Archive.

p. 185: 'not an intellectual but he was stylish . . .', Billy Apple quoted in Livingstone and Lo Iacono, *When Britain Went Pop: British Pop Art: The Early Years* (London: Christie's, 2013), p. 277.

p. 186: 'devoted to finding a personal voice . . .', Livingstone in ibid., p. 16.

p. 187: '[h]e didn't see himself as part of a group . . .', Lisa Tickner, 'Pop Goes the Easel: Derek Boshier in 1962', in Paul Gorman (ed.), *Derek Boshier: Rethink/Re-entry* (London: Thames & Hudson, 2015), p. 76.

p. 187: 'Barrie Bates has made a very considerable . . .', J. R. P. Moon, letter to New Zealand High Commission, 7 August 1962. Barrie Bates's student file, RCA Archives.

p. 189: 'The banality of these images...', Sophie Cras, 'An American in Paris', *Tate 'In Focus'* series, https://www.tate.org.uk/research/publications/in-focus/parts-of-the-face-french-vocabulary-lesson-larry-rivers/an-american-in-paris

pp. 189–90: 'One of the interesting things about . . .', George Butcher, 'The Anatomy of Pop', *Guardian*, 21 June 1962.

p. 190: 'Allen Jones, who was there ...', phone interview by the author with Allen Jones, 11 November 2019.

p. 192: 'I want to do something no one else . . .', Quin and Bates, 'B. B's

Second Manifesto'.

p. 193: 'It was a very exciting time . . .', conversation with Richard Smith in Marco Livingstone, *Richard Smith: The Green Gallery Years 1960–1963* (New York: Richard L. Feigen & Co., 1992), p. 37.

p. 194: 'In using this material . . .', Richard Smith, 'New Readers Start Here . . .', *ARK* 32, Summer 1962, p. 38.

pp. 194–95: For discussion of the ICA screening of *Trailer*, see Martin Gayford, *Modernists & Mavericks: Bacon, Freud, Hockney & The London Painters* (London: Thames & Hudson, 2018), p. 230.

p. 195: For discussion of Darwin changing Hockney's results, and Hockney's intervention on behalf of his classmates, see Webb, *Portrait of David Hockney*, pp. 48–49.

p. 199: 'Their sources are plain . . .', Nevile Wallis, '"Private-Eye" Painters', *Observer Weekend Review*, 19 August 1962.

p. 206: 'The brand was also a way to get away from . . .', Byrt, 'Brand, New', *frieze*, p. 137.

pp. 206–07: 'In London in 1962 I began an extended work . . .', Serpentine Gallery exhibition catalogue, *From Barrie Bates to Billy Apple, 1960–1974* (London: Arts Council of Great Britain, 1974), p. 11.

p. 207: 'art-political statement'. In 1979–80, Billy Apple carried out a series of interventions in New Zealand galleries and museums, collectively titled 'ALTERATIONS: The Given as an Art-Political Statement'.

p. 208: 'Today we live on the frontier . . .', Marshall McLuhan, *The Gutenberg Galaxy: The Making of Typographic Man* (Toronto: University of Toronto Press, 1962), p. 141.

p. 210: The following quotes come from Laing, *The Divided Self*, 'a man of twenty-five . . . ', p. 120, 'sever the ties', p. 131; 'The body clearly occupies . . .', ibid., pp. 131–32.

p. 211: 'The unstated essence of Hip . . .', Mailer, *Advertisements for Myself*, p. 284.

p. 213: 'the oddest [exhibition] London has seen for some time', Edward Lucie-Smith, 'Smile, Slim, We're Having Our Photo Taken,' *The Listener*, 4 April 1963.

Epilogue: America, 1964

p. 217: 'I could do with a dozen pep pills . . .', Quin, undated letter to Barrie Bates, early 1962, Billy Apple® Archive.
p. 219: 'I do feel some active acquaintance with writers . . .' and 'Taos where Lawrence stayed . . .', Ann Quin, letter to Robin Darwin, 1 November 1964, Quin's staff file, RCA Archives.
p. 220: See Ekbert Faas, *Robert Creeley: A Biography* (Montreal: McGill-Queen's University Press, 2001), p. 303.
p. 220: 'an Irish girl there, 27 years . . .', excerpt from Henry Williamson's diaries, February 1964, transcribed and provided by Anne Williamson of The Henry Williamson Society.
p. 220: 'while with A.Q. . . . ', ibid., 17 June 1964.
p. 220: 'On her single bed they had gone so far . . .', from Quin, 'A Double Room', in *The Unmapped Country: Stories and Fragments*, edited and introduced by Jennifer Hodgson (Sheffield: And Other Stories, 2018), p. 31.
p. 222: 'I seek stillness, as that is the vital reservoir . . .', Ann Quin, quoted in Sewell, *Like Black Swans*, p. 183.
p. 222: 'I don't know about the book I'm on at the moment . . .', ibid.

IMAGE CREDITS

Cover:

David Hockney and Barrie Bates in Cornwall, October 1961, photo: Ron Fuller, courtesy of the Ron Fuller estate

Image section:

1: Barrie Bates with his work *B.E.A. Flight Over East Berlin*, 1961, at the Royal College of Art, London, 1961, photo: Frank Apthorp, courtesy of the Billy Apple® Archive

2: Ann Quin, *c.* 1968, photo: Oswald Jones, private collection/Bridgeman Images

3: David Hockney and Derek Boshier at the Royal College of Art, London, 1961, photo: Geoffrey Raymond Reeve, private collection, photo © Geoffrey Raymond Reeve/Bridgeman Images

4: Frank Bowling, *c.* 1965, with his *Self-Portrait as Othello*, 1962, photo: Tony Evans/Timelapse Library Ltd, courtesy of Tony Evans/Timelapse Library Ltd/Hulton Archive/Getty Images

5: Pauline Boty (far left), Anthony Macley, Natalie Gibson and Peter Blake (far right), 1961, photo: Geoffrey Raymond Reeve, private collection, photo © Geoffrey Raymond Reeve/Bridgeman Images

6: Billy Apple, *Art Declared Found Activity* (Lathering, Alicante Spain, April 1960), 1960 (made while still Barrie Bates), courtesy of The Mayor Gallery, London

7: Billy Apple, *Drunk (Earls Court Road, London, Winter 1960)*, 1960 (made while still Barrie Bates), courtesy of the Billy Apple® Archive

8: David Hockney and Peter Crutch with Hockney's *Peter.C*, 1961, photo: Geoffrey Raymond Reeve, private collection, © Geoffrey Raymond Reeve/Bridgeman Images

9: David Hockney and Peter Crutch with Hockney's *The Second Tea Painting*, 1961, photo: Geoffrey Raymond Reeve, private collection, © Geoffrey Raymond Reeve/Bridgeman Images

10: Billy Apple, exhibition poster for 'The Ring' at Bilston Art Gallery, 1960 (made while still Barrie Bates), courtesy of the Billy Apple® Archive

11: Billy Apple, 'we all love tea', award-winning design campaign, 1961 (made while still Barrie Bates), courtesy of the Billy Apple® Archive

12–15: Barrie Bates and David Hockney, New York, summer 1961, photographer unknown, courtesy of the Billy Apple® Archive

16: David Hockney, *My Bonnie Lies Over the Ocean*, 1961–62, etching and aquatint in three colours with collage, edition of 50, approximately 18 x 17 ¾", © David Hockney, photo: Richard Schmidt

17: David Hockney, *The Arrival* from 'A Rake's Progress', 1961–63, etching, edition of 50, 15 ½ x 22 ½", © David Hockney

18–19: Wolfschmidt vodka campaign from 1960, by the agency Papert Koenig Lois, art-directed by George Lois, courtesy of George Lois

20–21: David Hockney and Barrie Bates in Cornwall, October 1961, photo: Ron Fuller, courtesy of the Ron Fuller estate

22: Larry and Clarice Rivers in Rivers' studio, 11 Impasse Ronsin, Paris, 1962, photo: Shunk-Kender, © J. Paul Getty Trust, Getty Research Institute, Los Angeles (2014.R.20). Gift of the Roy Lichtenstein Foundation in Memory of Harry Shunk and Janos Kender.

23: Barrie Bates with his work at 'Young Contemporaries 1962', February 1962, photographer unknown, courtesy of the Billy Apple® Archive

24–25: Barrie Bates at 'Young Contemporaries 1962', February 1962, with works by him and David Hockney, photographer unknown, courtesy of the Billy Apple® Archive

26: Billy Apple, *Relation of Aesthetic Choice to Life Activity (Function of the Subject)*, 1961–62 (made while still Barrie Bates), courtesy of the Billy Apple® Archive, Collection Tate, UK

27: Billy Apple, *Smile, Slim, We're Having Our Photo Taken*, 1962 (made while still Barrie Bates), originally purchased by E. J. Power, courtesy of the Billy Apple® Archive

28: David Hockney, *Life Painting for a Diploma*, 1962, oil on canvas with charcoal on paper, collage 70 7/8 x 70 7/8", © David Hockney

29: David Hockney, *The First Marriage (A Marriage of Styles I)*, 1962, oil on canvas, 72 x 84 ¼", © David Hockney, Collection Tate, UK

30: Billy Apple, *Billy Apple Bleaching with Lady Clairol Instant Crème Whip, November 1962*, 1962, original photograph by Richard Smith, courtesy of the Billy Apple® Archive

31: David Hockney, 1963, photo: Tony Evans/Timelapse Library Ltd, courtesy of Tony Evans/Timelapse Library Ltd/Hulton Archive/ Getty Images

Interlude:

Larry Rivers Times Four, photo: Peter Stackpole, Peter Stackpole/The LIFE Picture Collection/Getty Images

INDEX

ACKNOWLEDGEMENTS

The creation of this book has depended on the extraordinary generosity of so many people. First and foremost, those who were there and who so kindly responded to my questions: David Hockney; Derek Boshier; Allen Jones; John Craddock; Clarice Rivers; Geoff Reeve; Michael Adams; and George Lois. And of course, none of it would have been possible without the cooperation of Billy Apple – who let me into his story, his work and his archives. My conversations with Billy began almost twenty years ago; his friendship, openness and support over all that time has been unwavering, and a remarkable gift.

Many writers, curators, archivists and family members have provided invaluable help: Billy's partner Mary Morrison; Neil Parkinson at the Royal College of Art; Rose Jones of The Frank Bowling Archive; George Snyder and Julie Green of David Hockney, Inc; Anne Williamson of The Henry Williamson Society; Sasha Tochilovsky and Laura Mircik-Sellers of The Herb Lubalin Study Center of Design & Typography; Jennifer Hodgson; Alice Butler; Jake Fuller and his family; Luke Lois; and Chris Stephens.

Special thanks go to Christina Barton, a truly great art historian whose exhaustive work on Billy's art and life has laid the groundwork for the rest of us; to David Joel of The Larry Rivers Foundation, whose enthusiasm and support for this project was there from our very first email exchange and hasn't stopped since; and to Jeremy Ward, who was so generous in sharing his family history and his recollections of his extraordinary aunt, Ann Quin.

To Creative New Zealand for the much-needed financial support, and to the Michael King Writers Centre for the generous space and time to write.

To Barry Schwabsky, Thomas Crow and Matt Saunders for their immensely useful feedback on early drafts. And to the team at Auckland University Press: Sam Elworthy, for seeing the path ahead; Sophia Broom and Katharina Bauer, for keeping me on it; Jane Parkin, for her sensitivity and attention and for understanding so clearly what I was hoping to achieve; Sarah Ell, for proofreading; and Kalee Jackson, for her incredible book design.

To my friends Nick Jeffs, Awhina Fleming, Travis Murdoch, Noel Ivanoff, Judy Millar, Katharina Grosse, Simon Denny, Steve Toussaint, Eleanor Catton and Mark O'Connell for their company, conversation and morale-boosting brilliance through this whole ordeal. To my parents Neville and Lexie, for picking up James from school all those times I was stuck in an archive, or on a plane, or editing pages.

And finally to Kyra, my love. We'll always have London.